THE INFINITE MERIT OF CHRIST

THE INFINITE MERIT OF CHRIST

*The Glory of Christ's Obedience in the Theology of
Jonathan Edwards*

CRAIG BIEHL

Pilgrim's Rock Press

The Infinite Merit of Christ: The Glory of Christ's Obedience in the Theology of Jonathan Edwards

Copyright © 2014 by Craig Biehl

First published by Reformed Academic Press in 2009

Reprinted by Pilgrim's Rock Press in August of 2014
  PO Box 27
  Horsham, PA 19044

www.PilgrimsRock.com

All rights reserved. No part of this publication may be reproduced, stored in a retrieval system, or transmitted in any form or by any means without prior permission of the publisher, except for brief quotations in books, articles, and reviews.

Cover Design: Geoff Stevens

Text Design and Layout: Blair Reid

Printed in the United States of America

Library of Congress Control Number: 2014948720
ISBN: 9780990666608

To Angelica

TABLE OF CONTENTS

ABSTRACT	xi
ACKNOWLEDGMENTS	xiii
LIST OF PRIMARY SOURCE ABBREVIATIONS	xv
INTRODUCTION	1
CHAPTER 1: GOD'S ULTIMATE PURPOSE IS TO DISPLAY AND COMMUNICATE HIS GLORY THROUGH CHRIST'S PERFECT OBEDIENCE TO GOD'S RULE OF RIGHTEOUSNESS	25
GOD'S GLORY IS HIS EXCELLENCY AND HAPPINESS FLOWING FORTH	26
The Display of His Glory and Communication of His Happiness Are One Work of God	33
CHRIST'S OBEDIENCE IS GOD'S ULTIMATE MEANS TO DISPLAY HIS GLORY	38
CHRIST'S OBEDIENCE IS GOD'S ULTIMATE MEANS TO COMMUNICATE HIS GLORY	41
God Provides a Spouse for His Son to Communicate His Happiness and Glorify Himself	42
All God's Works Are for Christ's Work of Redemption	46
GOD'S PURPOSE IS COMPLETE IN THE HAPPINESS OF THE ELECT IN HEAVEN	48
The Saints' Happiness in Heaven Is Viewing and Loving God's Excellency as Displayed and Communicated by Christ	49
United to Christ, the Saints Enjoy All the Blessings of Christ's Exaltation and Glory	50
SUMMARY	52

CHAPTER 2: CHRIST ACCOMPLISHES GOD'S ULTIMATE PURPOSE ACCORDING TO THE TERMS OF THE PRE-TEMPORAL COVENANT OF REDEMPTION	55
THE COVENANT OF REDEMPTION IS ACCORDING TO THE NATURE AND ORDER OF THE PERSONS OF THE TRINITY	56
The Father Is the Initiator and Head of the Covenant	58
The Covenant Is by "Mutual Free Agreement"	61
Christ Is the Fit Mediator Between God and Man	64
The Holy Spirit Participates in Making and Executing the Covenant	66
THE FATHER FREELY SETS HIS LOVE UPON UNWORTHY SINNERS FROM ETERNITY	68
God's Initial Love to Sinners Is the Love of Benevolence, God's Love of Complacence Is Purchased by Christ	68
GOD DETERMINES TO REDEEM SINNERS WITHOUT INJURY TO HIS JUSTICE BY THE TERMS OF THE COVENANT OF REDEMPTION	70
The Covenant Is Between the Father and Christ Mystical	72
The Covenant Terms Accomplish Righteousness for the Elect	76
THE SON DISPLAYS HIS LOVE TO THE FATHER AND THE ELECT BY FREELY CHOOSING TO BE THE ELECT'S SUBSTITUTE AND SURETY	77
The Son Freely Binds Himself to the Terms of the Covenant	78
The Son Freely Binds Himself to Suffer Infinite Wrath	81
THE FATHER DISPLAYS HIS LOVE TO THE SON AND THE ELECT IN THE REWARDS PROMISED TO CHRIST FOR HIS OBEDIENCE	81
SUMMARY	83
CHAPTER 3: GOD'S RULE OF RIGHTEOUSNESS REQUIRES PERFECT OBEDIENCE FOR ETERNAL LIFE AND DEATH FOR DISOBEDIENCE	87
ADAM WAS TO HONOR GOD'S AUTHORITY AND LAW BY PERFECT OBEDIENCE TO GOD'S RULE OF RIGHTEOUSNESS	89
ADAM STOOD AS SURETY FOR ALL MANKIND	91

ALL COMMANDS ARE COMPREHENDED IN THE ONE GREAT LAW OF GOD	92
Perfect Obedience Is Required of Angels for Eternal Life	96
GOD'S UNALTERABLE RULE OF RIGHTEOUSNESS REFLECTS THE NATURE OF GOD	97
God Must Always Uphold the Honor of His Authority and Law	97
Perfect Obedience Is Owed to God as Creator	100
SUMMARY	101
CHAPTER 4: ADAM'S SIN MAKES CHRIST'S PERFECT OBEDIENCE THE ONLY BASIS OF SALVATION	103
ADAM'S SIN MAKES ALL MANKIND GUILTY SINNERS UNDER GOD'S WRATH ACCORDING TO THE STRICT NATURE OF GOD'S RULE OF RIGHTEOUSNESS	104
The Law Is Exceedingly Strict	106
The Law Has No Provision for Deliverance from Sin and Guilt	110
ALL SINNERS POSSESS INFINITE GUILT AND CANNOT OBTAIN ETERNAL LIFE BY OBEDIENCE	113
All Sin Bears Infinite Guilt Requiring Infinite Satisfaction	113
All Good Works Are Corrupt and Infinitely Hateful	117
ADAM'S SIN DOES NOT CANCEL OR ALTER GOD'S RULE OF RIGHTEOUSNESS	119
The Nature of God and His Law Will Not Allow It	119
God's Rule of Righteousness Is Eternal and Unaltered by Salvation by Grace	122
GOD'S UNALTERABLE RULE OF RIGHTEOUSNESS REQUIRES PERFECT POSITIVE RIGHTEOUSNESS FOR JUSTIFICATION	125
Pardon Gives Freedom from Punishment Only, Justification Requires Perfect Positive Righteousness	126
God's Law and Authority are Not Honored Without the Righteousness of Christ's Perfect Obedience	133
GOD AS A RIGHTEOUS JUDGE CANNOT FALSELY JUSTIFY IMPERFECT RIGHTEOUSNESS	135

Righteousness and Justification Concern Judgment According to Law	137
Justification Would Be a "False Sentence" Without Perfect Righteousness	139
The Purpose of God's Judgment is to "Glorify God's Righteousness"	140
CHRIST DIED NEEDLESSLY IF BELIEVERS ARE UNDER A LAW THAT ONLY REQUIRES IMPERFECT OBEDIENCE	142
GOD'S RULE OF RIGHTEOUSNESS PRECLUDES JUSTIFICATION BY ANY VIRTUE OR MERIT IN FAITH	144
Faith Unites to Christ That Salvation Might Be by Grace	145
JUSTIFICATION BY MAN'S RIGHTEOUSNESS INSULTS THE GLORY OF THE TRINITY	150
SUMMARY	154
CHAPTER 5: CHRIST INFINITELY SATISFIES GOD'S UNALTERABLE RULE OF RIGHTEOUSNESS ON BEHALF OF THE ELECT	157
CHRIST AS SECOND ADAM WAS UNDER GOD'S UNALTERABLE RULE OF RIGHTEOUSNESS, AS WAS ADAM	158
Christ Was Bound to Perfect Obedience Regardless of Specific Commands, as Was Adam	159
The Perseverance of Christ Remedies the Defect of the First Covenant with Adam	162
CHRIST JUSTIFIES SINNERS BY THE MERITORIOUS RIGHTEOUSNESS OF HIS OBEDIENCE ON THEIR BEHALF	164
Christ's Obedience Is Meritorious as Voluntary	165
Christ's Obedience Is Meritorious as Perfectly Fulfilling All Laws	167
Christ's Perfect Obedience to God's Rule of Righteousness Constitutes His Justifying Righteousness	170
Christ's Obedience as Surety Achieves the Two-Fold Righteousness Required for Justification of the Elect	179
Christ's Perfect Obedience Purchases a "Full Capacity," as Would Have Adam's Perfect Obedience	188

CHRIST'S OBEDIENCE TO DEATH IS INFINITELY MERITORIOUS AND THE "MOST EXALTED PART OF CHRIST'S POSITIVE RIGHTEOUSNESS"	195
Christ's Obedience to Death Makes Atonement and Merits Eternal Life	196
Christ's Obedience to Death Is an Infinite, Holy Act of Love and Honor to the Father and His Law	200
Christ's Death Is Infinitely Meritorious as Voluntary and "Active"	203
Christ's Obedience to Death Is Infinitely Meritorious by Virtue of Christ's Infinite Dignity and Worth	207
Christ's Obedience to Death Is Infinitely Meritorious as an Infinite Condescension	209
Christ Endured the Greatest Trial of Obedience Ever	213
Christ Exercised Perfect Virtue in His Greatest Trial of Obedience	218
Christ's Death Is His Highest Act of Love to the Elect	220
ALL CHRIST'S ACTS AS MEDIATOR ARE PROPITIATORY AND MERITORIOUS.	222
CHRIST'S OBEDIENCE MERITS THE REWARDS OF THE COVENANT OF REDEMPTION	226
Judgment over Mankind and Angels	232
The Renewal and Beautification of Heaven, Earth, and the Elect	237
CHRIST'S OBEDIENCE ACCOMPLISHES GOD'S ULTIMATE PURPOSE TO DISPLAY AND COMMUNICATE HIS GLORY	240
Union and Communion of Believers with the Trinity	241
Deliverance of the Kingdom to the Father	246
CONCLUSION	249
BIBLIOGRAPHY	251

ABSTRACT

The Merit of Christ's Obedience to God's Rule of Righteousness in the Theology of Jonathan Edwards

Historically, the tendency of scholars to modernize and distance Edwards from his biblicist, exclusivist, evangelical and Reformed tradition has resulted in relatively little attention being given to the importance of the person and redemptive work of Christ in Edwards' Trinitarian thought. The contention of this study is that the foundation, center, and unifying thread of Edwards' thought is the person and work of Christ in accomplishing God's ultimate purpose to display and communicate His glory to unworthy sinners by perfect obedience to God's unchanging rule of righteousness. Edwards' theology cannot be properly understood in abstraction from the person and redemptive work of Christ as revealing and communicating the glorious perfections of the Trinity, nor can revisionist interpretations of Edwards' soteriology as inclusivistic or Catholic be tenable without an overthrow and rewrite of the entirety of Edwards' theology. Salvation of a single soul apart from perfect conformity to God's rule of righteousness would render God unrighteous and prohibit the fulfillment of His ultimate purpose to display and communicate His glory. Indeed, God could not be God.

Chapter one examines the ultimate Trinitarian purpose to display and communicate His glory through the Father's gift of a bride for His Son, and the Son's purchase of His bride by His perfect obedience to God's rule of righteousness. Chapter two probes the pre-temporal Trinitarian and covenantal foundation of Christ's obedience, highlighting the Father's love in His purpose to save a people, and the Son's love in freely undertaking to accomplish that salvation. Chapter three examines the nature of the command to Adam as representative of God's unalterable rule of righteousness that requires perfect obedience for the obtaining of eternal life. Chapter four probes the absolute need for Christ's perfect obedience in light of Adam's sin as surety for mankind, the immutability of God's righteousness and law despite Adam's sin, the infinite guilt of sin and the need of an infinite remedy, God's requirement of a perfect positive righteousness and exclusion of an imperfect righteousness for justification, Christ's perfect satisfaction of God's unalterable rule of righteousness, and God's nature as a righteous judge to uphold eternally His rule of perfect righteousness. Chapter five examines the basis and infinite extent of the merit of Christ's perfect obedience as the righteousness by which sinners are justified, the free act of Christ giving His life as His greatest meritorious act, the propitiatory and meritorious nature of all of Christ's incarnate acts, and the rewards earned on behalf of the elect. All this is to the accomplishment of God's ultimate purpose to display and communicate His glory, consummated in heaven in the marriage of Christ to His bride, to the enjoyment of God's glory forever.

ACKNOWLEDGMENTS

I would like to thank my advisor, Dr. Samuel Logan, for his gracious assistance, excellent advice, and timely encouragement throughout the writing process; he was a great blessing to my wife and me. Thanks also to Dr. Doug Sweeney for his gracious and timely scholarly assistance, and his tremendous example of what it means to be a Christian scholar. The ever thoughtful and helpful Grace Mullen, along with Melvin Hartwick and Emily Sirinides of the Westminster library have always been there to provide whatever resources I have needed. The Jonathan Edwards Center at Yale has proven to be a most valuable resource for the present work, with special thanks to Dr. Michael McClenahan for introducing me to the Edwards Center and the Beinecke Rare Book and Manuscripts Library at Yale University, and for his excellent interaction and critical input, and to Dr. Kenneth Minkema and Caleb Maskell for their kind recommendation of the manuscript. I am most grateful to Dr. Ligon Duncan of Reformed Academic Press for his interest in the manuscript and his decision to publish it, while working closely with his first-rate assistant, Nicholas Reid, has been a delight. Thanks also to Jason Grabulis, Blair Reid, and Geoff Stevens for their part in bringing the manuscript to press. A special thanks to Jeff and Ruth Waddington, whose home has been a warm retreat for much theological discourse and hospitality, while Jeff has been a constant source of encouragement and excellent theological input over the years, for which I am most grateful.

No thanks are sufficient to my loving parents who never doubted that I might actually finish this, by God's grace. Finally, my lovely wife Angelica has been God's special gift to me this side of glory. I cannot adequately express my thanks for her love and support. To Angelica I dedicate this work. And above all, to our great God and Savior Jesus Christ, to whom we owe all thanks for every good gift, in whom is life everlasting, and in and by whom we see the glory of God.

LIST OF PRIMARY SOURCE ABBREVIATIONS

Works 2 *Religious Affections.* Edited by John Edwin Smith. Vol. 2 of *The Works of Jonathan Edwards.* New Haven: Yale University Press, 1959.

Works 3 *Original Sin.* Edited by Clyde A. Holbrook. Vol. 3 of *The Works of Jonathan Edwards.* New Haven: Yale University Press, 1970.

"EGCW"
Works 8 "Dissertation Concerning the End for Which God Created the World," in *Ethical Writings.* Edited by Paul Ramsey. Vol. 8 of *The Works of Jonathan Edwards.* New Haven: Yale University Press, 1989.

HWR
Works 9 *A History of the Work of Redemption.* Edited by John F. Wilson. Vol. 9 of *The Works of Jonathan Edwards.* New Haven: Yale University Press, 1989.

Works 10 *Sermons and Discourses, 1720-1723.* Edited by Wilson H. Kimnach. Vol. 10 of *The Works of Jonathan Edwards.* New Haven: Yale University Press, 1992.

Works 13 *The "Miscellanies," a-500.* Edited by Thomas A. Schafer. Vol. 13 of *The Works of Jonathan Edwards.* 2002; Corrected ed. New Haven: Yale University Press, 1994.

Works 14 *Sermons and Discourses, 1723-1729.* Edited by Kenneth P. Minkema. Vol. 14 of *The Works of Jonathan Edwards.* New Haven: Yale University Press, 1997.

Works 15   *Notes on Scripture.* Edited by Stephen J. Stein. Vol. 15 of *The Works of Jonathan Edwards.* New Haven: Yale University Press, 1998.

Works 16   *Letters and Personal Writings.* Edited by George S. Claghorn. Vol. 16 of *The Works of Jonathan Edwards.* New Haven: Yale University Press, 1998.

Works 17   *Sermons and Discourses, 1730-1733.* Edited by Mark Valeri. Vol. 17 of *The Works of Jonathan Edwards.* New Haven: Yale University Press, 1999.

Works 18   *The "Miscellanies," Entry Nos. 501-832.* Edited by Ava Chamberlain. Vol. 18 of *The Works of Jonathan Edwards.* New Haven: Yale University Press, 2000.

Works 19   *Sermons and Discourses, 1734-1738.* Edited M. X. Lesser. Vol. 19 of *The Works of Jonathan Edwards.* New Haven: Yale University Press, 2001.

Works 20   *The "Miscellanies," Entry Nos. 833-1152.* Edited by Amy Plantinga Pauw. Vol. 20 of *The Works of Jonathan Edwards.* New Haven: Yale University Press, 2002.

Works 21   *Writings on the Trinity, Grace, and Faith.* Edited by Sang Hyun Lee. Vol. 21 of *The Works of Jonathan Edwards.* New Haven: Yale University Press, 2003.

Works 22   *Sermons and Discourses, 1739-1742.* Edited by Harry S. Stout, Nathan O. Hatch and Kenneth P. Farley. Vol. 22 of *The Works of Jonathan Edwards.* New Haven: Yale University Press, 2003.

Works 23	*The "Miscellanies," Entry Nos. 1153-1360*. Edited by Douglas A. Sweeney. Vol. 23 of *The Works of Jonathan Edwards*. New Haven: Yale University Press, 2004.
Works 24	*The "Blank Bible"*. Edited by Stephen Stein. Vol. 24 of *The Works of Jonathan Edwards*. New Haven: Yale University Press, 2006.
Works 25	*Sermons and Discourses, 1743-1758*. Edited by Wilson H. Kimnach. Vol. 25 of *The Works of Jonathan Edwards*. New Haven and London: Yale University Press, 2006.
Works (Hickman)	*The Works of Jonathan Edwards*. With a Memoir by Sereno E. Dwight. 2 vols. Edited by Edward Hickman. Reprint; 1974. Edinburgh: Banner of Truth Trust, 1834.
MDM	*The Glory and Honor of God*. Vol. 2 of *Previously Unpublished Sermons of Jonathan Edwards*, ed. Michael D. McMullen. Nashville, Tennessee: Broadman & Holman Publishers, 2004.
WJEO	*Works of Jonathan Edwards Online*, eds. Harry S. Stout, Kenneth P. Minkema, Caleb J.D. Maskell, 2005. Typed transcripts of unpublished sermon manuscripts of the Beinecke Rare Book and Manuscripts Library, Yale University, posted online at http://edwards.yale.edu/archive/ (accessed October 28, 2007).
YMSS	Typed transcripts of unpublished sermon manuscripts of the Beinecke Rare Book and Manuscripts Library, Yale University. Transposed and typed by the Jonathan Edwards Center at Yale University.
M	"Miscellanies" entry.

INTRODUCTION

In 1981, M. X. Lesser published a list of 1,800 books, articles, and dissertations, noting that in the previous forty years the number of dissertations on Edwards had doubled every ten years.[1] In 2004, Ken Minkema noted that "secondary publications on Edwards fast approaches 4,000, making him one of the most studied figures in Christian thought and *the* most studied American intellectual figure before 1800."[2] Though interest in Edwards never entirely ceased in America since his death in 1758,[3] the middle of the 20th century has seen an astounding increase in scholarly interest fueled by the increasing availability of his printed works.[4]

---

[1] M. X. Lesser, *Jonathan Edwards: A Reference Guide*, A Reference Guide to Literature, ed. Everett Emerson (Boston, Mass.: G.K. Hall, 1981). For additional bibliographic information on secondary literature see also M. X. Lesser, *Jonathan Edwards: An Annotated Bibliography, 1979-1993*, Bibliographies and Indexes in Religious Studies, No. 30 (Westport, Conn.: Greenwood Press, 1994); Sean Michael Lucas, "Jonathan Edwards between Church and Academy," in *The Legacy of Jonathan Edwards: American Religion and the Evangelical Tradition*, ed. D. G. Hart, Sean Michael Lucas, and Stephen J. Nichols (Grand Rapids: Baker Academic, 2003); Nancy Manspeaker, *Jonathan Edwards, Bibliographical Synopses* (New York: E. Mellen Press, 1981). See Lesser and Lucas for useful summaries of the history of Edwards scholarship, while Manspeaker provides helpful annotations on individual works. Minkema and Lucas bring us up-to-date on the most recent literature through 2003. For a bibliography of Edwards' printed writings, see M. X. Lesser and Thomas Herbert Johnson, *The Printed Writings of Jonathan Edwards, 1703-1758: A Bibliography*, rev. ed. (Princeton: Princeton Theological Seminary, 2003).

[2] Kenneth P. Minkema, "Jonathan Edwards in the Twentieth Century," *Journal of the Evangelical Theological Society* 47 (2004), 678.

[3] William J. Scheick, *Critical Essays on Jonathan Edwards*, Critical Essays on American Literature (Boston: G. K. Hall, 1980), xiii. Scheick notes that "Edwards' theology was transmitted to our time without interruption" through various periodicals and printed articles on Edwards in the 19th century.

[4] The Yale edition of *The Works of Jonathan Edwards* has been a great success and boon to interpreters of Edwards, while on a more popular level, Banner of Truth Trust has made Edwards accessible to a predominantly evangelical audience through the publishing of many of his treatises and sermons, including Jonathan Edwards and Sereno Edwards Dwight, *The Works of Jonathan Edwards*, ed. Edward Hickman, 2 vols. (1974; repr., Edinburgh: Banner of Truth Trust, 1834).

Nonetheless, the history of Edwards' scholarship exhibits a relative dearth of interest in the person and redemptive work of Christ as Mediator, despite the critical and central importance of the same in the overall thought and ministry of Edwards. A brief examination of the recent history of Edwards scholarship will explain the present need for a systematic examination of his theology concerning the person and redemptive work of Christ and, more specifically, the merits of His obedience as Mediator in light of the unchanging rule of God's righteousness, the narrow theological topic to be addressed in this work.

To begin, despite the remarkable volume of literature published, a cohesive picture of Edwards' thought is only beginning to take shape, as scholars have often found difficulty in understanding the variety and volume of Edwards' writings as parts of a coherent and systematic whole. Moreover, contemporary scholarship has only recently (in the latter part of the 20th century) turned its predominant focus upon the biblical/theological foundation of his thought. Indeed, in 2006 a new chapter in Edwards scholarship has recently been opened with the publication of the Yale edition of *The "Blank Bible"*, Edwards' interleaved commentary on Scripture.[5] Additionally, over 25,000 pages of previously unpublished sermons and works, with more to come, have only recently been made available to the public on the website of the Jonathan Edwards Center at Yale.[6] Much remains to be done with this material alone.

Additional difficulties contribute to the need for further scholarship. William Scheick identifies the difficulty in interpreting Edwards in the complexity of his mind, and even as we know more of him, he will "continue to elude us" as he is more than the sum of his parts. Therefore, "his essential mystery and, as well, the enig-

---

John Piper's numerous works have also popularized the theology of Edwards among a broad audience of evangelicals.
[5] Jonathan Edwards, *The "Blank Bible"*, ed. Stephen J. Stein, vol. 24 of *The Works of Jonathan Edwards* (New Haven: Yale University Press, 2006). This is a magnificent two-volume work that will generate much fruitful Edwards scholarship.
[6] See http://edwards.yale.edu/ (accessed October 28, 2007).

matic source of the commentary" is largely attributed to Edwards himself.[7] Thus, the depth and complexity of his thought, as well as the sheer volume and variety of his works (published and unpublished) contribute to the problem.

The abundance of differing and conflicting interpretations can also be traced to the variety of perspectives and agendas brought to the task. Holbrook notes that some of the most common and familiar "polar interpretations" include "Edwards as either an incipient modernist or medievalist,[8] puritan or romantic, rationalist

---

[7] Scheick, *Critical Essays on Jonathan Edwards*, xxiii. De Prospo lists a group of "dialectical interpretations" where the polar tensions reside in Edwards himself. R. C. De Prospo, *Theism in the Discourse of Jonathan Edwards* (Newark: University of Delaware Press, 1985), 49. Per Lesser, "as Edwards continues to be the object of almost relentless pursuit, he remains elusive as ever." Lesser, *Jonathan Edwards: An Annotated Bibliography, 1979-1993*, xiii. May writes, "He seems both inexhaustible and impossible to pin down." Henry F. May, "Jonathan Edwards and America," in *Jonathan Edwards and the American Experience*, ed. Nathan O. Hatch and Harry S. Stout (New York: Oxford University Press, 1988), 30. Weber writes, "Edwards will likely still prove enigmatic and slippery." Donald Weber, "The Figure of Jonathan Edwards," *American Quarterly* 35, no. 5 (1983), 564.

[8] For example, per Peter Gay, Edwards is the "last medieval American," Miller's thesis regarding Edwards' modernity is "absurd," and Miller's *Jonathan Edwards* is "simply perverse." Peter Gay, *A Loss of Mastery; Puritan Historians in Colonial America*, Jefferson Memorial Lectures (Berkeley: University of California Press, 1966), 116, 154. Marsden sees Edwards as both modern and medieval. George M. Marsden, *Jonathan Edwards: A Life* (New Haven: Yale University Press, 2003), 213. De Prospo sees him as neither fully Puritan nor fully "enlightened," but "Janus-like in between past and future as potentially a link between." De Prospo, *Theism in the Discourse of Jonathan Edwards*, 35. Per Brand, he is the "last Puritan." David C. Brand, *Profile of the Last Puritan: Jonathan Edwards, Self-Love, and the Dawn of the Beatific*, ed. Susan Thistlewaite, American Academy of Religion Academy Series (Atlanta: Scholars Press, 1991). Edwards is viewed "from a dizzying array of perspectives." Lucas, "Jonathan Edwards between Church and Academy." Edwards is far too complex and nuanced to neatly and exclusively fit into any polar category. For example, with respect to Edwards as either "medieval" or "modern," perhaps he can *broadly* be described as modern in his eclectic use of sources scientific, philosophical, and theological, while Reformed and Augustinian in that all sources were appropriated to the service of his theocentric theology (the term "medieval" introduces additional confusion in describing a "Reformed" theologian). He was modern in his innovative and sometimes speculative approach to theological issues, though quite orthodox in

or mystic, empiricist or idealist."[9] Michael McClymond writes:

> Following Miller's lead, much of recent scholarship on Edwards tends toward a secularizing and naturalizing interpretation of his ideas. Thus Edwards's Christian sermonizing becomes rhetorical theory, while his reflections on the beauty of God translate into general aesthetics, and his typological worldview becomes semiotics....Decontextualizing and detheologizing Edwards's ideas may be a help in understanding the individual segments of the corpus. Yet such a procedure fails conspicuously to yield a sense of the whole.[10]

Daniel Shea notes that "Edwards has been seen as his readers needed to see him. Exegesis of Edwards has often been its antonym, eisegesis."[11] Iain Murray remarks that the wide disparity of opinions concerning Edwards reflects the wide disparity of opinions concerning the God of Edwards.[12] In describing the "Jona-

---

his adherence to the fundamental doctrines of his Reformed and Augustinian tradition and to the ultimate authority of Scripture in all matters. In any event, descriptive shortcuts may be useful in saving time and explanation, but, as is in the case of Edwards, can sometimes produce unhelpful and inaccurate caricatures that are difficult to dispel.

[9] Clyde A. Holbrook, *Jonathan Edwards, the Valley and Nature: An Interpretative Essay* (Lewisburg: Bucknell University Press, 1987), 127. Stephen Nichols identifies three schools of Edwards interpretation, "Edwards as a philosopher, first and foremost....as a theologian and pastor," and "as mediating theology and philosophy." Stephen J. Nichols, *An Absolute Sort of Certainty: The Holy Spirit and the Apologetics of Jonathan Edwards* (Phillipsburg, NJ: P & R Publishing, 2003). For an enlightening summary of the various schools of negative opinion toward Edwards up until the middle of the 20th century, see Clyde A. Holbrook, "Jonathan Edwards and His Detractors," *Theology Today* 10 (1953).

[10] Michael J. McClymond, *Encounters with God: An Approach to the Theology of Jonathan Edwards*, Religion in America (New York: Oxford University Press, 1998), 4.

[11] Daniel Shea, "Jonathan Edwards: The First Two Hundred Years," *Journal of American Studies* 14 (1980), 185.

[12] Iain H. Murray, *Jonathan Edwards: A New Biography* (Edinburgh: The Banner of Truth Trust, 1987; reprint, 1988), xxvi-xxvii. Allen is representative of many when he writes: "The great wrong which Edwards did, which haunts us as an evil dream throughout his writings, was to assert God at the expense of humanity."

than Edwards at 300" symposium, Douglas Winiarski writes: "The scholars attending his tercentennial birthday party shared little in the goals, methods, or outcomes of their research, and they seemed even less willing to discuss the diversity of interpretive approaches that their collective works represent."[13]

Henry May raises the following important question: "Is it possible to have a fruitful discussion of a great religious thinker with the frank participation of believers, rejecters, and agnostics? This seems to me a question which…needs to be faced head-on." Moreover, he states: "'Many modern scholars,' says Hoopes, 'have no idea what it feels like to perceive holiness [this seems to me a massive understatement[14]], and those who do can no more describe the sensation to the rest of us than one can tell a man blind since birth what it feels like to see.'"[15] For Edwards, the experience of the "new birth" and the attendant spiritual illumination to see and love the beauty of the holiness of the God of Scripture are foundational to a proper understanding of God, a spiritual sight and experience unknown to the unbeliever. Thus, May raises an important question: How does one who has not experienced this sight adequately understand and evaluate Edwards whose entire theology rests upon that sight?[16] Certainly one's view of the legitimacy or reality of such an experience, or the reality of the God of Edwards will effect one's interpretation of Edwards and his theology.

Moreover, Edwards was a biblicist and an exclusivist, posing no small problem for interpreters eager to make him acceptable

---

Alexander V. G. Allen, *Jonathan Edwards*, 1889 ed. (New York: Burt Franklin; reprint, 1974), 388.

[13] Douglas L. Winiarski, "Seeking Synthesis in Edwards Scholarship," *William and Mary Quarterly* 61, no. 1 (2004).

[14] May's words.

[15] May, "Jonathan Edwards and America," 31. May quotes James Hoopes, "Jonathan Edwards's Religious Psychology," *Journal of American History* 69 (1982-83), 861.

[16] May writes: "Who and what was Edwards *really*? It is impossible to answer that question without the divine and spiritual light to which I claim no access." May, "Jonathan Edwards and America," 20.

to modern scholarship. This, in part, may explain the tendency of modern scholars, such as Miller, to highlight the philosophical in Edwards to the neglect of his biblical and theological thought that is its foundation, resulting in lopsided and inaccurate interpretations. And though it is possible and legitimate to study Edwards' philosophy as a philosopher, it is difficult to impossible to accurately interpret his philosophy apart from his central theological concerns.[17]

Thus, many factors contribute to the disparity of interpretations and the difficulty scholars have found in discovering the essential thought of Edwards. Perhaps William Morris best summarizes that state of Edwards scholarship:

> What is the problem of Jonathan Edwards? Indeed, there are so many problems connected with his person and his

---

[17] Vernon Louis Parrington, one unsympathetic with Edwards' theology, writes: "to one cardinal principle Edwards was faithful—the conception of the majesty and sufficiency of God; and this polar idea provides the clue to both his philosophical and theological systems." May affirms Parrington's statement as "undeniable." See Vernon Louis Parrington, *Main Currents in American Thought; an Interpretation of American Literature from the Beginnings to 1920* (New York: Harcourt Brace and Co., 1930), I, 152. Quoted in May, "Jonathan Edwards and America," 30. Cherry writes: "For Edwards, as for his forefathers, most any subject could be studied to the glory of God; and to the degree that such subjects could strengthen the appeal of the great themes of Calvinist theology, they were bent to that purpose." Conrad Cherry, *The Theology of Jonathan Edwards: A Reappraisal*, 1990 ed. (Bloomington: Indiana University Press, 1966), 5. Noll writes that Edwards "exploit[ed] contemporary philosophy and sensibility on behalf of the traditional faith." Mark A. Noll, "Jonathan Edwards and Nineteenth-Century Theology," in *Jonathan Edwards and the American Experience*, ed. Nathan O. Hatch; Harry S. Stout (New York: Oxford University Press, 1988), 271. Holbrook writes, "I am inclined to hold with Douglas J. Elwood's contention that Edwards's primary emphasis was deposited upon the doctrine of God." Clyde A. Holbrook, *The Ethics of Jonathan Edwards; Morality and Aesthetics* (Ann Arbor: University of Michigan Press, 1973), vii. Regarding Edwards' early philosophic speculations, Riforgiato writes: "Edwards never actually abandoned his ontology but blended it into his theology. The link between the two appears to be his Trinitarian thought which served as the basic model for philosophy and theology alike." Leonard R. Riforgiato, "The Unified Thought of Jonathan Edwards," *Thought* 47 (1972), 59.

writings that the problem of the problem of Edwards has itself become something of a problem.[18][!]

The chief catalyst to contemporary scholarly interest in Edwards is Perry Miller, whose interpretive biography *Jonathan Edwards* generated no lack of positive and negative responses to his creative interpretations. Miller's Edwards was a modern, a disciple of John Locke, a lonely genius out of place and beyond his peers (indeed, he was "so much ahead of his time that our own can hardly be said to have caught up with him").[19] He rejected the "highly legalistic" "Federal Theology" of New England, but was nonetheless tragic[20] in his captivity to his Calvinistic tradition.[21] But as a philosopher, distanced from his biblical and God-centered focus, he was both

---

[18] William Sparkes Morris, *The Young Jonathan Edwards: A Reconstruction*, vol. 14 of *Chicago Studies in the History of American Religion* (Brooklyn, N.Y.: Carlson Pub., 1991), 4.

[19] Perry Miller, *Jonathan Edwards* (1981; repr., Amherst: The University of Massachusetts Press, 1949), xxxii. The view of Edwards' heavy dependence upon John Locke has its genesis in Hopkins' well known account of Edwards at Yale reading Locke with more pleasure "than the most greedy miser, when gathering up handfuls of silver and gold from some newly discovered treasure." Cited in Cherry, *The Theology of Jonathan Edwards: A Reappraisal*, 15. Per Winslow, Edwards' realm is the "realm of Locke, or Newton, and of all those to whom reality is primarily of the mind and spirit." Ola Elizabeth Winslow, *Jonathan Edwards, 1703-1758* (1975; repr., New York: Octagon, 1940), 73.

[20] Miller echoes Henry B. Parkes, who described Edwards' career as "the most tragic in American history." Henry Bamford Parkes, *Jonathan Edwards, the Fiery Puritan* (New York: Minton, Balch & Company, 1930), 254.

[21] Miller, *Jonathan Edwards*, 30-32, 47. Miller incorrectly interprets "Federal Theology" as a means of predestinarians to "offer rational men certain inducements for their attempting to open negotiations," providing "a way for human enterprise in the midst of a system of determinism," thus arguing for a split between Edwards, the lone defender of a more pure Calvinism, and New England Calvinists. Miller, *Jonathan Edwards*, 30, 47. Edwards was both a Federal theologian and was not alone in New England as a theologian of grace. See Carl W. Bogue, *Jonathan Edwards and the Covenant of Grace* (Cherry Hill, NJ: Mack Publishing Company, 1975); Brand, *Profile of the Last Puritan: Jonathan Edwards, Self-Love, and the Dawn of the Beatific*, 79-109; Cherry, *The Theology of Jonathan Edwards: A Reappraisal*.

brilliant and acceptable to modern scholarship.[22] Many followed Miller, who's *Edwards* held sway for three decades, and still stands as a seminal work for contemporary scholars.

Conrad Cherry's *Theology of Jonathan Edwards* marks the next significant milestone in Edwards scholarship, whose convincing treatment did much to correct Miller's unbalanced and often inaccurate portrait of Edwards. Cherry's Edwards was "a Calvinist theologian; and, as a Calvinist theologian, he claimed the heritage

---

[22] Miller's following comment typifies this view: "I agree that if one stops with the surface narrative, *A History of the Work of Redemption* sounds like a story book for fundamentalists, and is hardly to be mentioned with Gibbon, Marx, Spengler, or Toynbee. Measured against modern scholarship, textual criticism, archeology, and comparative religions, it is an absurd book....If Edwards' book be read as a study of this problem [problem of history], and the superficial narrative [i.e., biblical narrative] be stripped from the philosophical thesis, it becomes a pioneer work in American historiography." Miller, *Jonathan Edwards*, 310-11. In his introduction to Miller, Weber notes that *Jonathan Edwards* "marks a turning point in the history of Edwards criticism: here was an Edwards shaken loose from the weight of revival brimstone; no longer rebuked as the misanthropic author of 'Sinners in the Hands of an Angry God,' but presented as a 'modern,' better understood in the twentieth century than in his own time," vi. With respect to pre-Miller responses to Edwards, McClymond writes: "If Edwards was praised...he was praised for his resolute orthodoxy and unstinting Calvinism. If Edwards was condemned...he was condemned for negating human values, for asserting God at the expense of humanity. Perry Miller changed the rules of the game. One could learn from Edwards without adhering to his creed." McClymond, *Encounters with God: An Approach to the Theology of Jonathan Edwards*, 3. Or, as James Hoopes put it, "to so use Edwards [to attack modern liberals], Miller had to render him palatable to modern readers and rescue him from the liberals' image of an inhuman preacher of fiery hell." Hoopes, "Jonathan Edwards's Religious Psychology," 849. Sweeney notes, "in the words of historian Bruce Kuklick, Edwards proved far more attractive and serviceable to secular intellectuals when portrayed by Perry Miller as 'one of us—close to being an atheist for Niebuhr.' But now that Edwards has been unmasked as an evangelical supernaturalist and committed parish pastor (ironically—and regrettably for Kuklick—by Miller's Edition), his thought 'is not likely to compel the attention of intellectuals ever again. Indeed,' argues Kuklick, 'it is more likely to repel their attention.'" Douglas A. Sweeney, "A Plentiful Harvest," *Books and Culture*, (November/December 2003). See also Bruce Kuklick, "Review Essay: An Edwards for the Millennium," *Religion and American Culture* 11 (2001).

of his New England forefathers."[23] According to Stephen Stein, Cherry "challenged the hegemony" of Miller's account of Edwards,

> and thereby contributed to the opening of a new chapter in the study of this influential New England minister.... For Cherry there is no question that William Ames, Richard Sibbes, Thomas Shepherd, and other reformed theologians were substantially more significant for Edwards than John Locke and Isaac Newton. Edwards used the new philosophy of his day in the service of theology rather than as a primary pursuit in its own right.[24]

As Cherry put it, "his philosophical and scientific interests were bent to a theological purpose."[25] Subsequent to Cherry, Carl Bogue's extensively documented *Jonathan Edwards and the Covenant of Grace* removed any possible doubts that Edwards was a thoroughgoing covenantal theologian and a Calvinist.[26]

Increasingly, others challenged Miller's Lockean thesis. Norman Fiering posits an Edwards far more eclectic in his sources of philosophical thought and intimately acquainted with continental philosophical debates: "Many of Edwards's most characteristic philosophical ideas can be traced to intellectual principles and trends that long antedated Locke's *Essay* and in fact had essentially theological roots....To assume that Edwards was in some way derivative from Locke, either by direct positive influence of even by way of negative reaction against Locke, is a serious error...and gives rise to a profound misclassification of Edwards as

---

[23] Cherry, *The Theology of Jonathan Edwards: A Reappraisal*, 3.
[24] Stephen J. Stein, "Foreword" in Cherry, *The Theology of Jonathan Edwards: A Reappraisal*, ix.
[25] Cherry, *The Theology of Jonathan Edwards: A Reappraisal*, 4.
[26] Bogue, *Jonathan Edwards and the Covenant of Grace*. See also Schafer's "Editor's Introduction" in Jonathan Edwards, *The "Miscellanies," a–500*, ed. Thomas A. Schafer, 2002 Corrected ed., vol. 13 of *The Works of Jonathan Edwards* (New Haven: Yale University Press, 1994), 39-40.

a thinker."[27] For William Morris, Edwards borrowed from Locke and others, but in the Scholastic Calvinists Heereboord and Burgersdicius "found the structuring principles whereby he was able to relate his philosophy to his theology."[28] Others, such as Elwood, Ramsay, Helm, Anderson, and Bogue, admit to Edwards' use of Locke, but generally reject Miller's Lockean thesis.[29]

Neo-orthodox theologians represent a significant group of interpreters that typically see in Edwards a greater focus upon theology, with his philosophical thought as a compatible handmaiden to his overall God-centered focus. For instance, in a helpful "prolegomenon to the theology of Edwards," Haroutunian correctly writes, "His supreme passion was 'the glory of God in the face of

---

[27] "Edwards belongs not with Locke but with Locke's rivals, with Norris and Bishop Berkeley and Malebranche in a group that Louis Loeb in a fine recent book has called the 'theocentric metaphysicians,' a sub-branch of the so-called Continental school. It is significant that all the members of this group were clergymen and determined to introduce philosophy that not only was perfectly compatible with Christian dogma but that would deliberately employ philosophy, in Henry More's phrase, to build stronger fences around theology." Norman Fiering, "The Rationalist Foundations of Jonathan Edwards," in *Jonathan Edwards and the American Experience* (New York: Oxford University Press, 1988), 77. Fiering makes a compelling case.

[28] Morris, *The Young Jonathan Edwards: A Reconstruction*, 3. Morris' work is the most extensive single discussion of the sources of Edwards' thought available.

[29] For instance, Helm notes that "Edwards was not an empiricist, and it is too much to say that his philosophy was Locke-inspired; he draws on arguments from 'the new way of ideas' only when these serve his wider aims." Paul Helm, "John Locke and Jonathan Edwards: A Reconsideration," *Journal of the History of Philosophy* 8 (1969), 51. See also "Editor's Introduction" in Bogue, *Jonathan Edwards and the Covenant of Grace*; Jonathan Edwards, *Freedom of the Will*, ed. Paul Ramsey, vol. 1 of *The Works of Jonathan Edwards* (New Haven: Yale University Press, 1957); Jonathan Edwards, *Scientific and Philosophical Writings*, ed. Wallace E. Anderson, vol. 6 of *The Works of Jonathan Edwards* (New Haven: Yale University Press, 1980); Douglas J. Elwood, *The Philosophical Theology of Jonathan Edwards* (New York: Columbia University Press, 1960). "Editor's Introduction to 'Images of Divine things' and 'Types,'" in Jonathan Edwards, *Typological Writings*, ed. Wallace E. Anderson, Jr., Mason I. Lowance, and David H. Watters, vol. 11 of *The Works of Jonathan Edwards* (New Haven: Yale University Press, 1993); Paul Helm, "A Forensic Dilemma: John Locke and Jonathan Edwards on Personal Identity," in *Jonathan Edwards: Philosophical Theologian*, ed. Paul Helm and Oliver D. Crisp (Burlington, VT: Ashgate, 2003).

Jesus Christ'....and saw in Christ God's end and design in creating the world."[30] Nonetheless, neo-orthodox interpreters, in general, are often guilty of making Edwards after their own image.[31] H. Richard Niebuhr is representative of this group, of whom Weber writes, "Niebuhr's Edwards is not a Parrington anachronism but rather a fellow neo-orthodox social critic whose visions of humanity's limits and the tendencies of historical 'progress' spoke powerfully to the religious sensibility of the 1950s."[32] Douglas Elwood rightly places Edwards' philosophical thought in its proper relationship with his theology, and correctly sees Edwards as a "Calvinist with a difference,"[33] while overstating a perceived discontinuity between Edwards and his theological tradition in viewing him as the "first real Augustinian Calvinist in America."[34] Insightfully, he sees that Edwards' "purpose was not to reformulate eighteenth-century ideas in terms of Christian thought but to

---

[30] Joseph Haroutunian, "Jonathan Edwards: Theologian of the Great Commandment," *Theology Today* 1 (1944), 368. This concise article is an excellent summary of the overall thought of Edwards. In what Sweeney calls a "widely influential neo-orthodox jeremiad against New England's alleged declension after Edwards," Haroutunian's neo-orthodox read of Edwards is more evident in Joseph Haroutunian, *Piety Versus Moralism: The Passing of the New England Theology* (1964; repr., New York: Harper & Row Publishers, 1932). For Sweeney's revisionist view of New England Theology after Edwards, see Douglas A. Sweeney, *Nathaniel Taylor, New Haven Theology, and the Legacy of Jonathan Edwards* (New York: Oxford University Press, 2003).

[31] To better understand the grid through which neo-orthodox interpreters often view Edwards, it helps to understand their interpretation of Calvin and Protestant Scholasticism in general. Broadly speaking, neo-orthodox theologians often view Protestant Scholasticism as deviating from their perception of Calvin's more warm and pristine doctrine of grace into a colder legalistic frame, with Karl Barth, and neo-orthodoxy in general, representing a return to the more pure orthodoxy of Calvin (though some also see problems with Calvin). Edwards is often enlisted into their ranks by a remake into the image of Barth and by viewing him as breaking ranks with the Protestant Scholastic theological tradition. Additionally, he is often shorn of his more fundamentalist and exclusivist trappings.

[32] Donald Weber, "The Recovery of Jonathan Edwards," in *Jonathan Edwards and the American Experience*, ed. Nathan O. Hatch; Harry S. Stout (New York: Oxford University Press, 1988), 65.

[33] Elwood, *The Philosophical Theology of Jonathan Edwards*, 155.

[34] Ibid., 153.

restate Christian thought in terms of eighteenth-century ideas."[35] Nonetheless, he gives a neo-orthodox slant to Edwards' doctrine of Scripture and illumination, and sees in Edwards a neo-orthodox universal and inclusivistic triumph of grace, in viewing Edwards' ontology as "more compatible with a theory of universal restoration in which God's sovereignty is fully and finally realized." Additionally, Edwards' sermons on condemnation are "an experiment in evangelism," both symbolic and an expression of "the experience of the threat of self-exclusion from eternal life in God," but of no real and ultimate eternal judgment.[36] Robert Jenson's *America's Theologian* is also reflective of this category of interpretation. According to Marsden, "Jenson, in his enthusiasm to make Edwards relevant to 20th-Century America, wants to create a new Edwards. To put it briefly, he wants to make Edwards into Karl Barth....we often cannot tell where Edwards ends and where Barth or Jenson begins."[37] Harold Simonson does the same.[38] Stephen R. Holmes' analysis and critique of Edwards from a Barthian perspective rightly sees the glory of God in all things as central to Edwards' thought, while avoiding much of the neo-orthodox tendency to remake Edwards into Barth as noted above.[39]

Therefore, while neo-orthodox interpreters did much to remedy an unbalanced focus on Edwards' philosophy as separate from his God-centered theology, they were often guilty of superimposing 20th century neo-orthodox perspectives upon his 18th century Calvinistic thought. And while Haroutunian correctly identified

---

[35] Ibid., 159.
[36] Ibid., 79-80.
[37] George M. Marsden, "The Edwardsian Vision," *The Reformed Journal* 39, (June 1989), 24.
[38] While helpful in directing his focus to the theology of Edwards, he nonetheless enlists Edwards as a neo-orthodox critic of Protestant Scholasticism: "In bringing new life to this nonlegalistic covenant of grace, Edwards struck at the foundations of New England Covenant Theology, which for generations had favored the logic of works." Simonson appears to see Edwards as Barth at almost every turn. Harold Peter Simonson, *Jonathan Edwards, Theologian of the Heart* (Grand Rapids: W.B. Eerdmans, 1974), 43.
[39] Stephen R. Holmes, *God of Grace and God of Glory: An Account of the Theology of Jonathan Edwards* (Grand Rapids: W.B. Eerdmans., 2001).

"the glory of God in the face of Jesus Christ" as Edwards' supreme passion, an adequate treatment of Christ's redeeming satisfaction of God's perfect justice as the display of that glory remains wanting in neo-orthodox Edwardsean scholarship.

Progress toward a fundamental unifying notion within Edwards' thought advanced with the publication of several pioneering works. Roland Delattre's comprehensive *Beauty and Sensibility in the Thought of Jonathan Edwards*[40] analyzes the meaning and interrelatedness of Edwards' *True Virtue, Religious Affections* and *The End for Which God Created the World*, positing beauty as the sole organizing principle in Edwards' thought. Holbrook, while granting the centrality and importance of beauty, argues that beauty is "an ingredient in Being itself," so "being, not beauty, was to be foundational to true virtue."[41] Similarly, Fiering argues that "the moral perfection of willing (or loving or consenting to) the diversity of existence created and unified by God (called by Edwards "excellency") is the primary quality in Edwards's ethical ontology, not beauty."[42] For Fiering, the Trinity was the ground of Edwards' moral theology.[43] Leonard Riforgiato summarizes, "Edwards' on-

---

[40] Roland André Delattre, *Beauty and Sensibility in the Thought of Jonathan Edwards: An Essay in Aesthetics and Theological Ethics* (New Haven: Yale University Press, 1968). See also Terence Erdt, *Jonathan Edwards: Art and the Sense of the Heart* (Amherst: University of Massachusetts Press, 1980).
[41] "The term 'beauty' by itself explains nothing unless it is considered not only in terms of both proportion and symmetry, but also in terms of certain spiritual attitudes. Beauty is thus not simply beauty, but holiness, charity, loving kindness, glory, etc., as numerous passages of the *Religious Affections* show." Holbrook, *The Ethics of Jonathan Edwards; Morality and Aesthetics*, 171-2.
[42] Norman Fiering, *Jonathan Edwards's Moral Thought and Its British Context* (Chapel Hill: Published for the Institute of Early American History and Culture, Williamsburg, Virginia, by the University of North Carolina Press, 1981), 81.
[43] "The best model, perhaps, by which to comprehend Edwards's conception of excellency and the 'consent of being to being' is the idea of the Trinity. The Trinity for Edwards was never an inert dogma. His entire moral theology is logically deductible from his theology of the Trinity alone, although unquestionably it worked the other way, too, and some of Edwards's insights into moral psychology contributed to his understanding of the Trinity. It is possible that Edwards arrived at a profound understanding of the Trinity only after formulating the salient ideas of his moral thought, but in terms of logical order in Edwards's

14 *The Infinite Merit of Christ*

tology, derived from his cosmology, harmonized with his theology. All three, moreover, were derived from his Trinitarian model."[44] Thus a Trinitarian theocentrism is increasingly being viewed as the unifying ground of Edwards thought.[45]

In his influential *Philosophical Theology of Jonathan Edwards,* Sang Hyun Lee argues that in "a thoroughgoing metaphysical reconstruction, a reconception of the nature of reality itself," Edwards "departed from the traditional western metaphysics of substance and form and replaced it with a strikingly modern conception of reality as a dynamic network of dispositional forces and habits." For Lee, "dispositional ontology" is "the key to the particular character of Edwards' modernity as well as the interpretive clue for the underlying logic, the original vision, in terms of which Edwards' thought can be seen as a unity."[46] Morimoto and McDermott utilize Lee's dispositional ontology as a point of departure

---

system, the Trinity comes first." Fiering, *Jonathan Edwards's Moral Thought and Its British Context*, 82.

[44] Riforgiato, "The Unified Thought of Jonathan Edwards," 610.

[45] Amy Plantinga Pauw's 1990 doctoral dissertation provided a significant treatment of Edwards and the Trinity, later published in 2002, see Amy Plantinga Pauw, *The Supreme Harmony of All: The Trinitarian Theology of Jonathan Edwards* (Grand Rapids: W.B. Eerdmans, 2002). For a noteworthy critique of Pauw's interpretation and use of Western and Eastern Trinitarian "paradigms," Edwards' trinitarianism, and her contention that Edwards often departed from the traditional doctrine of divine simplicity, see Steven Michael Studebaker, "Jonathan Edwards' Social Augustinian Trinitarianism: A Criticism of and an Alternative to Recent Interpretations" (Marquette University, 2003). Other notable works related to Edwards' trinitarianism include Robert W. Caldwell, III, *Communion in the Spirit: The Holy Spirit as the Bond of Union in the Theology of Jonathan Edwards*, Studies in Evangelical History and Thought (Carlisle, U.K.: Paternoster, 2007); William J. Danaher, Jr., *The Trinitarian Ethics of Jonathan Edwards*, Columbia Series in Reformed Theology (Louisville: Westminster John Knox Press, 2004); Jonathan Edwards, *Writings on the Trinity, Grace, and Faith*, ed. Sang Hyun Lee, vol. 21 of *The Works of Jonathan Edwards* (New Haven: Yale University Press, 2003); Jasper Reid, "The Trinitarian Metaphysics of Jonathan Edwards and Nicolas Malebranche," *The Heythrop Journal* 43, no. 2 (2002); Richard M. Webber, "The Trinitarian Theology of Jonathan Edwards: An Investigation of Charges against Its Orthodoxy," *Journal of the Evangelical Theological Society* 44 (2001).

[46] Sang Hyun Lee, *The Philosophical Theology of Jonathan Edwards* (Princeton: Princeton University Press, 1988), 3-4.

for their more inclusivistic interpretations of Edwards' doctrine of justification. Morimoto and Hunsinger argue that Edwards held to a kind of justification via congruent merit.[47] McDermott, introducing "a strange new Edwards," argues that Edwards, in his use of the *Prisca Theologia* to refute Deism, moved to a broader view of the extent of revelation as compared to Calvin, as well as to a potentially wider view of salvation through his application of his "dispositional ontology" to soteriology.[48] For Holmes, Lee's thesis is "mistaken" and "Edwards did not need a dispositional ontology, and he did not use a dispositional ontology."[49] While granting some of Lee's insights, Bombaro sees "a theocentrism of ends" as "the foremost regulative principle" of Edwards' "philosophical theology," not dispositional ontology.[50] He argues that Morimoto and McDermott go astray in three ways: 1) in their "unqualified acceptance of Lee's explanation of Edwardsean dispositions," 2) in "their refusal to read Edwards according to his admittedly...confessional theological position," and 3) "perhaps most importantly, they fail to work with deference to the grand scale and organic nature of Edwards' theocentric and telic-oriented theological and metaphysical system."[51]

---

[47] See Anri Morimoto, *Jonathan Edwards and the Catholic Vision of Salvation* (University Park: Pennsylvania State University Press, 1995). George Hunsinger, "Dispositional Soteriology: Jonathan Edwards on Justification by Faith Alone," *The Westminster Theological Journal* 66, Part 1 (2004).
[48] Gerald R. McDermott, *Jonathan Edwards Confronts the Gods: Christian Theology, Enlightenment Religion, and Non-Christian Faiths* (New York: Oxford University Press, 2000).
[49] Stephen R. Holmes, "Does Jonathan Edwards Use a Dispositional Ontology? A Response to Sang Hyun Lee," in *Jonathan Edwards: Philosophical Theologian*, ed. Paul Helm; Oliver D. Crisp (Burlington: Ashgate, 2003), 110.
[50] John Bombaro, "The Formulation of Jonathan Edwards' Theocentric Metaphysics: Part One of Four," *The Clarion Review* 1 (2004), 10.
[51] Bombaro, "The Formulation of Jonathan Edwards' Theocentric Metaphysics: Part One of Four," 10. See also John J. Bombaro, "Jonathan Edwards's Vision of Salvation," *Westminster Theological Journal* 65 (2003), 48. Here he effectively argues that "Morimoto and McDermott misinterpret Edwards' philosophy of dispositions and, consequently, his soteriology, evangelistic engagement with unbelievers, and vision of the history of the work of redemption." Bombaro concludes that Edwards, "in no uncertain terms, resolutely denies that non-Christians have gracious dispositions and therefore epistemological access to

McClymond, in a speculative stretch, also sees in Edwards a possible inclusivistic tendency, noting "striking" similarities (despite "differences, far too numerous to indicate") between the "unfinished *History of the Work of Redemption* alongside these mid- to late-twentieth-century trends in American theology" as typified by Tillich's "theology of cultures."[52] Peter Gay is more on the mark, however: "We can only speculate how Edwards would have transformed his sermons on redemption into a book of history. This much is certain: he would not have discarded, or modified, their classical Puritan theology....In the midst of the greatest revolu-

---

truly moral and spiritual dimensions of reality. In a word, no gracious disposition means no regeneration, no salvation, no spiritual data, and no justification. Second, his soteriology does not permit a hard and fast distinction between regeneration and conversion; indeed, he often uses the terms interchangeably. Third, Edwards does not divorce regenerating grace from the divinely ordained means of special revelation—the word of God. There may be extraordinary cases, but on the whole Edwards remains skeptical and restrictivistic. To him, unregenerates cannot access regenerating grace in natural revelation because the oral tradition of the *prisca theologia* (a) was never intended to redeem, that is, it was not an 'ends' but a 'means'; (b) was superseded by special revelation in a covenantal context; and (c) was contextualized within the history of redemption as being merely preparatory for that which does facilitate regenerative salvation—the gospel means of Christ," 48. Building on Lee's interpretation of Edwards' dispositional ontology, Morimoto and McDermott interpret Edwards soteriologically where Lee would not go. See Lee's "Editor's Introduction" in *Works* 21:1-106, and Sang Hyun Lee, "Grace and Justification by Faith Alone," in *The Princeton Companion to Jonathan Edwards*, ed. Sang Hyun Lee (Princeton: Princeton University Press, 2005). See also Greg D. Gilbert, "The Nations Will Worship: Jonathan Edwards and the Salvation of the Heathen," *Trinity Journal* 23NS (2002); Gerald R. McDermott, "Response to Gilbert: 'the Nations Will Worship: Jonathan Edwards and the Salvation of the Heathen,'" *Trinity Journal* 23NS (2002). Pauw follows Lee's "dispositional ontology" interpretation in her treatment of Edwards' trinitarianism. Pauw, *The Supreme Harmony of All: The Trinitarian Theology of Jonathan Edwards*, 80-89.

[52] Michael J. McClymond, "A Different Legacy?" in *Jonathan Edwards at Home and Abroad: Historical Memories, Cultural Movements, Global Horizons*, ed. David William Kling; Douglas A. Sweeney (Columbia: University of South Carolina Press, 2003), 33-34. Allen saw Edwards as "the forerunner of the later New England transcendentalism quite as truly as the author of a modified Calvinism" and saw universalists such as Thomas Erskine, McLeod Campbell, and Bishop Ewing as "the true continuators of the work of Jonathan Edwards." Allen, *Jonathan Edwards*, 388-389.

tion in the European mind since Christianity had overwhelmed paganism, Edwards serenely reaffirmed the faith of his fathers."[53]

Increasingly, contemporary scholars are more attentive to the theological foundations and nuances of his thought, with philosophy more accurately seen as doing service to his God-centered agenda.[54] For instance, greater attention is being given to Edwards' sermons as forming an important part of his chief theological concerns,[55] and though relatively scant attention has been given by modern interpreters to Edwards' exegesis of Scripture,[56] there ap-

---

[53] Gay, *A Loss of Mastery; Puritan Historians in Colonial America*, 91.

[54] Fiering notes, "Edwards was an Enlightenment figure only in the limited sense that he entered fully into dialogue with some of the philosophers of the British Enlightenment; his purpose, contrary to that of the *philosophe*, was to turn the best thought of his time to the advantage of God." Fiering, *Jonathan Edwards's Moral Thought and Its British Context*, 61.

[55] Of the numerous recent publications of Edwards' sermons, the six Yale *Works* volumes are the most significant, including Jonathan Edwards, *Sermons and Discourses, 1720-1723*, ed. Wilson H. Kimnach, vol. 10 of *The Works of Jonathan Edwards* (New Haven: Yale University Press, 1992); Jonathan Edwards, *Sermons and Discourses, 1723-1729*, ed. Kenneth P. Minkema, vol. 14 of *The Works of Jonathan Edwards* (New Haven: Yale University Press, 1997); Jonathan Edwards, *Sermons and Discourses, 1730-1733*, ed. Mark Valeri, vol. 17 of *The Works of Jonathan Edwards*, (New Haven: Yale University Press, 1999); Jonathan Edwards, *Sermons and Discourses, 1734-1738*, ed. M. X. Lesser, vol. 19 of *The Works of Jonathan Edwards* (New Haven: Yale University Press, 2001); Jonathan Edwards, *Sermons and Discourses, 1739-1742*, ed. Harry S. Stout, Nathan O. Hatch, and Kyle P. Farley, vol. 22 of *The Works of Jonathan Edwards* (New Haven: Yale University Press, 2003); Jonathan Edwards, *Sermons and Discourses, 1743-1758*, ed. Wilson H. Kimnach, vol. 25 of *The Works of Jonathan Edwards* (New Haven and London: Yale University Press, 2006). Wilson Kimnach's "General Introduction" in volume 10 is an excellent introduction to this critical part of Edwards' ministry. Also, the extensive posting of previously unpublished sermon material on the Jonathan Edwards Center website is likely to increase scholarly interest in this area.

[56] Sweeney writes, "Jonathan Edwards was a biblicist—one whose world revolved around the words of Scripture…modern scholars have yet to come close to understanding the ways in which Edwards's life was animated by what he deemed God's word. Three hundred years after Edwards's birth, and a half a century into what some have called the Edwards renaissance, few have bothered to study Edwards's extensive exegetical writings. While preoccupied with his roles in America's 'public' life and letters, and failing to see the public significance of his biblical exegesis, we have neglected the scholarly work that he took most seriously."

pears to be a growing consideration of Edwards' dependence upon Scripture as the first and last authority in all matters metaphysical, philosophical, and theological.[57] The recent Yale publication of *The Blank Bible* will likely contribute to a greater understanding of the importance of Edwards' interpretation of Scripture as central to his thought and his relationship to his theological tradition, as Edwards and his Calvinist peers and predecessors shared a mutual dependence upon Scripture as the authoritative source for their theology. Furthermore, as the interpretive grid through which Edwards' writings are viewed is increasingly adjusted to reflect the worldview of Edwards himself, specific works will be more accurately interpreted in light of the whole of his thought. The process is slow and labor-intensive, but hopeful and fruitful nonetheless, for Edwards is far less "enigmatic" and "elusive" when the various aspects of his thought (philosophical, scientific, pastoral, ethical, political, theological, *et al*) are seen in light of his God-centered focus and concerns.[58]

Douglas A. Sweeney, "'Longing for More and More of It'? The Strange Career of Jonathan Edwards's Exegetical Assertions," in *Jonathan Edwards at 300: Essays on the Tercentenary of His Birth*, ed. Harry S. Stout, Kenneth P. Minkema, and Caleb J. D. Maskell (Lanham, MD: University Press of America, 2005), 25-26.

[57] For instance, see Thomas F. Atchison, "Towards Developing a Theology of Christian Assurance from 1 John with Reference to Jonathan Edwards," *DAI* 65, no. 02A (2004); Robert E. Brown, *Jonathan Edwards and the Bible* (Bloomington: Indiana University Press, 2002); Jonathan Edwards, *Notes on Scripture*, ed. Stephen J. Stein, vol. 15 of *The Works of Jonathan Edwards* (New Haven: Yale University Press, 1998); Edwards, *The "Blank Bible"*; Samuel T. Logan, "The Hermeneutics of Jonathan Edwards," *Westminster Theological Journal* 43 (1980); Allyn Lee Ricketts, "The Primacy of Revelation in the Philosophical Theology of Jonathan Edwards," *DAI* 56, no. 05A (1995); Stephen J. Stein, "Quest for the Spiritual Sense: The Biblical Hermeneutics of Jonathan Edwards," *Harvard Theological Review* 70 (1977); Stephen J. Stein, "The Spirit and the Word: Jonathan Edwards and Scriptural Exegesis," in *Jonathan Edwards and the American Experience*, ed. Nathan O. Hatch; Harry S. Stout (New York: Oxford University Press, 1988); Ralph G. Turnbull, *Jonathan Edwards the Preacher* (Grand Rapids: Baker Book House, 1958); Brandon G. Withrow, "'Full of Wondrous and Glorious Things': The Exegetical Mind of Jonathan Edwards in His Anglo-American Cultural Context," *DAI* 68, no. 10A (2007).

[58] When apologetics is viewed as both a subset and application of theology, Nichols is correct in positing, "the key to understanding Edwards is to understand

The primary purpose of the present work is to contribute to a further understanding of Edwards' coherent, systematic, and God-centered worldview by an exposition of a central Christological and redemptive facet of his Trinitarian thought. As noted above, recent scholarship has seen a growing identification of the Trinity as the interpretive key and foundation to Edwards' thought; however, despite progress in understanding Edwards' Trinitarian thought, relatively little work has been done with respect to his theology of the person and redemptive work of Christ, the second person of the Trinity.[59] It is likely that this aspect of his theology has been neglected, in part, for the same reason his philosophical thinking has been over-emphasized or treated in abstraction from his theology, for in Edwards' doctrine of Christ one is brought face-to-face with the facet of his narrow biblical and exclusivist thought that is disagreeable to modern sensibilities, as is evident in the brief survey of Edwards scholarship above. Such, however, is central to Edwards' pastoral and theological concerns (as predominantly reflected in his sermons), and to his understanding of the overall Trinitarian purpose of God in displaying His excellence in and through creation and the person and redemptive work of Christ.[60] For Edwards, "the infinite excellency, greatness, and glory of God is the foundation of all religion,"[61] and "never were God's perfections manifested so gloriously as they have been manifested in the work of redemption; never did his infinite glories so

---

him as an apologist. By its nature, apologetics brings together philosophy and theology, theory and practice....His concern for apologetics explains his various roles as theologian, philosopher, and pastor....Edwards's theology is philosophically informed, and his philosophy is theologically informed; both enrich each other." Nichols, *An Absolute Sort of Certainty: The Holy Spirit and the Apologetics of Jonathan Edwards*, 18.

[59] Kimnach, in introducing Edwards' sermon on 1 Corinthians 11:3, "Of God The Father," rightly notes that the center of Edwards' theology is the Trinity, "his favorite theological mystery," and the work of redemption, "his favorite paradigm of theology," *Works* 25:143.

[60] "Dissertation Concerning the End for Which God Created the World," in Jonathan Edwards, *Ethical Writings*, ed. Paul Ramsey, vol. 8 (New Haven: Yale University Press, 1989), 433, 439, 441, 443, 452, 459, 467-536.

[61] "God's Excellencies," *Works* 10:425. Schafer dates this sermon to the summer of 1722, see *Works* 10:645.

brightly shine forth as in the face of Jesus Christ,"[62] the defense of which motivated much of his polemical works, the proclamation of which filled his sermons, and the understanding of which formed the focal point of his interpretation of history.[63] Indeed, Edwards describes his intended but never completed *magnum opus* on the history of redemption as

> a Body of Divinity in an entire new method, being thrown in the form of a history, considering the affair of Christian theology, as the whole of it, in each part, stands in reference to the great work of redemption by Jesus Christ; which I suppose is to be the grand design, of all God's designs, and the summum and ultimum of all the divine operations and degrees; particularly considering all parts of the grand scheme in their historical order.[64]

Thus, from the time of his earliest sermons until the end of his life, the person and redemptive work of Christ were the foundation of Edwards' Trinitarian theology. In this modest and narrow exposition of Edwards' understanding of the merits of Christ's obedience, I intend to show that this Christological and redemptive aspect of Edwards' theology is central to his overall God-centered and Trinitarian thought and the key to understanding his view of the nature, purpose and acts of the Triune God. For the ultimate purpose of God to display and communicate His glory is accomplished through the person and redemptive work of Christ.

---

[62] "God's Excellencies," *Works* 10:415. "The gospel is by far the most glorious manifestation of God's glory that ever was made to man." "Glorious Grace," *Works* 10:396.

[63] As most notably seen in Jonathan Edwards, *A History of the Work of Redemption*, ed. John F. Wilson, vol. 9 of *The Works of Jonathan Edwards* (New Haven: Yale University Press, 1989).

[64] Samuel Hopkins, *The Life and Character of the Late Reverend Mr. Jonathan Edwards* (Boston: 1765), 77. Quoted by Schafer in the "Editor's Introduction" in *Works* 10:72. For the full text of Edwards' comments, see Edwards' letter, "To the Trustees of the College of New Jersey," in Jonathan Edwards, *Letters and Personal Writings*, ed. George S. Claghorn, vol. 16 of *The Works of Jonathan Edwards* (New Haven: 1998), 727-8.

Moreover, this Christological and redemptive facet of Edwards Trinitarian thought is the key to understanding Edwards' doctrine of justification, for "the highest glory of the gospel and the delight of the Scriptures is this very doctrine of justification through the righteousness of Christ obtained by faith."[65] For example, speculation with respect to perceived inclusivistic tendencies based on a narrow survey of particular passages, or in Edwards' interest in non-Christian religions, must take into consideration the broader Christological and redemptive aspects of Edwards Trinitarian thought. Bombarro correctly identifies deficiencies in the interpretations of Morimoto and McDermott in this regard in that they refuse "to read Edwards according to his admittedly…confessional theological position," and "fail to work with deference to the grand scale and organic nature of Edwards' theocentric and telic-oriented theological and metaphysical system."[66] While the present work does not directly respond to Morimoto or McDermott, it does further elucidate Christological and redemptive aspects of Edwards' theology that should be considered in any interpretation of his thought, for the Christological and redemptive aspects of Edwards' Trinitarian theology are at odds with inclusivistic reads of Edwards' doctrine of justification. An inclusivistic doctrine of justification is incompatible with the center and foundation of his thought, as with the interdependent fabric of his theology derived from that foundation. For Edwards,

> God's design of glorifying his free grace by Jesus Christ.... is the design which God has had upon his heart from all eternity…for which indeed he made this world and in subordination to which he orders and disposes all things. In this way, God always intended to glorify himself and

---

[65] "A Sinner is Not Justified in the Sight of God Except Through the Righteousness of Christ Obtained by Faith," otherwise known as and hereafter referred to as Edwards' *Quaestio*, preached on the occasion of his M.A. commencement at Yale, in *Works* 14:60.
[66] Bombaro, "The Formulation of Jonathan Edwards' Theocentric Metaphysics: Part One of Four," 10.

his Son. They therefore that think to be saved by their own righteousness…overthrow this whole design.[67]

For Edwards, the doctrine of justification by grace is founded upon the absolute necessity of perfect conformity to God's unchanging rule of righteousness for the attaining of eternal life. As will be seen below, Edwards understood the only possible means by which God can justify the ungodly to be the merits of Christ's perfect fulfillment and satisfaction of God's unchanging rule of righteousness, accomplished through His entire life of perfect obedience to the Father, to the infinite extent of death, to the honor and fulfillment of God's justice, applied to believers via union with Christ by faith.

The discussion of Edwards' understanding of the merits of Christ's obedience in light of God's unchanging rule of righteousness will proceed as follows: Chapter one examines the ultimate Trinitarian purpose of God to display and communicate His glory through the Father's gift of a bride for His Son. God's purpose will be accomplished through Christ's redemption of sinners by perfect obedience to God's rule of righteousness. Chapter two examines the pre-temporal Trinitarian and covenantal arrangement that is the foundation of Christ's obedience, highlighting the love of the Father in His purpose to save a people, the love of the Son in His purpose to save a people and willingly undertake to accomplish that salvation, and the love of the Father in promising great rewards to the Son for His voluntary obedience to the terms of the covenant. Chapter three examines the temporal covenantal basis of Christ's perfect obedience, including the necessity of Adam's obedience to obtain eternal life, the command to Adam as representative of God's unalterable rule of righteousness, and the requirement of God to always uphold the honor of His authority according to His unchanging nature. Chapter four looks at the absolute need for Christ's perfect obedience in light of Adam's sin as surety for mankind, the immutability of God's righteousness despite Adam's sin, the infinite guilt of sin and the

---

[67] "None Are Saved by Their Own Righteousness," *Works* 14:336-7.

need of an infinite remedy, God's requirement of a perfect positive righteousness and exclusion of an imperfect righteousness for justification, Christ's perfect satisfaction of God's unalterable rule of righteousness, and God's nature as a righteous judge to uphold His rule of perfect righteousness always, despite Christ having met its requirement. Chapter five examines the voluntary nature of Christ's perfect obedience as the basis of its merit, the extent of the merit as infinite, the righteousness of Christ's perfect obedience as the righteousness by which sinners are justified, the willful act of Christ laying down His life as the greatest and infinitely meritorious act of Christ, the nature of all of Christ's acts in His humiliation as both propitiatory and meritorious, the rewards earned by Christ on behalf of those for whom He was surety, all to the accomplishment of God's ultimate purpose to display and communicate His glory.

In presenting a narrow, systematic, theological picture of Edwards' view of the merits of Christ's perfect obedience, I will rely primarily upon published and unpublished sermons and discourses, as well as *The "Miscellanies," The "Blank Bible", A History of the Work of Redemption*, and *The End for Which God Created the World*, with attention given to Edwards' biblical support for the doctrine. And while historical and contextual concerns are important, their consideration will necessarily be constrained by the limited scope and purpose of this work. Nonetheless, every attempt will be made to avoid the eisegesis of modern, Reformed, or other thought into his mind or context. In light of the history of Edwards scholarship as described above, the great need is for Edwards to speak for himself. Erroneous views of Edwards have been passed from decade to decade as scholars build upon each other's work, while the critical need for detailed exposition of Edwards himself is often neglected. The most egregious example is Perry Miller's *Jonathan Edwards*, where his interpretations held sway for decades without a single footnote. In light of these concerns, this work will be heavily documented, with Edwards being allowed to speak for himself as much as possible, with interaction with secondary interpreters within the body of the work self-consciously kept to a minimum. Those Edwards scholars familiar with the history of Edwards' scholarship, particularly of the last sixty years, will have no problem seeing the implications of this exposition with respect to many of the soteriological and Trinitarian interpretations of Edwards. To those new to the field, my hope is that this approach will provide a fair exposition of Edwards' Christ-centered Trinitarian thought. Additionally, in taking a systematic approach to the subject I do not deny progress in Edwards' understanding of the topic, as there is indeed progress, though primarily with respect to the depth and breadth of his exposition. Many of the basic theological principles of the doctrine at hand can be found in his early sermons, including his M.A. *Quaestio* of 1723,[68] and in a more comprehensive and detailed form in his 1729 discourse, *The Threefold Work of the Holy Spirit*. Nonetheless, the subtle and often profound nuances of Edwards' thought concerning the glory of God in Christ's obedience are best seen in a broad and comprehensive look at his works. Accordingly, my exposition may appear repetitious or redundant at times as I attempt to capture subtle and highly nuanced distinctions concerning a rather narrow topic. My hope, however, is that this approach will provide the reader with a more complete picture of the depth of Edwards' thinking concerning the interrelated and mutually dependent facets of the person and work of Christ in the fulfillment of God's ultimate purpose.

---

[68] See *Works* 14:47-66.

CHAPTER ONE

God's Ultimate Purpose Is To Display And Communicate His Glory Through Christ's Perfect Obedience To God's Rule of Righteousness

In his introduction to Edwards' sermon on 1 Corinthians 11:3, Wilson Kimnach makes the following observation:

> Edwards links the doctrine of the Trinity to that of the work of redemption, identifying his favorite theological mystery with his favorite paradigm of theology. Having arrived, as it were, at the center of his theology, Edwards introduces the metaphor of the family, the controlling metaphor of the entire sermon.[1]

What Kimnach describes as Edwards' "favorite theological mystery" is indeed the foundation of the entirety of Edwards' theological thought concerning the nature, purpose, and works of God, while his "favorite paradigm" is the means by which God accomplishes His ultimate purpose in all things. That purpose is to display His glory in the person and work of Christ and communicate

---
[1] *Works* 25:143.

His glory in redeeming sinners to a participation in the love and glory of the Trinity. Indeed, in the work of Christ in redemption, in His meritorious obedience to God's unalterable rule of righteousness, in His accomplishment of the ultimate Trinitarian purpose of the display and communication of God's glory, we have arrived at the center of Jonathan Edwards' theology.

In the present chapter, the following aspects of Edwards' theology relating to God's ultimate purpose in displaying and communicating His glory through the person and redemptive work of Christ will be examined. First, God's glory is defined as the flowing forth of His excellence and happiness, while His ultimate purpose in all things concerns His glory in the display and communication of His excellence and happiness to His creatures. Second, Christ's perfect obedience is the ultimate Trinitarian work to *display* God's glory. Third, Christ's obedience is the ultimate Trinitarian work to *communicate* God's glory in the purchase of His bride, the elect. And last, God's ultimate purpose will be complete in the happiness of the elect in their viewing and enjoying God's excellence forever in heaven. Thus, in the present chapter, Edwards' view of the Trinitarian foundation of Christ's work in the ultimate purpose of God will provide the basis for understanding his view of Christ's redemptive work as the fulfillment of God's unchanging rule of righteousness in chapters two and following.

God's Glory Is His Excellency and Happiness Flowing Forth

The glory of God, as it relates to God fulfilling His ultimate purpose in the meritorious obedience of Christ in the redemption of sinners, provides the foundation and unifying thread throughout the entirety of Edwards' theology.[2] "God's glory, as it is spoken of in Scripture," is "the end of all God's works."[3] Defined briefly,

---

[2] Edwards most complete and in-depth treatment of God's glory and ultimate purpose is found in "EGCW," *Works* 8:405-536.

[3] M 1266[a], Jonathan Edwards, *The "Miscellanies," 1153-1360*, ed. Douglas A. Sweeney, vol. 23 of *The Works of Jonathan Edwards* (New Haven: Yale University Press, 2004), 213.

God's glory is the "the excellency of God flowing forth," like the "*shechinah* of old,"[4] an "emanation" of "the fullness of God,"[5] "the flowing out of his goodness, or the communication of his fullness of happiness."[6]

> Glory is a shining forth, an effulgence; so the glory of God is the shining forth or effulgence of his perfections, or the communication of his perfections, for effulgence is the communication of light....So that the glory of God is the shining forth of his perfections; and the world was created that they might shine forth, that is, that they might be communicated.[7]

Moreover, the glory of God in the shining forth of His excellent perfections to the created world has its source in the glory displayed and communicated between the persons of the Trinity in their intra-Trinitarian relationships (in the theological terms used by Edwards, the display of the perfections of God *ad extra*, literally "to outside," has its source in the display and communication of the perfections of God *ad intra*, literally "to within").[8]

> God is glorified within himself these two ways: (1) by appearing or being manifested to himself in his own perfect idea, or, in his Son, who is the brightness of his glory; (2) by enjoying and delighting in himself, by flowing forth in

---

[4] M 1082, Jonathan Edwards, *The "Miscellanies," 833-1152*, ed. Amy Plantinga Pauw, vol. 20 of *The Works of Jonathan Edwards* (New Haven: Yale University Press, 2002), 465.
[5] M 1266[a], *Works* 23:213.
[6] M 1094, *Works* 20:482. In support, Edwards cites the parallel use of the term "glory" in Ephesians 2:16, Romans 9:22-23, and Philippians 4:19, with the use of the terms "grace" and "goodness" in Ephesians 1:7, 2:4, 2:7, and 3:8. Citing Exodus 33:18-19, he writes: "When Moses besought God to show him his glory, God answered, 'I will make all my goodness to pass before thee,'" 483.
[7] M 247, *Works* 13:361.
[8] Discussion of Edwards' doctrine of the Trinity will be brief and limited to showing his understanding of the inseparability and dependence of the person and redemptive work of Christ to the nature and ultimate purpose of the Trinity. For Edwards' most comprehensive treatment of the Trinity in a single work, see "Discourse on the Trinity," *Works* 21:113-144.

> infinite love and delight towards himself, or, in his Holy Spirit.[9]

In other words, as the glory of God in the excellent perfections of the Son is displayed to the understanding of the Father, and as the Father, by the Holy Spirit, loves and rejoices in the display of His perfections in the Son, so also God is glorified in His display of His perfections to the understanding of His creatures, and in their love and rejoicing in the sight of His glory. Thus God is glorified toward his creatures *ad extra* as a reflection of His *ad intra* glory, in that the souls created in His image also have "understanding and will, idea and love, as God hath," differing only "in perfection of degree and manner." Thus, in displaying and communicating His glory to His creatures, he manifests Himself to their understanding, and communicates himself to their heart.[10]

> So God glorifies himself toward the creatures also two ways: (1) by appearing to them, being manifested to their understandings; (2) in communicating himself to their hearts, and in their rejoicing and delighting in, and enjoying the manifestations which he makes of himself. They both of them may be called his glory in the more extensive sense of the word, viz. his shining forth, or the going forth of his excellency, beauty and essential glory *ad extra*.[11]

Accordingly, the display and communication of God's *ad intra* glory *ad extra* is according to the procession and economic nature of the persons of the Trinity.

> This twofold emanation or communication of the divine fullness *ad extra* is answerable to the twofold emanation or going forth of the Godhead *ad intra*, wherein the internal and essential glory and fullness of the Godhead consists,

---

[9] M 448, *Works* 13:495.

[10] "Discourse on the Trinity," *Works* 12:113.

[11] M 448, *Works* 13:495. Citing John 1:14, "And we beheld his glory as of the only begotten of the Father, full of grace and truth," Edwards associates "manifestation" with "truth," and "communication" with "grace." M 1094, *Works* 20:483.

> viz. the proceeding of the eternal Son of God, God's eternal idea and infinite understanding and wisdom and the brightness of his glory, whereby his beauty and excellency appears to him; and the proceeding of the Holy Spirit, or the eternal will, temper, disposition of the Deity, the infinite fullness of God's holiness, joy, and delight.[12]

Moreover, included in the display and communication of God's perfections is "all that is great and good in the Deity," including His "excellent sweetness and blessedness" and "infinite fountain of happiness," often described in Scripture as "the fountain of life, the water of life, the river of God's pleasures, God's light, etc."[13] In other words, as the glory of God includes the happiness and joy of God in the "proceeding" of the Holy Spirit in the intra-Trinitarian relationship of the Father, Son, and Holy Spirit, so in communicating His glory, God makes His creatures happy in communicating to them His own happiness by giving them the Holy Spirit.

> Happiness is very often in Scripture called by the name of glory, or included in that name in Scripture. God's eternal glory includes his blessedness, and when we read of the glorifying of Christ, and the glory which the Father has given him, it includes his heavenly joy. And so when we read of the glory promised to or conferred on the saints, and their being glorified, the unspeakable happiness is a main thing intended. Their joy is full of glory, and they are made happy in partaking of Christ's glory. The fullness of the saints' happiness is the riches of God's glory in the saints. Therefore the diffusing the sweetness and blessedness of the divine nature is God's glorifying himself, in a Scripture sense, as well as his manifesting his perfection to their understandings.[14]

---

[12] M 1266[a], *Works* 23:213. See also M 1082, *Works* 20:465-6. Edwards cross references M 1084 and 1094.

[13] M 1082, *Works* 20:465. See also "Discourse on the Trinity," *Works* 21:129.

[14] M 1082, *Works* 20:466.

Therefore, as God is glorified *ad intra* in the *display* of His perfections in the Son, as well as in the *communication* of His glory in the flowing forth of the infinite love of Himself in His Holy Spirit, so also God manifests His glory to the understanding of His creatures in the revelation of the excellence of His perfections in the Son, and in communicating His glory to the hearts of His creatures in making them participants in His holiness and happiness by the Holy Spirit.

> God communicates himself to the understanding in the manifestation that is made of the divine excellency and the understanding, idea or view which intelligent creatures have of it. He communicates his glory and fullness to the wills of sensible, willing, active beings in their rejoicing in the manifested glory of God, in their admiring it, in their loving God for it, and being in all respects affected and disposed suitably to such glory…and in their being themselves holy, and having the image of his glory in their hearts, and as it were partaking of God's brightness, and in their being happy in God, whereby they partake of God's fullness of happiness.[15]

Moreover, "the Holy Ghost is God's love and delight, because the saints' communion with God consists in their partaking of the Holy Ghost."[16] In communion with the Father and Son, the saints "partake with the Father and Son of their good, which is their excellency and glory." They partake of God's divine nature (His holiness and happiness), by "partaking of the same Holy Spirit."[17]

---

[15] M 1266[a], *Works* 23:213.

[16] "Discourse on the Trinity," *Works* 21:129. Edwards cites 1 John 1:3. See also M 330, *Works* 13:409: "It appears that the Holy Spirit is the holiness, or excellency and delight of God, because our communion with God and with Christ consists in our partaking of the Holy Ghost (II Cor. 13:14; I Cor. 6:17; I John 3:24, and 4:13)."

[17] "Discourse on the Trinity," *Works* 21:129-30. Edwards cites 2 Peter 1:4, "Ye are made partakers of the divine nature"; Hebrews 12:10, "That we might be partakers of His holiness"; John 17:22-23, "And the glory which thou hast given me I have given them; that they may be one, even as we are one: I in them, and thou in me"; and John 17:13, "That they may have my joy fulfilled themselves."

God's people "derive their holiness from Christ as the fountain of it. He gives it by his Spirit, so that 'tis Christ's holiness communicated, 'tis the light of the sun reflected."[18] "It is the office of the person that is God's idea and understanding to be the light of the world, to communicate understanding, so 'tis the office of the person that is God's love to communicate divine love to the creature."[19]

> Whatsoever in the work of redemption is done immediately in or upon men's souls is the work of the Spirit, whether it be actually making them partakers of this redemption, by converting them and uniting them to Christ, and carrying on {grace in their hearts}[20] and making them perfect in holiness in heaven, and filling them with happiness.[21]

---

[18] "None Are Saved by Their Own Righteousness," *Works* 14:340-1. "There is a two-fold righteousness that the saints have: an imputed righteousness, and 'tis this only that avails anything to justification; and an inherent righteousness, that is, that holiness and grace which is in the hearts and lives of the saints. This is Christ's righteousness as well as imputed righteousness: imputed righteousness is Christ's righteousness accepted for them, inherent holiness is Christ's righteousness communicated to them. They derive their holiness from Christ as the fountain of it. He gives it by his Spirit, so that 'tis Christ's holiness communicated, 'tis the light of the sun reflected. Now God takes delight in the saints for both these: both for Christ's righteousness imputed and for Christ's holiness communicated, though 'tis the former only that avails anything to justification."

[19] "Discourse on the Trinity," *Works* 21:123. See 121-131 for Edwards' biblical support for his understanding of the Holy Spirit as God's holiness, love, and joy.

[20] Brackets are used in the Edwards text taken from *Works* 14 and *Works* 25 and are used by the editor to identify repeated phrases in the sermon manuscripts identified by Edwards by a long dash. See *Works* 14:xiii or *Works* 25:xiii.

[21] "The Threefold Work of the Holy Ghost," *Works* 14:378. An adequate treatment of the *application* of redemption is beyond the present scope, as this work concerns the *accomplishment* of redemption, though both are ultimately the work of Christ. As will be discussed below, Christ "merits" or "purchases" the Holy Spirit by the perfection of His redemptive work, and it is Christ who gives the Holy Spirit to those whom He redeemed. It is by Christ giving the Holy Spirit that the elect are united to Him, and it is the Holy Spirit Himself that is the very bond of that union. See M 341 and M 376, *Works* 13:415, 448.

Moreover, not only is the Holy Spirit He who communicates the divine holiness, love and happiness of God to the creature, "the sum of all that Christ purchased for man was the Holy Ghost" Himself.[22]

> Christ purchased for us that we should have the favor of God and might enjoy his love; but this love is the Holy Ghost. Christ purchased for us true spiritual excellency, grace and holiness, the sum of which is love to God, which is but only the indwelling of the Holy Ghost in the heart. Christ purchased for us spiritual joy and comfort, which is in a participation of God's joy and happiness; which joy and happiness is the Holy Ghost, as we have shown. The Holy Ghost is the sum of all good things.[23]

Therefore, God is glorified to a greater degree when His creatures not only see the display of His glory, but "rejoice" and "delight" in His glory, as that very delight is the Holy Spirit dwelling within the believer. God communicates His glory "that it might [be] received both by the mind and heart."[24]

> God is glorified not only by his glory's being seen, but by its being rejoiced in, when those that see it delight in it: God is more glorified than if they only see it; his glory is then received by the whole soul, both by the understanding and by the heart. God made the world that he might

---

[22] "Discourse on the Trinity," *Works* 21:136.
[23] "Discourse on the Trinity," *Works* 21:136.
[24] M 448, *Works* 13:495. This is consistent with Edwards' description of the nature of the soul in *The Religious Affections*, wherein he describes the soul's faculties as *understanding* and *heart* or *will*. For Edwards, unregenerate people may see and understand God's glory, but according to their fallen nature are nonetheless "disinclined" or "averse" to it in not seeing and loving its beauty. The regenerate believer, according to his or her new nature, by virtue of the indwelling Holy Spirit, both understands and loves the sight of God's glory, seeing and loving its beauty for what it is. Jonathan Edwards, *Religious Affections*, ed. John Edwin Smith, vol. 2 of *The Works of Jonathan Edwards* (New Haven: Yale University Press, 1959), 96-7, 253-266.

communicate, and the creature receive, his glory, but that it might [be] received both by the mind and heart.[25]

The love that is the Father's delight in the Son and the Son's delight in the Father is the very same love that is God's delight in the believer as the Holy Spirit dwells and manifests within the believer His holiness, love, and delight in God. To summarize:

> God communicates himself to the understanding of the creature, in giving him the knowledge of his glory; and to the will of the creature, in giving him holiness, consisting primarily in the love of God: and in giving the creature happiness, chiefly consisting in joy in God. These are the sum of that emanation of divine fullness called in Scripture, "the glory of God."[26]

And that glory, displayed and communicated to the believer in the giving of the Holy Spirit, is purchased by the redeeming work of Christ.

The Display of His Glory and Communication of His Happiness Are One Work of God

As Edwards understood the glory of God to include both the *display* and *communication* of the perfections and happiness of God, so he did not consider the glory of God and the happiness of His creatures as contrary, separate, or distinct purposes of God; rather, they are of one and the same ultimate purpose of God in the shining forth of His "internal glory or fullness" to His creatures.[27]

> These two things ought [not] to be separated when we speak of God's end in the creation of the world, as the assembly of divines in speaking of the chief end for which man was created have judiciously united glorifying and

---

[25] M 448, *Works* 13:495.
[26] "EGCW," *Works* 8:529.
[27] "EGCW," *Works* 8:530-1.

enjoying {God}. Indeed, God's communicating himself and glorifying {himself} ought not to be looked upon as though they were two distinct ends, but as what together makes one last end, as glorifying God and enjoying {God} make one chief end of man.[28]

"God and the creature, in this affair of the emanation of the divine fullness, are not properly set in opposition," nor are "God's glory and the creature's good to be spoken of as if they were properly and entirely distinct," for they are "implied one in the other."[29]

God in seeking his glory, therein seeks the good of his creatures: because the emanation of his glory (which he

---

[28] "Approaching the End of God's Grand Design," *Works* 25:116-7. See also M 1218, *Works* 23:150-3. This particular "Miscellanies" entry is source material for Edwards' treatise *The End for Which God Created the World* and reflects Edwards' mature thought with respect to God glorifying Himself and communicating His happiness to the creature as one ultimate purpose of God. In contrast, in the early entry M 243 he stated, "God's glory is a good independent of the happiness of the creature." *Works* 13:358-9. Additional early entries identifying the happiness of the creature as an ultimate end of God include M 3, *Works*, 13:199; M 104, *Works* 13:272; M 106, *Works* 13:276; M 332, *Works* 13:410. Ramsey notes that M 1080 "marked the beginning of JE's mature and thorough study of the meaning of glory in Scripture and soon rendered untenable the notion of 'fellow' ends expressed in those early Miscellanies" [M 243 and M 247]. See "The End for which God Created the World," *Works* 8:519, fn 5. In M 1066 Edwards posits that "language seems to be defective and to want a proper general word to express the supreme end of the creation and of all God's works, including both those two as branches of it, viz. God's glorifying himself or causing his glory and perfection to shine forth, and his communicating himself or communicating his fullness and happiness.... Both are sometimes in Scripture included in one word, namely, God's being glorified.... Both these things are plainly signified by God's glory in Is. 6:3." M 1066, *Works* 20:446. Also, with respect to God's purpose in creation, Edwards' writes: "The Spirit of God don't seem to be to represent God's ultimate end as manifold, but as one. For though it be signified by various names, yet they appear not to be names of different things, but various names involving each other in their meaning; either different names of the same thing, or names of several parts of one whole, or of the same whole viewed in various lights, or in its different respects and relations. For it appears that all that is ever spoken of in the Scripture as an ultimate end of God's works is included in that one phrase, 'the glory of God.'" "EGCW," *Works* 8:526. See also, 527-8.

[29] "EGCW," *Works* 8:458-9.

> seeks and delights in, as he delights in himself and his own eternal glory) implies the communicated excellency and happiness of his creature. And that in communicating his fullness for them, he does it for himself: because their good, which he seeks, is so much in union and communion with himself. God is their good. Their excellency and happiness is nothing but the emanation and expression of God's glory: God in seeking their glory and happiness, seeks himself: and in seeking himself, i.e. himself diffused and expressed (which he delights in, as he delights in his own beauty and fullness), he seeks their glory and happiness.[30]

In rejoicing in the happiness He communicates to His creatures in giving them the Holy Spirit, God rejoices in His own glory as the excellence and happiness of His creatures display His very own excellence.

> 'Tis easy to conceive how God should seek the good of the creature, consisting in the creature's knowledge and holiness, and even his happiness, from a supreme regard to himself; as his happiness arises from that which is an image and participation of God's own beauty; and consists in the creature's exercising a supreme regard to God and complacence in him; in beholding God's glory, in esteeming and loving it, and rejoicing in it, and in his exercising and testifying love and supreme respect to God: which is the same thing with the creature's exalting God as his chief good, and making him his supreme end.[31]

Further, as the holiness and happiness of the creature and the glory of God cannot be viewed as separate purposes of God, and as the excellence in the creature is the excellence of God communicated to the creature, God has no need of the creature.

---

[30] "EGCW," *Works* 8:459.
[31] "EGCW," *Works* 8:533.

> God stands in no need of creatures, and is not profited by them; neither can his happiness be said to be added to by the creature. But yet God has a real and proper delight in the excellency and happiness of his creatures. He hath a real delight in the excellency and loveliness of the creature, in his own image in the creature, as that is a manifestation, or expression, or shining forth of his own loveliness. God has a real delight in his own loveliness, and he also has a real delight in the shining forth or glorifying of it.[32]

Thus, God delights in His creatures insofar as they display His own holiness and happiness communicated to them.[33] For God, "there is his delight in the act, and in the fruit. The act is the exercise of his own perfection, and the fruit is himself expressed and communicated."[34] Hence, it is from a "regard to Himself that inclines him to seek the good of his creature" and "disposes him to diffuse and communicate himself," in which "exhibitions, expressions, and communications" of His glory He delights.[35]

---

[32] M 679, Jonathan Edwards, *The "Miscellanies," 501-832*, ed. Ava Chamberlain, vol. 18 of *The Works of Jonathan Edwards* (New Haven: Yale University Press, 2000), 237-8.

[33] While a treatment of the nature of the creature's renewal to a proper sight and love of the excellence of God at salvation is beyond the present scope of this work, it is worthwhile to note that this renewal is the foremost effect of the Holy Spirit taking permanent residence in the believer at the point of faith (replacing the hostility of the unregenerate unbeliever). It constitutes the chief foundation for all genuine fruit of a true salvation or conversion, as presented in Edwards' treatise *The Religious Affections*. Thus, in light of the ultimate Trinitarian purpose as understood by Edwards, there can be no fulfillment of that purpose of glorifying Himself in manifesting *and* communicating his perfections to His creatures without the renewal or "regeneration" of the creature and the fruit of sight and love to the excellence of God. See *Works* 2:197-291. See also Atchison, "Towards Developing a Theology of Christian Assurance from 1 John with Reference to Jonathan Edwards." Atchison examines Edwards' understanding of regeneration bringing the believer into a loving relationship with the Father, Son, and Holy Spirit with respect to contemporary discussions of assurance.

[34] M 679, *Works* 18:239. See also Edwards' *Discourse on the Trinity* for an in-depth discussion of this point in *Works* 21:129-30, 136-7, 141-3. See also "EGCW," *Works* 8:446-7.

[35] "EGCW," *Works* 8:452, see also 532.

> The emanation of communication of the divine fullness, consisting in the knowledge of God, love to God, and joy in God, has relation indeed both to God and the creature: but it has relation to God as its fountain, as it is an emanation from God; and as the communication itself, or thing communicated, is something divine, something of God, something of his internal fullness; as the water in the stream is something of the fountain; and as the beams are of the sun....In the creature's knowing, esteeming, loving, rejoicing in, and praising God, the glory of God is both exhibited and acknowledged; his fullness is received and returned.[36]

"All our good is of God the Father; 'tis all through God the Son; and all in the Holy Ghost, as he is himself all our good."[37] Further, in creating a union of love with His creatures, the interest of the creature becomes the interest of God.

> God's respect to the creature's good, and his respect to himself, is not a divided respect; but both are united in one, as the happiness of the creature aimed at is happiness in union with himself. The creature is no further happy with this happiness which God makes his ultimate end than he becomes one with God.[38]

To summarize the discussion so far, Edwards defines the glory of God as the shining forth of His excellent perfections. Internally, the glory of God is displayed and communicated among the persons of the Trinity in the Son reflecting the excellent perfections of the Father, in the Father viewing His own excellence in the perfections of the Son, and in the Father's joy and love of those perfections by the Holy Spirit, the love between the persons of the Trinity. In the same manner, God accomplishes His ultimate purpose to display and communicate His glory to His creatures in His glory displayed in the person and redeeming work of Christ, and

---
[36] "EGCW," *Works* 8:531.
[37] "Discourse on the Trinity," *Works* 21:137.
[38] "EGCW," *Works* 8:533. See also 534-5.

in the giving of the Holy Spirit to believers by whom they love and rejoice in the excellence of the Son and the Father. Consequently, God's ultimate purpose to glorify Himself is one and the same with His purpose to communicate His happiness to His creatures, the whole of which is accomplished in and through the person and redeeming work of Christ.

Christ's Obedience Is God's Ultimate Means to Display His Glory

The person and work of Christ is the "grand medium" by which the ultimate purpose of God to display and communicate His glory is accomplished.

> God's work from the beginning of the universe to the end, and in all parts of the universe, appears to be but one. 'Tis all one design carried on, one affair managed in all God's dispensations, towards all intelligent beings, viz. the glorifying and communicating himself in and through his Son Jesus Christ as God-man and by the work of redemption of fallen man.[39]

Christ, in His incarnation, life, death, and exaltation, is God's great instrument in the manifestation and communication of His excellent perfections.[40] Christ is "the greatest instrument of glorifying God that ever was," and the "great means or author of the glory of God."[41] For Edwards, such is the clear testimony of Scripture.[42] For instance, in commenting on John 17:4-5, concerning

---

[39] M 744, *Works* 18:388.

[40] Regarding the wisdom of God in the incarnation, see M 392 and M 395 in *Works* 13:455, 461.

[41] M 526, *Works* 18:70.

[42] In a section entitled "'Tis manifest from Scripture that God's glory is the last end of that great work of providence, the work of redemption by Jesus Christ," Edwards lists the following verses in support: John 17:18, 12:27-28, 29-31, 23-24, 17:4-5, 13:31-32; Philippians 2:6-11; Ephesians 1:3-14; 2 Corinthians 4:14-15; Psalm 79:9; Isaiah 44:23, 48:10-11, 49:3. "EGCW," *Works* 8:485-489.

Christ's prayer to the Father before His betrayal and crucifixion, he writes:

> "I have glorified thee on earth: I have finished the work which thou gavest me to do. And now, O Father, glorify thou me with thine own self." Here 'tis pretty plain that declaring to his Father that he had glorified him on earth, and finished the work God gave him to do, meant that he had finished the work which God gave him to do for this end, viz. that he might be glorified. He had now finished that foundation that he came into the world to lay for his glory. He had laid a foundation for his Father's obtaining his will, and the utmost that he designed. By which it is manifest that God's glory was the utmost of his design, or his ultimate end in this great work.[43]

The foundation laid by Christ in His incarnation and earthly ministry was to reach its zenith in His suffering and death, where the glory of God will be manifest in its greatest light.

> This design is great and wonderful, and attended with such great difficulties that require the exceeding display of the infinite fullness of the divine nature to accomplish it. The design is of that nature that it contains such difficulties that no finite wisdom could conceive of a way, because of the nature of the subject pitched upon, especially to answer this great design—fallen man, ruined mankind—difficulties in the way of the invention of any finite wisdom, innumerable and altogether insurmountable, requiring an extraordinary display of divine power. But more especially, an extraordinary display of divine grace: here is a great occasion for the manifestation of the fullness of God's heart. In the creatures' unworthiness and misery is [an] extraordinary occasion for opening the treasury of infinite riches and fullness of the divine nature.[44]

---

[43] "EGCW," *Works* 8:486.
[44] "Approaching the End of God's Grand Design," *Works* 25:119.

The work of redemption was to be the greatest display of the excellent perfections of God, including His divine wisdom, power, and grace. "Mercy and justice do gloriously and wondrously illustrate one another in the work of redemption," for thereby is God's grace manifest in giving His only Son to suffer the full weight of the punishment for sin to maintain His "immutable justice."[45] In the vindication of God's justice, the infinite love of the Father and Son is displayed and God's glory is "advanced."

> Hereby was most clearly manifested to men and angels the distinction of the persons of the Trinity. The infinite love of the Father to the Son is thereby manifested, in that for his sake he would forgive an infinite debt, would be reconciled with and receive into his favor and to his enjoyment those that had rebelled against him and injured his infinite majesty, and in exalting of him to that high mediatorial glory; and Christ showed his infinite love to the Father in his infinitely abasing himself for the vindicating of his authority and the honor of his majesty. When God had a mind to save men, Christ infinitely laid out himself that the honor of God's majesty might be safe and that God's glory might be advanced.[46]

In dying for sinners, Christ "manifested an infinite regard to the glory of God," for "all God's perfections have their most glorious display in that way of salvation."[47] Even Satan's attempt to destroy mankind in Adam resulted in the exaltation of the elect to higher glory through the redemptive work of Christ,[48] for the wisdom of God turned the fall of man into "an occasion of manifesting the Glory of his Grace."[49] In all things, Christ is the means by which God manifests His glory.

---

[45] M 759, *Works* 18:405-6.
[46] M 327[a], *Works* 13:406.
[47] "Christ's Sacrifice an Inducement to His Ministers," *Works* 25:667.
[48] M 809, *Works* 18:515.
[49] "Romans 6:14," *Works of Jonathan Edwards Online*, eds. Harry S. Stout, Kennth P. Minkema, Caleb J. D. Maskell, 2005-, L. 7v. Note, I have cited the "manuscript view" of the sermons transcripts posted on *WJEO*. Accordingly, I have made my

The one grand medium by which he glorifies himself in all is Jesus Christ, God-man. All the tribute of his glory comes through his hands; in this eminent manner does the Son glorify the Father, which is what Christ has respect [to in] John 17:1, "Father, glorify thy Son, that thy Son also may glorify thee." "The only begotten that is in the bosom of the Father, he it is that declares the Father" (John 1:18). This person who is the "brightness of his glory" [Heb. 1:13] is he by whom God's glory shines forth, or by whom God has his declarative glory both in heaven and earth.[50]

Christ's Obedience Is God's Ultimate Means to Communicate His Glory

In addition to *displaying* the excellent perfections of God, Christ is the "grand medium" by which God achieves His ultimate purpose in *communicating* His glory.

> For God glorifies himself in communicating himself, and he communicates himself in glorifying himself. Jesus Christ, and that as God-man, is the grand medium by which God attains his end, both in communicating himself to the creatures and [in] glorifying himself by the creation.[51]

---

own small technical adjustments to the text for modern readability, including slight changes to punctuation, capital letters, the spelling out of abbreviations, spelling of words, and some minor grammatical adjustments.

[50] "Approaching the End of God's Grand Design," *Works* 25:116. Additional Scripture cited by Edwards in support of the doctrine that creation was for the purpose of the glory of God includes Isaiah 44:6, 48:12; Revelation 1:8,11,17, 21:6, 22:13; Romans 11:36; Colossians 1:16; Hebrews 2:10; Proverbs 16:4. "EGCW," *Works* 8:467. See also M 1080 for an extensive list of Scriptural support, *Works* 20:462-4.

[51] "Approaching the End of God's Grand Design," *Works* 25:117.

God Provides a Spouse for His Son to Communicate His Happiness and Glorify Himself

As the glory of God in creation reflects the glory of God in the intra-Trinitarian relations between the persons of the Godhead, so the Father's infinite love for the Son is central in God's ultimate purpose in manifesting and communicating His glory. In the Father's love and desire to bless and glorify the Son, He provides the gift of a pure and beautiful spouse to whom the Son can be united, through whom both He and the Son will be glorified.

> God's design in all the work {of creation} is to glorify his Son, and through him to glorify himself….God hath an infinite love to his [Son and] delights to put honor upon him….And the principal means by which God glorifies his Son in the world that is created is by providing him a spouse, to be presented [to] him in perfect union, in perfect purity, beauty and glory.[52]

As "the Son is the adequate communication of the Father's goodness" and "an express and complete image of him," so "the Son has also an inclination to communicate himself, in an image of his person that may partake of his happiness."[53] As the Father displays and communicates His glory to and through the Son, so also through the Father's gift of a spouse will the Son manifest and communicate His glory to and through His spouse.

> The way in which the eternal Son of God is glorified in the creation is by communicating himself to the creatures, not by receiving anything from the creatures. God the Son, having the infinite goodness of the divine nature in him, desired to have a proper object to whom he might communicate his goodness: to have this object in the nearest, strictest union with himself, and therefore desires (to speak of him after the manner of men) a spouse to be brought and presented to himself in such a near relation

---

[52] "Approaching the End of God's Grand Design," *Works* 25:117.
[53] M 104, *Works* 13:272.

and strict union as might give him the greatest advantage to communicate his goodness to her.[54]

The spouse to be chosen would be in a "fallen, miserable, helpless state," unable to give any good to the Son, one for whom Christ needed to suffer, and for whom Christ would willingly suffer in order to obtain her as His spouse, "because suffering is the greatest expression of goodness and manifestation of kindness." In this "great design" Christ would "bring her to come to him, present her to himself and make her perfectly beautiful, perfectly and unspeakably happy."[55] God created the world for this very purpose. Citing Ephesians 5:25, Edwards writes:

> "[Christ] loved the church and gave himself for it." And this is the way that God the Father intended to glorify his Son: the world was created that from thence Christ might obtain this spouse. This was God's portion and inheritance, [his] first fruits, his jewel, [his] darling. This was the great gift of God to the Son in the eternal work of redemption, the great promise of God to Christ, the joy set before him. These things seem very manifest by the holy Scripture, and God the Father in this way glorifies himself by thus glorifying his Son, Jesus Christ. This spouse of Christ is that part of the creation which God has made for his glory in an eminent manner. Is. 43:7, "Everyone that is called by my name: for I have created [him] for my glory." This is the way in which God presents elect men to him, viz. by presenting them to Christ. Being presented to Christ in perfect glory, Christ will present them to the Father. In subserviency to this design of thus presenting {the elect} are all things in heaven and earth managed, and that through all the varieties of God's dispositions.[56]

For Edwards, there is but "one great design in all," one scheme of God of which "all his manifold and various dispensations" and

---
[54] "Approaching the End of God's Grand Design," *Works* 25:117.
[55] "Approaching the End of God's Grand Design," *Works* 25:118.
[56] "Approaching the End of God's Grand Design," *Works* 25:118.

"various and manifold" works are intended, in which they all have their end, and "by which he will obtain his glory."

> The grand design and scheme and work of God in all his manifold works and dispensations is one.
>
> *Inq.* What is this one great design that God has in view in all his works and dispensations?
>
> *Ans.* 'Tis to present to his Son a spouse in perfect glory from amongst sinful, miserable mankind, blessing all that comply with his will in this matter and destroying all his enemies that oppose it, and so to communicate and glorify himself through Jesus Christ, God-man.[57]

God's "eternal purpose of creating the world, and of the sum of his purposes with respect to creatures, was to procure a spouse, or a mystical body, for his Son," that Christ might love them, and make them holy and happy.[58]

> The creation of the world seems to have been especially for this end, that the eternal Son of God might obtain a spouse, towards whom he might fully exercise the infinite benevolence of his nature, and to whom he might, as it were, open and pour forth all that immense fountain of condescension, love and grace that was in his heart, and that in this way God might be glorified.[59]

To rescue and obtain His bride, he left His glory in heaven to become a man and conquer the terrible enemies holding her captive.

---

[57] "Approaching the End of God's Grand Design," *Works* 25:116.
[58] M 1245, *Works* 23:178. See also "Approaching the End of God's Grand Design," *Works* 25:116, wherein Edwards cites Ephesians 1:10, 22.
[59] "The Church's Marriage to Her Sons, and to Her God," *Works* 25:187. In his comments on Psalm 136, Edwards writes: "This Psalm confirms me that an ultimate end of the creation of the world and of all God's works is his goodness, or the communication of his good, to his creatures. For this Psalm sufficiently teaches that all God's works, from the beginning of the world to the end of it, are works of mercy to his people, yea, even the works of his vindictive justice and wrath." *Works* 24:537.

God's Ultimate Purpose   45

For the "joy set before Him," the reward of her eternal happiness, He paid the ultimate price of suffering unto death, performing a greater work than His creation of the world.[60]

> But Christ had done greater things than to create the world, to obtain his bride and the joy of his espousals with her: for he was incarnate, and become man for this end; which was a greater thing than his creating the world. For the creator to *make* the creature was a great thing; but for him to *become* a creature was a greater thing. And he did a much greater thing still to obtain this joy; in that for this he laid down his life, and suffered even the death of the cross: for this he poured out his soul unto death, and he that is the Lord of the universe, God over all, blessed for evermore, offered himself a sacrifice, in both body and soul, in the flames of divine wrath. Christ obtains his elect spouse by conquest: for she was a captive in the hands of dreadful enemies, and rescue her out of their hands, that she might be his bride.[61]

And as a reward for Christ's perfect obedience to the Father in fulfilling the requirements for the purchase of His bride, God created the heavens for the wedding celebration and eternal glory of the bride and Bridegroom.

> And as God built the whole of the upper world to be an habitation for his dear Son, so when the time comes that God shall reward his Son for his perfect and great obedience, and finishing his great work appointed him to do, when the work he was appointed to in his office is all finished at the end of the world, and the time comes for him to receive his full reward, to be glorified with his complete and highest glory in the head and all his members, and all enter into heaven together at Christ's last and greatest ascension thither, the house shall be garnished and beau-

---

[60] Christ's spouse as "reward" will be discussed further in chapters two and five.
[61] "The Church's Marriage to Her Sons, and to Her God," *Works* 25:187.

> tiful exceedingly to make it fit for his reception in this his highest glory....The house shall be garnished to prepare it for the glorious Bridegroom, who shall enter into it with his blessed bride in her complete and perfect beauty, when they shall enter into heaven to celebrate the solemnity, and to partake of the glorious entertainments and joys of an eternal wedding.[62]

All God's Works Are for Christ's Work of Redemption

Further, as all of God's works are for the purpose of obtaining a spouse for the Son, and as the spouse is obtained by the Son through His work of redemption, so also all of God's works, including creation, providence, and the incarnation, life and death of Christ are for the purpose of Christ's work of redemption.

> Indeed, all the works of God that were before the fall of men were parts of the work of preparation for the work of redemption. The creation itself was so, and for this reason the creation of the world was committed into his hands. And there is no reason to suppose that part of this work of preparation was committed into Christ's hands, because it was a preparation for his work, and not other parts of the preparation for the same work. All things are for Christ for his use; and therefore God left it with him to prepare all things for his own use that in everything he might have the preeminence, and that in him might all fullness dwell, a perfect sufficiency every way for the design that he had to accomplish.[63]

"Christ was to be the great means of God's glory" by His work of redemption, "to which all other works, and even the creation of the world itself, were subordinate,"[64] rendering Christ's in-

---

[62] M 952, *Works* 20:212-3.
[63] M 833, *Works* 20:43-4.
[64] See Edwards' comments on Ephesians 3:9-10 wherein he also references Revelation 1:18 and Proverbs 8:27-31, *Works* 24:1100-1.

carnation a greater event than the creation of the world.[65] All things done until the time of Christ's incarnation were "preparatory" for Christ's humiliation (the period from His birth until His resurrection),[66] including all of God's works of providence, both "material and immaterial." "All other works of providence may be looked upon as *appendages* to this great work, or *things* which God does to subserve that grand design."[67] And as the gospel reveals the ultimate purpose of Christ entering the world, it also reveals the "grand mystery of all God's counsels and works" and "the treasures and divine wisdom and knowledge in God's proceedings," including "that infinite wisdom aimed [at] in the creation of the world, and the great things that he accomplishes in it from age to age."[68] Thus, the mystery of God's ultimate purpose in all things is revealed in Christ.

Further, God not only purposed all things for the redemptive work of Christ, He purposed all things in Christ and for the sake of Christ. "All things that God ever decreed he decreed for the sake of his beloved. And all was decreed to be brought to pass by his Son."[69] "All his purposes are included in the work of redemption and all that [he] has done or will do in fulfillment of those purposes, is done in and by Christ,"[70] including the creation and the consummation of the world, and all things between, culminating in the wedding and wedding feast of Christ and His spouse, the church.[71] For this reason Christ Himself created the world, for all things were created *by* Christ because all things were cre-

---

[65] *HWR, Works* 9:299.
[66] *HWR, Works* 9:294.
[67] M 702, *Works* 18:284.
[68] M 982, *Works* 20:301-2. Edwards cites Colossians 2:2-3 as support, "to the acknowledgment of the mystery of God, even of the Father and of Christ, in whom or in which are hid all the treasures of wisdom and knowledge."
[69] M 1245, *Works* 23:178.
[70] M 702, *Works* 18:297.
[71] M 702, *Works* 18:298. "The wedding feast is eternal; and the love and joys, the songs, entertainments and glories of the wedding never will be ended. It will be an everlasting wedding day."

ated *for* Christ and His work of redemption.[72] God gave to Christ to accomplish all that concerned salvation, that all should look to Him in complete trust, "that the faith of God's people might be encouraged and strengthened…and that Christ might have all the glory."[73] "He being the end of all God's works *ad extra*, therefore the accomplishment of all was committed to him."[74] Moreover, both the manner of Christ's creating the world, as well as the world itself as it exists in history, foreshadow and "point to" Christ and His redemptive work. Thus, in a most comprehensive sense, all things exist by and for Christ and His work of redemption for God's one and ultimate purpose of manifesting and communicating His glory.[75]

God's Purpose Is Complete in the Happiness of the Elect in Heaven

The display and communication of God's glory will ultimately be complete in heaven, the eternal home of Christ and His bride. Such will be the great reward for Christ in completing His redemptive work in perfect obedience to the Father. He "shall pos-

---

[72] See Edwards' commentary on Ephesians 3:9-10 wherein he also references Revelation 1:18 and Proverbs 8:27-31, *Works* 24:1100-1.

[73] "The Threefold Work of the Holy Ghost," *Works* 14:380-1. "For this end, God the Father appointed him ruler of the world, head over all things to the church, [and] gave the kingdom of providence into his hands. John 17:2, he gave him 'power over all flesh, that he should give eternal life to as many as he hast given him.' And for this end, the Holy Ghost became in the work subordinated to the Son, that Christ might [have] the whole work of salvation in his hands," 381.

[74] M 1245, *Works* 23:178. Edwards cites Colossians 1:15-19, "'Who is the image of the invisible God, the first born of every creature: for by him were all things created, that are in heaven,' etc., 'all things were created by him, and for him: and he is before all things, and by him all things consist. And he is the head of the body, the church: who is the beginning, the firstborn from the dead; that in all things he might have the preeminence. For it pleased the Father that in him should all fullness dwell.'"

[75] See M 702, *Works* 18:283-297, for a detailed discussion of this and Edwards' biblical support for the same. For Edwards' most comprehensive treatment of creation and history pointing to Christ and His work of redemption, see *A History of the Work of Redemption, Works* 9.

sess his church…made perfect, without spot or wrinkle, or any such thing, all in their consummate beauty, as a bride adorned for her husband, and all in their consummate happiness."[76] All that precedes this is preparatory to the consummation of all things in "the marriage of the Lamb," when the Son "shall obtain and bring home His wife," when the entire church, including each member, shall be "perfectly redeemed." And as all God's works are for this purpose, this is "in a sense the last of God's works."[77]

The Saints' Happiness in Heaven Is Viewing and Loving God's Excellency as Displayed and Communicated by Christ

As God is glorified in the display and communication of His holiness and happiness, and as that display and communication is by the grand medium of Christ in His redemptive work, so the saints' happiness in heaven will be as participants in God's ultimate purpose in viewing and loving Christ and His redemptive work. "The beatifical vision of God in heaven consists mostly in beholding the glory of God in the face of Jesus Christ, either in his work or in his person as appearing in the glorified human nature."[78] The saints will view God's glory in Christ as "the image of the invisible God," whose perfections shine forth most prominently in the acts and fruits of His redemptive work.[79] The souls of the saints in heaven will be "ravished" in beholding the "beauty and amiable

---

[76] M 742, *Works* 18:376. See also M 804, *Works* 18:506.

[77] M 946, *Works* 20:203.

[78] M 1137, *Works* 20:515. See also "True Saints, When Absent from the Body, Are Present with the Lord," *Works* 25:238. Edwards included the view of the ongoing works of redemption on earth as viewed by the saints already in heaven as part of the happiness of the saints in heaven. See M 917 and M 1061, *Works* 20:166, 429-30.

[79] M 777, *Works* 18:431. See also M 1137, *Works* 20:515, wherein Edwards notes that the rest of Christ into which saints enter, per Hebrews 4:4-11, "seems to argue…1. that the way that the saints will be happy in the beholding the glory of God will be very much in beholding the glory of his perfections in his works; 2. that the happiness of the saints in heaven, especially since Christ's ascension, consisting in beholding God's glory, will consist very much in seeing his glory in the work of redemption."

excellency of Christ as appearing in his virtues," in viewing the "height" and "sum" of His glory, "appearing in and by the exercise of dying love to them." In viewing Christ "they see the transcendent greatness of his love shining forth in the same act that they see the transcendent greatness of his loveliness shining forth."[80]

> They see everything in Christ that tends to kindle and enflame love, and everything that tends to gratify love, and everything that tends to satisfy them: and that in the most clear and glorious manner, without any darkness or delusion, without any impediment or interruption.[81]

What is seen by saints in their earthly body is mingled with darkness and the spiritual deformity of sin, but the vision of their "glorious redeemer," the "Sun of righteousness," will be seen "without clouds" and in full light in heaven.[82]

Moreover, the saints "have the additional pleasure of considering that this lovely virtue is imputed to them. 'Tis the lovely robe, and robe of love, with which they are covered."[83] Thus the glory of Christ's righteousness by which they are overwhelmed with joy is the righteousness in which they are covered, providing an additional basis of their great happiness in Christ.

United to Christ, the Saints Enjoy All the Blessings of Christ's Exaltation and Glory

In union with the head of the body, the happiness of Christ in heaven is the happiness of the saints in heaven. The bride of Christ, the church, has her happiness in union with the Bridegroom, in the perfection of "this mutual rejoicing of Christ and

---

[80] M 791, *Works* 18:494-5.
[81] "True Saints, When Absent from the Body, Are Present with the Lord," *Works* 25:230.
[82] "True Saints, When Absent from the Body, Are Present with the Lord," *Works* 25:230-1.
[83] M 791, *Works* 18:495.

his saints," in entering into marriage with Him at the time of their "glorification with Christ in heaven."[84]

> The church shall be brought to the full enjoyment of her bridegroom, having all tears wiped away from her eyes; and there shall be no more distance or absence. She shall then be brought to the entertainments of an eternal wedding feast, and to dwell eternally with her bridegroom; yea to dwell eternally in his embraces. Then Christ will give her his love; and she shall drink her fill, yea she shall swim in the ocean of his love.[85]

United to Christ in marriage, they participate in the joy of Christ's "exaltation and glory," His "enjoyment of the Father," His heavenly and earthy kingdom reign, the joy of the success of His redemptive work in His "justifying many by his righteousness, his conquering his enemies, his subduing and triumphing over Satan and Antichrist and all other enemies."[86] As the body of Christ, they enjoy what Christ enjoys.

> They are with him in his honor and advancement. They are with him in his pleasures; they are with him in his enjoyment of the Father's love, the love wherewith the Father loves him is in them, and he in them [John 17:22]. They are with him in the joy of his success on earth. They are with him in his joy at the conversion of one sinner.[87]

---

[84] "The Church's Marriage to Her Sons, and to Her God," *Works* 25:182. Edwards cites Matthew 25:10 and Psalm 45:15.

[85] "The Church's Marriage to Her Sons, and to Her God," *Works* 25:182, see also 183-4.

[86] M 1089 *Works* 20:469. See also "True Saints, When Absent from the Body, Are Present with the Lord," *Works* 25:236-41, wherein Edwards cites the following biblical support: Daniel 7:13-14; Psalm 37:11, 72:7, 149:5; Jeremiah 33:6; Micah 4:3; Isaiah 2:4, 11:6-9, 53:10-12, 57:1-2; Matthew 5:5, 19:28-9; Luke 15:4-6; Romans 8:17; 1 Corinthians 3:21-23; 2 Timothy 2:12; Hebrews 1:14, 11:39-40; Revelation 2:26-7, 3:21, 5:10, 11:15, Ch. 19.

[87] M 1089, *Works* 20:469, also 470-1. In support, Edwards cites Luke 15:5-6; Canticles 3:11; Isaiah 62:5; Zephaniah 3:17; Revelation 3:12, 7:9, 19:1-9, 14; Romans 16:20; Daniel 7:13-14; Psalm 110:1-3, 6, Colossians 1:24. See also "2 Thessalonians 2:14," *Works* 24:1123-4.

Thus, as God's ultimate purpose to manifest and communicate His perfections and happiness is complete in His marriage to His bride, so in union with Christ does the bride participate in the intimate union and love of the Father and the Son. The Son's enjoyment of the Father is the bride's enjoyment of the Father, unhindered by sin and possessed with an infinite capacity to enjoy the Father in union with Christ.[88] As the "friends and spouse" of Christ, saints will "have fellowship with him in the infinite pleasure and joy he has in the enjoyment of his Father," in a full and everlasting sight of the Father's "beauty and brightness,"[89] and in "partaking with him of that joy that he has in the enjoyment of his Father's love."[90] Christ is for the saints in heaven the "grand medium of enjoyment of the Father."[91] Further, enjoyment of the Father consists "not only in contemplation" of the Father's excellence, but also "in actively serving and glorifying God" in "fellowship with Christ, in his blessed and eternal employment of glorifying the Father."[92]

Summary

The foundation and center of Edwards' thought is the glory of the person, purpose, and work of the great Triune God of Scripture. The glory of God, as manifest and communicated among the persons of the Trinity, is manifest and communicated in the person and work of Christ, the perfect image of the Father, and the grand medium in whom God accomplishes His ultimate purpose in displaying and communicating His glory to undeserving creatures. The glory of God is the excellence of His perfections shining forth, displayed and communicated to His creatures by the person and redemptive work of Jesus Christ. God's glory is manifest and communicated by the Father giving His Son a bride, to whom the

---

[88] M 1072, *Works* 20:455.
[89] "True Saints, When Absent from the Body, Are Present with the Lord," *Works* 25:243.
[90] "Matthew 25:21," *Works* 24:870.
[91] M 957, *Works* 20:233-4.
[92] "True Saints, When Absent from the Body, Are Present with the Lord," *Works* 25:242. Edwards cites Revelation 2:3, 15:2-3, 19:5; John 17:1.

Son displays the excellence of His perfections in His perfect work of her rescue and purchase. He communicates His holiness and happiness in giving them the Holy Spirit, whom Christ purchased by His perfect redeeming work, that the saints may see and love the excellence of God's perfections and participate in His eternal happiness. And as Christ accomplished God's ultimate purpose in purchasing the bride promised by the Father, so the glory of God and the holiness and happiness of the redeemed are one and the same ultimate purpose of God. God the Father delights in the display of His own glory in the perfect redeeming work of the Son, and in His own glory communicated to the saints by the giving of the Holy Spirit to dwell within them. All God's works in creation and providence are by and for Christ purchasing His bride for heaven where, united to Christ, they will share in the eternal and infinite happiness of the Son as He views and rejoices in the excellence and beauty of the Father. In heaven, the eternal abode of the bride and Bridegroom, the saints will share in every blessing of the exaltation of the Son, rejoicing with the Son in the glory of the Father, while rejoicing in the greatest display of the excellence of the perfections of God in the person and redemptive work of Christ. Thus, Christ's redemption of sinners is the ultimate Trinitarian work to both display and communicate God's glory, and the inseparable heart and soul of Edwards' Trinitarian theology. Further, as will be explained at length in the following chapters, Christ's obedience to death in fulfillment of God's unchanging rule of righteousness is the meritorious basis of that redemption, and therefore inseparable and foundational to God's ultimate purpose. Accordingly, the heart of Edwards' Trinitarian theology is the person and work of Christ in His obedience to God's unchanging rule of righteousness in the redemption of sinners, by which the ultimate purpose of God to display and communicate His glory is accomplished. Edwards summarizes this chapter best:

> [He will] glorify his majesty, power [and] justice before his elect that they might behold the glory and so be happy in the sight of this glory of God, and that they might give

God the glory due to him on this account, and that they might be the more sensible of the worth of {their}[93] happiness and of the wonderfulness and sovereignty of God's grace. Thus the grand design of God in all his works and dispensations is to present to his Son a spouse in perfect purity, beauty and glory from amongst [mankind], blessing all [the elect] and destroying those [that oppose], and so to glorify himself through his Jesus Christ, God-man; or in one word, the work of redemption is the grand design of [history], this the chief work of God, [the] end of all other works, so that the design of God is one. Hence all the decrees of God are spoken of in Scripture as one purpose which God purposed in Christ Jesus (Eph. 1:9-11). All decrees may one way or other be referred to the covenant of redemption: the grand subject of [the] revelations that God hath made, [the] subject of the words of God, [the] subject of prophecy, [the] great things insisted on in the contemplations and praises of saints and angels, and will be to all eternity.[94]

We turn now to Edwards' doctrine of the covenant of redemption, the pre-temporal arrangement between the Father and Son and the appointed means by which Christ would merit eternal life for His bride.

---

[93] The sermon editor used curly brackets to indicate "repeated phrases sometimes represented by Edwards with a long dash." "Note to the Reader," *Works* 25:xiii.
[94] "Approaching the End of God's Grand Design," *Works* 25:118-9.

CHAPTER TWO

Christ Accomplishes God's Ultimate Purpose According to the Terms of the Pre-Temporal Covenant of Redemption

In briefly examining Edwards' theology of God's ultimate purpose to display and communicate His glory through the person and redemptive work of Christ, we noted the Trinitarian foundation of the nature and purpose of Christ's work. In the present chapter and following, we will examine further the essential nature of Christ's redemptive work as the fulfillment of God's unchanging rule of righteousness, as founded upon and inseparable from its Trinitarian foundation in God's ultimate purpose.

The following aspects of Edwards' theology concerning Christ's perfect obedience to the pre-temporal covenant of redemption between the Father and the Son will be examined. First, the nature and terms of the covenant of redemption are according to the nature and order of the persons of the Trinity. All persons participate and share equally in the glory of redemption according to the covenant terms, while the direct parties of the covenant are the Father and the Son, with the Father as the initiator and head of the covenant, and the Son as the voluntary and appointed mediator to fulfill its terms. Second, the redemption proposed in the covenant is according to the free and benevolent (unconditional) love of the Father set upon sinners from all eternity. Third, the Father determined to redeem sinners without injury to His justice. The parties to the covenant are the Father and Christ mystical, namely, Christ and those united to Him, or those for whom Christ will act as substitute and surety (the elect). Perfect obedience to God's unchanging rule of righteousness according to the terms of the covenant is the necessary and sufficient condition for the redemption of the elect in a manner consistent with God's justice. Fourth, the Son displays His great love to the Father and the elect in freely binding Himself to fulfill the covenant terms on behalf of the elect by suffering God's infinite wrath in satisfaction of His perfect and unchanging justice. And last, God the Father displays His great love to the Son and the elect in the promise of great rewards for perfect obedience to the requirements of the covenant.[1]

The Covenant of Redemption Is According to the Nature and Order of the Persons of the Trinity

God's ultimate purpose to display and communicate His glory is most conspicuously accomplished by the saving work of Christ, but is nonetheless Trinitarian in both its accomplishment and glory. For as God purposed to glorify Himself, and as all of the

---

[1] Reformed theologians have traditionally employed the terms "active" and "passive" to describe Christ's obedience, the former with reference to Christ's life, and the latter with reference to His obedience unto death. The distinction has been utilized to maintain the unity and merit of Christ's obedience in life and death in contradistinction to interpretations rendering Christ's life of obedience as merely an example of piety, separate from the substitutionary nature of His death. As will be discussed in chapter five, Edwards rejects the terminology of "passive" and "active" obedience, viewing all of Christ's redemptive work in life and death as "active." Nonetheless, in so doing, he affirms the original intent of the distinction, namely, the unity of the redemptive and substitutionary nature of Christ's obedience in both life and death. For a helpful summary of the history and intent of the use of "passive" and "active" to describe Christ's redemptive work, see G. C. Berkouwer, *The Work of Christ*, trans. Cornelius Lambregtse (Grand Rapids: W. B. Eerdmans, 1965).

persons of the Trinity "are equal in their eternal glory," so each is "equally worthy to be glorified."[2] Thus, "the whole Trinity is concerned in the affair of our redemption," and each person glorified in it.[3] Redemption "is a work designed for the glory of each of the persons."[4] As noted above, all God's works concern the redeeming work of Christ to purchase His bride, so also every work of the Father, Son, and Holy Spirit relate to this great work.[5] Indeed, the concern of each person of the Trinity in the ultimate purpose of God's glory is seen and understood most clearly in the work of redemption.

> 'Tis because of this that when this work came to be clearly revealed, the doctrine of the Trinity was also clearly revealed. And hence, the doctrine of the Trinity becomes so fundamental an article of the Christian faith, viz. by reason of the concern that each person [has in the work of redemption]; so that we can't have any distinct knowledge of that affair, or any proper exercise of faith in that revelation that is made concerning it, without some knowledge

---

[2] "Of God the Father," *Works* 25:144-5. Also, though "there is a subordination of the persons of the Trinity...particularly in what they act in the affair of man's redemption....'Tis very manifest that the persons of the Trinity are not inferior one to another in glory and excellency of nature." M 1062, *Works* 20:430. See also "The Threefold Work of the Holy Ghost," *Works* 14:379.

[3] "Of God the Father," *Works* 25:144. "The glory of it [redemption] equally belongs to each of them." M 402, *Works* 13:467. See also "The Threefold Work of the Holy Ghost," *Works* 14:435: "Now I think it can hardly be said which of the persons in the Trinity has the greatest share in this work of redemption: it's all from every one of them. It's all from God the Father, for he is the person that determines whether or no there shall be any salvation at all: he provides the Savior, by whom all salvation is procured, and he accepts him, and he sends the Spirit; so that it is all originally from the Father. It is also all from the Son, for he procures it all; he is the medium of it all. And it is all from the Holy Ghost, for he applies it all; he possesses of it all. Therefore the glory of all that happiness which we have by redemption is to be given to each of them, and our absolute dependence in the whole affair is to be upon each of them."

[4] "Of God the Father," *Works* 25:144.

[5] "Of God the Father," *Works* 25:145.

of the concern that each person [has in it], and so the knowledge and belief of the doctrine of the Trinity itself.[6]

So, not only is the doctrine of the Trinity revealed by the work of each person of the Trinity in the work of redemption, but the knowledge of the doctrine of the Trinity itself is thereby fundamental to a proper exercise of faith. Thus, the knowledge of the Trinity as revealed in the work of redemption is necessary for a proper exercise of faith. So again, as seen in chapter one, Edwards' doctrine of the Trinity and his doctrine of the person and redemptive work of Christ are mutually dependent and inseparable.

The Father Is the Initiator and Head of the Covenant

All persons of the Trinity are involved in the great work of redemption and each has a distinct part to play according to an order of subordination. The Father is head of all, the Son is "second in the affair," while the Holy Spirit acts as "dependent" upon the Father and the Son.[7] God the Father, as the head of the Trinity, having determined to display and communicate His glory through the redemptive work of His Son, conceived and initiated the covenant of redemption as the means by which the Son would accomplish His ultimate purpose.[8] The determination of the particular method by which God would accomplish His ultimate purpose follows the inclination of His nature to glorify Himself in the shining forth of His goodness.[9] And though the nature and terms of the covenant are suitable to "the natural order of the eternal and necessary subsistence of the persons of the Trinity,"[10] the "economy of the persons of the Trinity is diverse from all that

---

[6] "Of God the Father," *Works* 25:145.
[7] "Of God the Father," *Works* 25:146.
[8] M 1062, *Works* 20:432-3. M 1062, *Works* 20:430-443, is entitled "Economy of the Trinity and Covenant of Redemption" and is a lengthy and detailed discussion of the same.
[9] M 1062, *Works* 20:432-3.
[10] M 1062, *Works* 20:432.

[is] established in the covenant of redemption, and prior to it."[11] The covenant of redemption is a "new" arrangement that will ultimately be consummated and fulfilled, while the economy of the persons of the Trinity will remain "after the work of redemption is finished, and everything appertaining to it brought to its ultimate consummation."[12] Further, as will be seen below, though the terms of the covenant are consistent with the economic order of the persons of the Trinity, the terms of the covenant are not required by that order. Nonetheless "the persons of the Trinity all consent to this order, and establish it by agreement, as they all naturally delight in what is in itself fit, suitable and beautiful," and "agreeable to the order of their subsisting."[13]

As head of the "society" or "family" of the Trinity, the Father "acts as one that is higher in authority than the other persons," though He does not have this authority "naturally." Rather, His authority is "established by agreement in the society of the persons of the Trinity."[14] Indeed, the authority of the Father in the work of redemption is so absolute that Christ, who possesses equal authority as God, has no authority in His appointed office as Mediator.[15] The authority of Christ as Mediator is only that which has been given Him as appointed by God, or in His Father's name, "but it is God the Father that is by the original agreement vested with the authority of this supreme Lord and Rector of the universe."[16]

---

[11] M 1062, *Works* 20:434.
[12] M 1062, *Works* 20:434.
[13] M 1062, *Works* 20:431. Also, "whatsoever is done concerning man's redemption, is done as it were by consultation and agreement amongst the persons of the Trinity. There was as it were an eternal consultation and agreement about it, and whatsoever is done by each person is done by the consent and concurrent of all." "The Threefold Work of the Holy Ghost," *Works* 14:380.
[14] "Of God the Father," *Works* 25:148.
[15] "Of God the Father," *Works* 25:148-9. Edwards cites John 14:28, "My Father is greater than I," and John 5:19, "The Son can do nothing of himself," and others, including John 10:18 and Isaiah 42:1, 19-20.
[16] "Of God the Father," *Works* 25:148-9. Edwards cites Psalm 2:6; Luke 22:29; Hebrews 12:2; Acts 5:31; 1 Corinthians 15:27; John 5:43, 10:25; Matthew 11:25; Ephesians 4:6.

God the Father is the supreme lawgiver to all creatures, and to Christ Himself in His office of mediator. The Father, "by the agreement of the persons of the Trinity" must "sustain the authority and maintain the rights of the Godhead," while all authority of the Son and the Holy Spirit in their offices in the work of redemption is derived from the Father by that same agreement.[17] Thus, the Father is identified as the party offended by sinful men, whose justice must therefore be satisfied.

> God the Father, by the original establishment and eternal agreement of the persons of the Trinity, thus is vested with all the authority of the Godhead, and maintains the rights of the Godhead in the affair of our redemption, that the price is offered up to him [by the] Mediator between him and sinful men, as though he only were offended. His justice is satisfied [and] he accepts; God the Son acts in his office as being no way originally concerned in the offense. 'Tis not properly his justice that is satisfied: 'tis the justice of his being and essence, but not properly of his person in his office. But 'tis the justice of the person of the Father that is satisfied.[18]

As the party offended and the one who sustains the dignity of the Godhead, any "mediator between God and man...must be appointed by the Father and the whole affair must be of God's ordering,"[19] including whether or not there should be redemption, the way of redemption, who should be redeemed, who should be

---

[17] "Of God the Father," *Works* 25:149-50. Edwards cites John 5:22, 30, 15:26; Hebrews 1:6, 2:5; Philippians 2:9; John 3:34; Colossians 1:19. Hence, Edwards notes, "God the Father is oftentimes called God in Scripture in a peculiar manner, as though he were God in some peculiar sense that the other persons of the Trinity are not." "Of God the Father," *Works* 25:149-50. Edwards cites Ephesians 4:6; 2 Corinthians 13:13, 5:19; 1 Timothy 2:5; Psalm 89:26, 22:1; Matthew 27:46; John 20:17; 1 Corinthians 3:23.

[18] "Of God the Father," *Works* 25:151.

[19] "Even As I Have Kept My Father's Commandments," Jonathan Edwards, *The Glory and Honor of God*, ed. Michael D. McMullen, vol. 2 of *Previously Unpublished Sermons of Jonathan Edwards* (Nashville: Broadman & Holman Publishers, 2004), 212.

redeemer, and what should be the redeemer's office, work, and reward. The Father, therefore, chooses, authorizes, anoints, and sends the redeemer.[20] Moreover,

> [He] invests him with all his offices: [as] prophet: appoints him what he shall say (John 12:49), what miracles he shall work (John 5:19); [as] priest: what commands he shall obey; [he] appoints him his trials: how much he shall suffer, and what cup he shall drink. [He] determines when he has done and suffered enough; appoints his release, when he shall rise. God raises him up [and] gives him his reward. The price is paid [by] him to him, and he gives him the thing purchased: [Christ's] kingly office. [The] redeemed are finally brought and presented to him: thus the head of Christ is God the Father; he is the head of all authority in the affair. [He is] the first disposer, the first fountain. Though the Son has an all-sufficiency in his office, yet [it is] derived. John 5:26, "[The] Father hath life in himself, and hath given to the Son to have life in himself."[21]

Thus, the Father is not only the initiator of the covenant, but is the head of the covenant in all of its aspects, from its inception to its fulfillment and consummation. Nevertheless, the Father as head of the covenant is contingent upon the acceptance of the terms of the covenant by the Son.

The Covenant Is by "Mutual Free Agreement"

The eternal Son is equal with the Father in glory and excellence of nature, and under no obligation to accept the terms of the covenant.[22] Acceptance of the terms is purely voluntary.

---

[20] "Of God the Father," *Works* 25:151. See also M 1062, *Works* 20:433.
[21] "Of God the Father," *Works* 25:151-2.
[22] Edwards held to the eternal Sonship of Christ. See M 1062, *Works* 20:443.

> Christ was not obliged on his own account, to undertake to obey. Christ in his original circumstances, was in no subjection to the Father, being altogether equal with him: he was under no obligation to put himself in man's stead, and under man's law, or to put himself into any state of subjection to God whatsoever.[23]

Therefore, the Father approaches the Son with respect to the terms of the covenant of redemption and Christ's part in it, as follows:

> He *proposes* the matter unto him, *offers* him authority for the office, *proposes* precisely what he should do as the terms of man's redemption, and all the work that he should perform in this affair, and the reward he should receive, and the success he should have.[24]

Should the Son accept the terms of the covenant, He thereby becomes obligated to the Father to keep the terms of the covenant, and place Himself as mediator under the authority of the Father (as delineated above). Thus, the covenant of redemption is undertaken by "mutual free agreement." Nonetheless, all persons of the Trinity possess the "same divine essence, perfection, and so the same glory." No one person of the Trinity "is by nature above another" or has "natural superiority."[25] "Independence is an essential property of the divine nature," so there can be no "natural subjection" of one person of the Trinity to another. The Father cannot "prescribe" to the Son or Holy Spirit anything below their "economical character," or "divine dignity," including Christ's humiliation as mediator, without their free and voluntary agreement. Indeed, if the Son of God were in natural subjection and obligation to the Father, His life and offering of Himself as a sacrifice would not be meritorious, as the merit of His life and sacrifice is

---

[23] "Justification by Faith Alone," *Works* 19:192. See chapter two above.
[24] M 1062, *Works* 20:435-6 (my italics). Christ was "pitched upon to be the purchaser." "The Threefold Work of the Holy Ghost," *Works* 14:380.
[25] "Of God the Father," *Works* 25:147.

founded on Christ voluntarily undertaking the tasks of mediator (as discussed in chapter five).[26]

Therefore, the Father's appointment of the Son to undertake the work of redemption, according to the terms of the covenant of redemption, followed the Son's voluntary undertaking to stand as surety for His bride (the elect) in salvation. The Son freely "undertook to stand in the stead of his elect people as their surety," and the Father "accepted his undertaking" and appointed Him to the office of mediator.[27] In assuming the office, as man's representative, the Son voluntarily placed Himself in a "new" subjection to the Father as the creature is subject to the Father.[28]

> There is a new kind of subordination and mutual obligation between two of the persons, arising from this new establishment the covenant of redemption: the Son undertaking and engaging to put himself into a new kind of subjection to the Father, far below that of his oeconomical station, even the subjection of a proper servant to the Father and one under his law—in the manner that creatures, that are infinitely below God and absolutely dependent for their being on the mere will of God, are subject to his preceptive will and absolute legislative authority—engaging to became a creature, and so to put himself in the proper circumstances of a servant. From which engagements of the Son the Father acquires a new right of headship and authority over the Son, to command him and prescribe to him and rule over him as his proper lawgiver and judge; and the Father also comes under new obligation to the Son, to give him such success, rewards, etc.[29]

---

[26] "Of God the Father," *Works* 25:147.
[27] "Hebrews 9:28," *WJEO*, L. 2v. Preached 1750. See also M 1062, *Works* 20:436.
[28] "Even As I Have Kept My Father's Commandments," *MDM*, 212.
[29] M 1062, *Works* 20:437.

Thus, the Father acquires new rights with respect to the Son, according to the Son's free agreement to the terms of the covenant of redemption on behalf of His bride.

Christ Is the Fit Mediator Between God and Man

The Son, as the person "between" the Father and the Holy Spirit, was fit to be the mediator between the Father and fallen man. The Father could not be mediator, "because he sustained the rights of Godhead and was the person offended and to be appeased by a mediator." No fallen man could be the mediator, as he is in need of a mediator.[30] Indeed, no creature "in heaven and earth was found worthy to undertake the work of redemption of sinners."[31] The mediator could not be the Father, as the mediator was between the Father and fallen man, and could be neither of them.[32] The Holy Spirit could not be the mediator, for such was needed between the Father and the Spirit as the "principal of life and action in fallen creatures."[33] The Son alone could be the mediator between the Father and the Holy Spirit in fallen man.

---

[30] M 614, *Works* 18:146.

[31] "Hebrews 1:5," Yale Collection of Edwards' Manuscripts, Beinecke Rare Book and Manuscript Library, Yale University, L. 5v. Note, I have made slight technical adjustments to the text of the unpublished sermon manuscripts utilized in this work to conform to a more modern readability. Revisions include punctuation, capital letters, the spelling out of abbreviations, spelling of words, and some minor grammatical adjustments.

[32] M 614, *Works* 18:146.

[33] "In being mediator between the Father and the saints, he is mediator between the Father and the Spirit. The saints as saints act only by the Spirit in all their transactings with God, they act by the Spirit, or rather it is the Spirit of God that acts in them. They are the temples of the Holy Ghost. The Holy Spirit dwelling in them is their principle of life and action. There is need of a mediator between God and the Spirit, as the Spirit is a principle of action in a fallen creature. For even those holy exercises that are the actings of the Spirit in the fallen creature, can't be acceptable nor avail anything with God as from the fallen creature, unless it be by a mediator. The Spirit in the saints is it that seeks blessings of God through a mediator, that looks to him by faith and depends on him for it." M 614, *Works* 18:146. Moreover, Edwards' understanding of the Holy Spirit as the love the Father and Son have for each other, excludes the Holy Spirit as a possi-

He only of the persons of the Trinity is fit, being the middle person between the Father and the Holy Ghost, and so only is fit to be a mediator between the Father and sinners, in order to their holiness and happiness. For in so being, he is a middle person between the Father and the Holy Ghost in them, in that he is the means or middle person by which holiness and happiness is purchased for them of the Father, or which is the same thing, by which the Holy Ghost is purchased for them: for the conferring of holiness and happiness consists in conferring the Holy Ghost. The purchaser and the price are intermediate between the person of whom the purchase is made, and the thing purchased of him. So he acts intermediately as between the Father and the Holy Ghost not only as he is the person by whom the Holy Ghost is purchased of the Father, but also by whom it is conferred on sinners from the Father.[34]

Thus, as God is glorified in the display and communication of the excellence of His attributes, and as the communication of the same is by the redemptive work of the Mediator in the purchase of the Holy Spirit from the Father to give to dwell within His bride (the elect) forever, so the Mediator can be none other than the Son.

---

ble mediator: "This was necessary that so the Mediator might be a person beloved of God. The third person may be said to be beloved of God, but not so properly, because he is the infinite love of God itself. He is the delight that the Father and the Son have in each other. A person may be said to love the delight he has in a person that he loves, but not so properly as he loves that person, because this would make love to that love, and delight in that delight, and again delight in the delight that he has in that delight, and so on in infinitum. It was above all things necessary in a mediator between God and his enemies that were justly the objects of his wrath, that he should be a person beloved of God. The success of everything in his mediation depends upon that." M 737, *Works* 18:363-4.
[34] M 772, *Works* 18:419-0.

The Holy Spirit Participates in Making and Executing the Covenant

"The covenant of redemption is only between the Father and the Son," whereas the Holy Spirit "is never represented as a party in this covenant." "Neither is there any intimation in Scripture of any such thing as any covenant, either of the Father or the Son, with the Holy Ghost."[35] The covenant was made with the "second Adam…after the covenant with the first Adam was broken."

> The covenant of redemption…was made only between God the Lawgiver and man's surety and representative, as the first covenant, that was made with the first Adam, was. The covenant of redemption was the covenant in which God the Father made over an eternal reward to Christ mystical, and therefore was made only to Christ, the head of that body. No proper reward was promised or made over in that covenant to the Holy Ghost, although the end of it was the honor and glory of all the persons of the Trinity.[36]

Nonetheless, "the Holy Spirit is infinitely concerned in the affair of our redemption as well as the Father and the Son, and equally with them." And as all of the persons of the Trinity were intimately involved in the creation of the world, though not according to a covenantal arrangement, so also all the persons are involved in the covenant of redemption, though the covenant itself was made between the Father and the Son.[37]

The Holy Spirit is involved with respect to the covenant of redemption as follows:

> (1) As his nature is the divine love that is between the Father and the Son, he is the bond of union between the two covenanting persons, whereby they with infinite sweetness

---

[35] M 1062, *Works* 20:442.
[36] M 1062, *Works* 20:442.
[37] M 1062, *Works* 20:442.

agree, and are infinitely strongly united as parties joined in covenant.

(2) As the Holy Ghost is the infinite love of God to himself and to the creature, so he is the internal spring of all that the other persons do in covenanting, and [the] moving cause of the whole transaction, as it was a marvelous transaction of love, the greatest that ever was.

(3) As the Holy Spirit is the infinite riches and fullness of the Godhead to be communicated in the work of redemption, so he is the great good covenanted for, and the end of the covenant.[38]

Moreover, as discussed in chapter one, the Holy Spirit is the holiness and happiness of God communicated to believers in God's ultimate purpose to display and communicate His glory.[39] And as the love of the Father and Son in redemption is revealed in the Father giving His Son, and the Son in freely giving His life, yet "the Holy Ghost *is* that wonderful love."[40]

God's giving his dear Son, and the Son's suffering so much, glorifies the Holy Ghost, as it shows the worth of the Holy Ghost, that the Father should give his Son, and the Son pay so great a price that the Holy Spirit might be purchased.[41]

Therefore, as the Father and the Son glorify themselves in their great display of "love and grace, just so much they glorify that love and grace, who is the Holy Ghost."[42] Accordingly, though the Holy Spirit is not a party to the covenant of redemption, He is equally a participant in redemption according to the terms of the covenant and equally glorified in its accomplishment.

---
[38] M 1062, *Works* 20:442-3.
[39] See also M 364, *Works* 13:436; M 537, *Works* 18:83; M 539, *Works* 18:84.
[40] M 402, *Works* 13:467 (emphasis his).
[41] M 402, *Works* 13:467. See also M 1065, *Works* 20:445-6.
[42] M 402, *Works* 13:467. See also M 1065, *Works* 20:445-6; "2 Corinthians 13:14," *Works* 24:1078.

The Father Freely Sets His Love upon Unworthy Sinners from Eternity

The redemption of sinners, according to the arrangement of the covenant of redemption, had its genesis "from all eternity"[43] in the love of the Father, the "first mover, and head, and fountain of all in the affair of our redemption."[44]

God's Initial Love to Sinners Is the Love of Benevolence, God's Love of Complacence Is Purchased by Christ

Edwards defines the love of "benevolence" as the desire for the good of another for the mere good of the object of this love, and not for any benefit received or love of the beauty or goodness in the object so loved.[45] In contrast, the love of "complacence" consists of "pleasure and delight" for some inherent or imputed good in the person loved.[46] God's benevolent love toward sinners, a love that is "particular" toward specific individuals,[47] is a love to "enemies" and precedes His love of complacence. In contrast, the latter was purchased by Christ and is for Christ's sake, a delight in the elect for the "beauty and excellency he has given them."[48] In this way, God is able to communicate His happiness to sinful creatures consistent with His manner of doing all things beautifully.

> But because God does everything beautifully, he brings about this their happiness which he determined, in an excellent manner; but it would be a grating, dissonant and deformed thing for a sinful creature to be happy in God's love. He therefore gives them holiness, which holiness he really delights in—he has really complacence in them after he has given them beauty, and not before—and so

---

[43] "Isaiah 53:10," *YMSS*, L. 2v.
[44] "2 Corinthians 13:14," *Works* 24:1078.
[45] "1 John 4:19," *WJEO*, L. 2v. – 3r.
[46] "1 John 4:19," *WJEO*, L. 3r.
[47] "Luke 2:14 (Christ's Appearing)," *WJEO*, L. 2r. – 2v.
[48] "Luke 2:14 (Christ's Appearing)," *WJEO*, L. 1r.

the beauty that he gives, when given, induces God in a certain secondary manner to give them happiness. That is, he wills their happiness antecedently, of himself, and he gives them holiness that he may be induced to confer it; and when it is given by him, then he is induced by another consideration besides his mere propensity to goodness. For there are these two propensities in the divine nature: to communicate goodness absolutely to that which now is nothing, and to communicate goodness to that which is beautiful and holy, and which he has complacence in. He has a propensity to reward holiness, but he gives it on purpose that he may reward it; because he loves the creature, and loves to reward, and therefore gives it something that he may reward.[49]

According to God's ultimate purpose to display and communicate His holiness and happiness to His creatures, God set His benevolent love on the undeserving and unlovable, making them lovable by the redemptive work of Christ. Having redeemed them, He loves them for the beauty of the holiness of Christ to whom they are united as His bride. In other words, God makes the unlovable lovable that He may communicate to them His happiness. He was moved by no merit in the creature, as there was none to move Him,[50] and expected no profit or gain from His goodness toward them, as none could be gained from them.[51] "God loved his saints before ever they were born or had done either good or evil or were capable either of loving or hating him." Indeed, "there is no beginning of God's love to his saints," for "from all eternity God's heart entertained a love to his people."[52] Thus, God the Father

---

[49] M 314, *Works* 13:395-6.
[50] "Romans 6:14," *WJEO*, L. 4v. – 5v. See also "Luke 2:14 (Christ's Appearing)," *WJEO*, L. 2r. – 2v, wherein Edwards writes: "Twas this love of God that moved God to create the creature and to make him excellent. His loveliness is the effect of God's love and therefore can't be the foundation of it. Eph 1:4, According as he hath chosen us in him before the foundation of the world. 1 John 4:19, he loved us first."
[51] "Romans 6:14," *WJEO*, L. 4r. - 4v.
[52] "1 John 4:19," *WJEO*, L. 4v. Edwards cites Romans 9:11-13.

entered into the covenant of redemption with the Son "from all eternity," based upon His desire to communicate His happiness to a bride for the Son, according to His benevolent love to unlovable sinners.[53]

Further, as will be explained at length below, God's benevolent love in communicating happiness to sinners is a positive favor beyond the appeasement of His anger and deliverance from the deserved penalty for sin.[54] As noted in chapter one, the objects of God's love also participate in His glory, a favor above and beyond the pardon of sin alone.

God Determines to Redeem Sinners Without Injury to His Justice by the Terms of the Covenant of Redemption

Having set His benevolent love upon unlovable sinners from eternity for the purpose of their redemption, God determined the means by which He would accomplish redemption in a manner consistent with His holiness and perfect justice (the strict nature of that justice will be discussed at length in chapter three below). For God's holiness is such that He "will by no means have to do with the fallen creature in any way of mercy…[but] through a mediator."[55] Redemption required a mediator to "unite the two distant parties" of God and fallen man, a "middle party" to "transact" for both parties, to stand in God's place to transact with

---

[53] "1 John 4:19," *WJEO*, L. 5v. Note, Edwards was supralapsarian with respect to the salvation of sinners, but sublapsarian with respect to reprobation. "God, in the decree of election, is justly to be considered as decreeing the creature's eternal happiness antecedent to any foresight of good works, in a sense wherein he does not, in reprobation, decree the creature's eternal misery antecedent to any foresight of sin: because the being of sin is supposed in the first things in order in the decree of reprobation, which is that God will glorify his vindictive justice; but the very notion of revenging justice simply considered supposes a fault to be revenged." M 700, *Works* 18:282-3. See also M 704, *Works* 18:314-317; "Romans 9:11-17," *Works* 24:1023.
[54] "Luke 2:14 (Christ's Appearing)," *WJEO*, L. 1r.
[55] "Job 33:6-7," *WJEO*, L. 2r. – 2v.

man, and in man's place to transact with God.[56] And though the Son, as God, was sufficient for the task, His "absolute and infinite perfection" precluded His standing in the place of sinful people to purchase their redemption. As God alone, He was incapable of the obedience and suffering required for the salvation of sinners.[57] "'Tis as impossible that one that is only God should obey the law that was given to man as 'tis that he should suffer man's punishment."[58] Therefore:

> It was requisite that Christ in order to redeem man should take on him the very nature of man and not any other created nature. If he had took on him the nature of an angel and had obeyed and suffered in that, it would not have been sufficient, for obeying the commands of God in an angelical nature would [not] have answered the law that was given to man. Man's law required the obedience of that nature, an obedience performed with the strength and under the circumstances [and] imperfections of that nature, and the temptations that it is liable to. It was therefore essential that Christ should be in the same nature, because the law could not be properly answered unless the ends for which God gave the law are answered; which was, that his authority might be submitted to and honored, by his commands being perfectly obeyed and authority perfectly yielded to in such a nature, in a nature of that strength and those circumstances.[59]

"Man's law" or the "moral law," in which "all positive precepts" are included, could not be satisfied by Christ unless He perfectly obeyed it "in man's nature."[60] Accordingly, the Father would covenant with the Son to take upon Himself a human nature that

---

[56] "Job 33:6-7," *WJEO*, L. 2v. – 3r.
[57] *HWR*, *Works* 9:295.
[58] *HWR*, *Works* 9:296.
[59] M 615, *Works* 18:147.
[60] M 615, *Works* 18:147. The nature of the "moral law" will be discussed in chapter five.

He might be qualified to be the mediator between the Father and sinners.

The Covenant Is Between the Father and Christ Mystical

God's infinite holiness prevents His interaction with sinners apart from a mediator, precluding a covenant relationship between God and sinners directly. Notwithstanding, God can and does enter into a covenant relationship with sinners by entering into a covenant relationship with Christ *mystical*.

> The promises that God, in the covenant of redemption, made to his Son of benefits to be given to him and his people jointly, such as justification, the privileges and benefits of his children, the eternal inheritance and kingdom, were properly made to Christ mystical. For they were made to Christ as a public person, as virtually containing the whole future church that he had taken as it were into himself, having taken their names on his heart, and having undertaken to stand as representing them all. And therefore the promises are in effect not only made to Christ, but his members. For they were made to the whole mystical Christ, and though the whole of Christ mystical was not yet in being, only the head of the body as yet is in being, and the members only existing in God's decree.[61]

In "covenanting with the Father to be for us and in our stead," Christ "made himself one with us by his own voluntary act from all eternity." In so doing He "assume[d] mankind into an union with himself," such that the covenant with Christ is a covenant with His bride, as if "they were all but one person."[62] Thus, if the covenant of grace is understood as the covenant "between God the Father and man," it is "in some respect, the same with the cov-

---

[61] M 1091, *Works* 20:475.
[62] "John 1:16," *WJEO*, L. 3v.

enant of redemption between the Father and the Son."⁶³ In this way Edwards treats the covenant between the Father and Christ and between the Father and believers as the same covenant of redemption.⁶⁴

---

⁶³ M 919, *Works* 20:167.

⁶⁴ Edwards distinguishes as different covenants the covenant between God and believers, which has Christ as mediator and Christ's righteousness as the condition of the covenant, and the covenant between Christ and believers, which has no mediator and has faith as uniting to Christ as the proper condition. "The due consideration of these things may perhaps reconcile the difference between those divines that think [the covenant of redemption] and the covenant of grace the same, and those that think 'em different. The covenant that God the Father makes with believers is indeed the very same with the covenant of redemption made with Christ before the foundation of the world, or at least is entirely included in it. And this covenant has a mediator, or is 'ordained in the hand of a mediator' [Gal. 3:19]. But the covenant by which Christ himself and believers are united, one with another, is properly a different covenant than that, and is not made by a mediator. There is a mediator between sinners and the Father to bring about a covenant union between them, but there is no mediator between Christ and sinners to bring about a marriage union between Christ and their souls." M 1091, *Works* 20:477-8. Also, "these things may also tend to reconcile the difference between those divines that [think] the covenant of grace is not conditional as to us, or that the promises of it are without any proper conditions to be performed by us, and those that think that faith is the proper condition of the covenant of grace. The covenant of grace, if thereby we understand the covenant between God the Father and believers in Christ, the covenant that he 'ordains in the hand of [a] mediator,' and the promises given us in him, is indeed without any proper conditions to be performed by us. Faith is not properly the condition of the covenant, but the righteousness of Christ. Faith is no more properly the condition of this covenant made with the second Adam, for himself and believers in him, than a coming into being by descent from Adam would properly have been the condition of the covenant God made with Adam, and the promises made to his posterity in him. Adam's righteousness was the alone proper condition, not only of Adam's eternal life but of his posterity's, according to the tenor of that covenant. So Christ's righteousness is the alone proper condition of eternal life to the second Adam and his spiritual seed, according to the tenor of the new covenant made with him. But the covenant of grace, if thereby we understand the covenant between Christ himself and his church or his members, is conditional as to us: the proper condition of it, which is a yielding to Christ's wooings and accepting his offers and closing with him as a redeemer and spiritual husband, is to be performed by us. A proper condition of a covenant is that qualification or act of the party with whom the covenant is made by which, according [to] the tenor of the covenant, the part is interested in the benefits therein promised. But

> If God the Father, before the foundation of the world, makes a covenant with his Son concerning him and his future spouse, and gives promises to both, considered as those that are to be one, and afterwards when his spouse is obtained, and he is united to her, he brings this covenant and these promises in his hand, and delivers it to her as a covenant made with them jointly, this don't make it now to become another covenant, anymore than if Christ's spouse had actually been with Christ when the covenant was first made, and both had appeared in actual union before the Father in that transaction.[65]

Thus, in the Father's covenanting with the Son in eternity past, He thereby also chooses those united to Christ. God in "foreowning" certain persons chooses them "to be actually his…by being in Christ, or being members of his Son." In foreknowledge He gives certain persons to Christ, and then predestines them "to be conformed to the image of his Son, both in his holiness and blessedness."[66]

---

the party with whom God the Father, as supreme Lord, ruler and disposer of all, makes his covenant in favor of fallen men is Christ mystical, containing both head and members, and will have nothing to do in any such friendly transaction with fallen men any otherwise but as in and under Christ, and considered as one party with him. But that in this party by which alone, according to the tenor of the covenant, the party, both head and members, is interested in eternal life is Christ's righteousness. But in the covenant between Christ and his member or spouse, she is by herself a party in the covenant, and that in this party by which alone, according to the tenor of the covenant, she is interested in the benefit of union and propriety in Christ (which is the benefit directly conveyed in this covenant) is her believing in Christ, or her soul's active union with him." M 1091, *Works* 20:478-9. See also M 1064, *Works* 20:445, and M 825, *Works* 18:536-7. For an in-depth treatment of Edwards on the Covenant of Grace, see Bogue, *Jonathan Edwards and the Covenant of Grace*.

[65] M 1091, *Works* 20:476. Also, "Christ is the Mediator of the new covenant, viz. the eternal covenant of grace made with him before the foundation of the world, in due time to be delivered to his people, called the new covenant, as revealed by Christ to his church when he came down from heaven," 477.

[66] M 769, *Works* 18:418. Edwards cites Ephesians 1:4.

> For God having in foreknowledge given us to Christ, he thenceforward beheld us as members or parts of him; and so ordaining the head to glory, he therein ordained the members to glory. Or, in destining Christ to eternal life, he destined all parts of Christ to it also, so that we are appointed to eternal life in Christ, being in Christ his members from eternity. In his being appointed to life, we are appointed.[67]

Therefore, "Christ's election is the foundation of ours, as much as his justification and glorification are the foundation of ours."[68]

Also, as God's initial pre-covenant and benevolent love toward sinners was particular to specific individuals, so also God's love is particular to those made beneficiaries of the covenant of redemption by being united to Christ from all eternity.

> The love of Christ to you was no new thing…it was a thing of old standing when the foundation of the heavens and the earth were laid. Christ had a book written, the Lamb's Book of Life, wherein your names had been written from all eternity. God the Father and the Son did as it were consult together from the days of eternity about the redemption of lost men and made a covenant together, and then was your name mentioned as one of those that should be redeemed.[69]

The love of God to the elect precedes creation and the existence of the elect in the created world. "The Father has given all believers to Jesus Christ before they come to him," for "every particular believer was given to Christ in that eternal covenant of redemption."[70]

---

[67] M 769, *Works* 18:418.
[68] M 769, *Works* 18:418.
[69] "Galatians 2:20," *WJEO*, L. 9r.
[70] "Galatians 2:20," *WJEO*, L. 2v. Edwards cites John 6:37, 17:2, 9; 10:16; 2 Timothy 1:9, 2:19; Romans 8:29; Revelation 21:27.

The Covenant Terms Accomplish Righteousness for the Elect

The terms of the covenant of redemption proposed by the Father stipulated that Christ as Second Adam would merit eternal life for sinners by honoring God's authority and law through perfect obedience. Christ would succeed where Adam failed in the trial of his obedience and honor to God's authority and law. Further, Christ would achieve more than a return to Adam's state of innocence and probation.

> And seeing that when Christ, in uniting himself to sinners, or assuming them by love into union with himself, he did not only seek that they might be restored to a state of indifference and probation, such a state as they were in before they fell, but that they should be brought to a sure title to eternal life, such as they would have had [had they] acquitted themselves well in their probation, and had honored God's authority by a perfect obedience; therefore, it was judged meet that Christ himself should do that honor to God's authority, which God at first required of man as the condition of his having a title to eternal life.[71]

Christ would render the perfect obedience required to satisfy God's law for obtaining the reward of eternal life.

> God saw meet to place man at first in a state of trial, and not to give him a title to eternal life as soon as he had made him, because it was his will that man should first give honor to his authority by perfectly obeying his law; and therefore still it is God's will, that man should not have eternal life without this honor to his authority being done.[72]

In accordance with the terms of Adam's trial of obedience, if eternal life was given to a sinner without the "active righteousness" of perfect obedience to God's law, "the honor of his law would not

---

[71] M 483, *Works* 13:526.
[72] M 483, *Works* 13:526.

be sufficiently vindicated."[73] Christ, according to the terms of the covenant of redemption with the Father, would therefore become "subject to God's authority" and "do that honor to God's authority by his obedience, the principal instance of which was his laying down his life."[74]

Thus, in the redemptive work of the Son, in His satisfaction and perfect obedience according to the terms of the covenant of redemption, "God has found out a way for making the freedom of grace consistent with the honour of his holiness, justice, majesty, and authority."[75] Moreover, He has done so to particular individuals in accordance with His equitable justice, as He is infinitely merciful to some, "but he is necessarily just to all."[76]

The Son Displays His Love to the Father and the Elect by Freely Choosing To Be the Elect's Substitute and Surety

Thus far in the discussion concerning the covenant of redemption, we have seen that the parties and terms of the covenant are in accord with the nature and order of the persons of the Trinity, with the Father as the head and initiator of the covenant, the Son as the fit mediator between God and man, and the Holy Spirit as the one purchased by the redemptive work of the Son to be given to the bride of Christ, to whom God communicates His happiness. The covenant is by mutual free agreement, as each of the persons of the Trinity are of equal essence and glory and under no necessity to subordinate themselves to each other as required by the terms of the covenant. The Father moves first in establishing the covenant by freely setting His benevolent love upon sinners from all eternity and making provision to give them holiness that He might love them still more on account of the beauty of that holiness. Further, God determined to redeem sinners without injury to His justice

---

[73] "Justification By Faith Alone," *Works* 19:188.
[74] M 483, *Works* 13:526.
[75] "Romans 6:14," *WJEO*, L. 3r.
[76] "Deuteronomy 32:4," *WJEO*, L. 2r.

by providing that Christ, as Second Adam, would honor God's authority and law through the perfect obedience required for the obtaining of eternal life. Accordingly, the parties to the covenant are the Father and Christ mystical, the latter including all those united to Christ as the chosen bride of Christ. Christ would accomplish for His bride what Adam failed to accomplish for his posterity. We turn now to Edwards' understanding of Christ's display of love to the Father and the elect in His voluntary acceptance of the terms of the covenant of redemption as the substitute and surety for the elect.

The Son Freely Binds Himself to the Terms of the Covenant

Christ's perfect obedience to the Father and His law displays His great love for the Father and the elect in that it was voluntary. Had Christ been obligated to take upon Himself the role of servant, to subject Himself to the rigors and requirements of the law, His obedience would not have displayed great love.[77] On the contrary, Christ freely undertook to submit to the law and "fulfill all righteousness" on behalf of the elect from "wonderful love to us," love to the Father, and love for the honor of God's authority and law (to be addressed at length in chapter five).

> It was for our sakes that Christ became subject to God's authority. He is naturally equal with God and not under his authority. It was for our sakes that he took upon himself the office and character of a mediator whereby he became subject. It was by putting himself in our stead and it was for our sakes that he took on him our nature and so was in the form of a servant and became subject to the same laws of God that we are subject to.[78]

Nevertheless, having bound Himself in His agreement to the covenant terms, Christ became obligated to keep the terms of the

---

[77] "Luke 2:14 (Christ's Appearing)," *WJEO*, L. 4r.
[78] "Even As I Have Kept My Father's Commandments," *MDM*, 218-9.

Christ Accomplishes God's Ultimate Purpose

covenant perfectly, subject to the penalties of the law for disobedience, and the rewards of the covenant for perfect obedience.

> When Christ had once undertaken with God, to stand for us, and put himself under our law, by that law he was obliged to suffer, and by the same law he was obliged to obey: by the same law, after he had taken man's guilt upon him, he himself being our surety, could not be acquitted, till he had suffered, nor rewarded till he had obeyed: but he was not acquitted as a private person, but as our head, and believers are acquitted in his acquittance; nor was he accepted to a reward for his obedience as a private person, but as our head, and we are accepted to a reward in his acceptance.[79]

In accepting the terms of the covenant, He freely agreed to condescend to take upon Himself a human nature.[80] In accepting His task as "the surety and substitute of his people," Christ not only became the Second Adam by whom the positive requirements of God's law would be fulfilled and the honor of God's authority upheld, He became the "prisoner of vindictive justice," the One who would bear the guilt and punishment of sinners.[81] The Son set His love upon unworthy sinners from eternity, "they were committed to him. He had taken their names." "He undertook to be their surety and so became obliged to answer for their sins from eternity in the eternal covenant."[82] Their sins and guilt would be imputed to Him, and He would pay their penalty. "It was impossible for Him to escape"; it was "impossible He should go to heaven in any other way."[83] "The great Physician has bound himself by his covenant perfectly to heal; but the nature of the disease requires some irksome medicine, which medicine is taken into the covenant."[84]

---

[79] "Justification By Faith Alone," *Works* 19:191.
[80] "Galatians 2:20," *WJEO*, L. 8r. – 8v.
[81] "Hebrews 9:28," *WJEO*, L. 3r.
[82] "Hebrews 9:28," *WJEO*, L. 4r. Edwards cites Titus 1:2; 2 Timothy 1:9.
[83] "Hebrews 9:28," *WJEO*, L. 3r. Edwards cites 2 Corinthians 5:21.
[84] M 335, *Works* 13:352.

This free and great love of Christ from all eternity was not only given at great cost, "it was pure disinterested love that moved him to all that he suffered." "He could receive no benefit by saving such poor miserable and wretched creatures," whom taken together are "in comparison of him…less than nothing and vanity."[85]

Having freely agreed to the terms of the covenant, Christ became "mediator and so subject to the Father before he came into the world,"[86] though He did not become subject to the "moral law" (or "man's law") until His incarnation.[87] As the incarnate mediator, Christ would be subject to the moral law, the ceremonial "Jewish law," in addition to the law to which He alone was subject, the command of the Father to fulfill the terms of the covenant of redemption, the most difficult task of all (to be covered in chapter five). As God-man, Christ would be the perfect mediator between God and man, possessing the nature and "circumstances" of both, including "the glory, majesty and happiness of the one, and the infirmity, meanness, disgrace, guilt and misery of the other."[88]

> He undertakes for each with the other. He undertakes for man with God. He becomes surety for him; he undertakes that the law shall be answered, God's majesty vindicated and glorified with respect to man. Yea, he so undertakes for sinners that he assumes them to himself; he puts himself before the Father in the sinner's stead, that whatever justice has to demand of the sinner, it may demand it of him. He takes the sinner's debt, becomes bound for him, so that justice no longer looks to the sinner for a discharge of the debt, but to Christ. And so he also undertakes for the Father with men, in order to their being reconciled to God, and resting in him as their sure and everlasting portion, that God will preserve them and keep them.[89]

---

[85] "Matthew 21:5," *YMSS*, L. 7r.
[86] "Even As I Have Kept My Father's Commandments," *MDM*, 214.
[87] "Even As I Have Kept My Father's Commandments," *MDM*, 213.
[88] M 722, *Works* 18:420.
[89] M 722, *Works* 18:420.

In binding Himself to the terms of the covenant, the Son bound Himself to those for whom He would suffer to satisfy God's justice, and to the authority of the Father in the accomplishment of God's ultimate purpose to display and communicate His glory to sinful creatures.

The Son Freely Binds Himself to Suffer Infinite Wrath

In freely accepting the terms by which His bride would be redeemed, the Son accepted to undertake the full extent of the punishment required by God's perfect justice on her behalf. Christ, therefore, would drink the cup of God's infinite wrath against sin.[90] His suffering would be "equivalent to the eternal suffering of all the elect," displaying a love equivalent to being "willing to undergo, for another, a whole eternity of such misery, as the damned do in hell, that he might in the meantime wholly escape and be made eternally happy."[91] His suffering would be infinite. And as the depth of the Son's love is displayed in the depth of suffering He is willing to undertake on her behalf, He displayed an infinite love to His bride in accepting the terms of the covenant.[92]

The Father Displays His Love to the Son and the Elect in the Rewards Promised to Christ for His Obedience

The terms of the covenant further display the love of the Father to the Son and His bride in the promise of rewards for the perfect obedience required by the covenant. The undertaking of such a costly and difficult task "should have a reward for it answerable to the merit and gloriousness of the work" and "to the difficulty and expense of it."[93] The Son's work would glorify God "in a peculiar and most distinguishing manner," while displaying a "superlative"

---

[90] Sermon on Luke 22:44, *Works* (Hickman) 2:867.
[91] M 898, *Works* 20:155.
[92] "Luke 2:14 (Christ's Appearing)," *WJEO*, L. 3r.
[93] "Isaiah 53:10," *YMSS*, L. 2r.

and "infinite" love to the Father in the voluntary undertaking of it.[94] The rewards promised to Christ before His work of redemption constituted the "joy that was set before Him" for which He "endured the cross,"[95] and include His mediatorial glory as surety for the elect, the power and authority to give the Holy Spirit to the elect, and the salvation and glorification of the elect.

Though the Son of God in His perfection is incapable of a reward, He is "capable of receiving honour and glory" in His state of humiliation as mediator.[96] As a reward for His voluntary humiliation and perfect obedience in keeping the terms of the covenant, Christ would be exalted to the right hand of the Father as "Lord and Judge of all." He would be exalted to a higher place than that which belonged to Him in His economic place as the second person of the Trinity, for the position of the ultimate and supreme ruler and judge of the universe belongs to the Father by virtue of the order of the persons of the Trinity.[97] Such was a "suitable reward" for Christ's suffering.[98] This "vicarious dominion and authority" will be "resigned at the end of the world" in order that "God may be all in all, and that things thenceforward may be dispensed only according to the order of the economy of the Trinity."[99]

Secondly, Christ would be given power and authority to give the Holy Spirit to the elect to communicate the happiness He purchased for His bride. "The Spirit was the inheritance that Christ as God-man purchased for himself and his church, or for Christ mystical, and it was the inheritance that he, as God-man, received of the Father at his ascension for himself and them." And as the Holy Spirit is the happiness of God to be eternally communicated to the church, the Spirit's subjection to Christ will "continue to

---

[94] "Isaiah 53:10," *YMSS*, L. 2v.
[95] "Isaiah 53:10," *YMSS*, L. 2r. – 2v. Edwards cites Hebrews 12:2.
[96] "Isaiah 53:10," *YMSS*, L. 4r. Edwards cites Psalm 110:1, 6; Philippians 2:9.
[97] M 1062, *Works* 20:439.
[98] "The Threefold Work of the Holy Ghost," *Works* 14:380. Edwards cites John 5:26-27, 17:2; Matthew 11:27.
[99] M 1062, *Works* 20:440.

eternity and never will be resigned up," for Christ as God-man will eternally be "the vital head and husband of the church."[100]

Thirdly, Christ will be rewarded with the salvation of His people. We noted earlier that the Son of God, in His perfection as God, cannot be benefited by sinful creatures. How, then, can the salvation of those of no benefit to the Son be construed as a reward, or as Edwards put it, "how can it be any reward for his suffering for us to be converted and saved" if He "has no need of us poor worms"?[101] The answer is that "Christ has so set his love upon men that the seeing this sight is what he earnestly desired and greatly delights in." His love for His sheep makes their salvation a reward.[102] Thus, seeing the salvation of the elect "was a great part of that joy that was set before him for which he endured His sufferings."[103]

Summary

The covenant of redemption, the pre-temporal arrangement of the persons of the Trinity for the redemption of sinners, was conceived by the Father as the great means by which the ultimate Trinitarian purpose to display and communicate His glory would be accomplished. As a "new" arrangement, the covenant

---

[100] M 1062, *Works* 20:440. Edwards cites Revelation 22:5.
[101] "Isaiah 53:10," *YMSS*, L. 4v.
[102] "Isaiah 53:10," *YMSS*, L. 4v. Edwards cites Proverbs 8:31 wherein wisdom personified, or Christ, delights in the sons of men; and Luke 15:4-6, wherein the Good Shepherd rejoices in finding the lost sheep. See also "Hebrews 12:2-3," *YMSS*, L. 9r.
[103] "Isaiah 53:10," *YMSS*, L. 4v. In commenting on Psalm 72:15, Edwards writes: "If we hold translation 'for him,' then it must be understood of the saints' praying for the Father's accomplishment of the promises made to the Son in the covenant of redemption, that his kingdom may come, his name glorified, and that he may see his seed, and that the full reward may be given him for his sufferings, and so that he may receive 'the joy that was set before him' [Heb. 12:2]." "Psalm 72:15," *Works* 24:509. Though his interpretation of this passage as a reference to the covenant of redemption appears as an interpretive stretch, it illustrates the centrality of the redemptive work of Christ in the accomplishment of the terms of the covenant of redemption in Edwards' theology.

was nonetheless according to the nature and order of the persons of the Trinity. The Father, first in the order of the persons and the person injured by sin, would initiate the covenant, determine the individuals to be redeemed, and the terms by which their redemption would be accomplished. And though the Father set His benevolent love on particular individuals to be the bride of His Son from eternity, consent to the covenant terms would need to be free and mutual, as the Son is equal to the Father in divinity and glory and under no necessity to consent to its terms. The Son, however, having set His benevolent love on the elect from eternity, agreed to be bound by the covenant stipulations from His great love of the Father and His bride. To mediate between God and man, the Son would condescend to take upon Himself a human nature and body. In His incarnation He would be bound to perfectly obey the requirements of the moral, ceremonial, and covenant commands of the Father (the latter to which He alone would be subject) and could only return to heaven by honoring God's authority and law by perfect obedience. The Father displayed His love for the Son and the elect in the promise of rewards for Christ's perfect obedience. Christ would be exalted to the Father's right hand, be given the Holy Spirit to give to those given Him by the Father, and receive His purchased bride to dwell with Him in holiness and happiness forever in their eternal home in heaven.

Thus, the ultimate purpose of God to display and communicate his glory is accomplished through the conception, undertaking, and fulfillment of the covenant of redemption, in which all members of the Trinity equally participate and are glorified, and in which Christ's performance of the terms of the covenant is the essential and central facet. In Christ's redeeming work we see the center of Edwards' Trinitarian theology, for the glory of God's perfections is most clearly displayed in Christ's perfect obedience to the covenant requirements. And by the success of His perfect obedience, Christ purchased the Holy Spirit to communicate God's holiness and happiness to His bride in the giving of the Holy Spirit to believers. Therefore, Edwards' Trinitarian theology is a tightly knit tapestry with the central thread of Christ binding it together, by whom the glory of the perfections of the Trinity are made known to His creatures, and by whom the holiness and happiness of God are communicated to the bride of Christ for all eternity. Accordingly, Edwards' theology cannot be properly understood and explained in abstraction from both the person and redemptive work of Christ and the glorious perfections of the Trinity as its center and foundation.

CHAPTER THREE

God's Rule Of Righteousness Requires Perfect Obedience for Eternal Life and Death for Disobedience

We turn now to a closer examination of Edwards' conception of the covenant stipulation of perfect obedience to God's unchanging rule of righteousness, that manifestation of the strict and exacting attribute of God's justice and unchanging requirement for the redemption of sinners. We have seen that the love of God the Father was manifest in giving His Son to uphold His justice by perfect obedience to the covenant stipulations, while the love of the Son was manifest in His free consent and accomplishment of the covenant stipulations. The essence of the covenant, however, is that God's strict justice, law, and supreme authority be honored and upheld by Christ's fulfillment of the covenant requirements. As will be seen in the following chapters, the covenant terms are summarized in God's unchanging rule of righteousness, the standard of God's strict justice and immutable requirement for obtaining eternal life. Thus, central to the accomplishment of God's ultimate purpose to display and communicate His glory is the requirement that the standard of God's rule of righteousness be fulfilled, that the honor to God's law and authority, required for eternal life in the trial of Adam, be performed.

> In assuming man to himself, he sought a title to this eternal happiness for him, after he had broken the law, that he himself should become subject to God's authority, and be in the form of a servant, that he might do that honor to God's authority for him, by his obedience, which God at first required of man, as the condition of his having a title to that reward. Christ came into the world to that end, to render the honor of God's authority and law, consistent with the salvation and eternal life of sinners; he came to save them, and yet withal to assert and vindicate the honor of the Lawgiver, and his holy law. Now if the sinner after his sin was satisfied for, had eternal life bestowed upon him, without active righteousness, the honor of his law would not be sufficiently vindicated.[1]

This was the intent of the covenant of redemption, that all might be accomplished in accordance with God's strict and unchanging standard of justice. God's purpose to display the excellence of His perfections could not be accomplished if His justice was compromised in the salvation of sinners, for His righteousness and justice are as much His perfections as His love and goodness. And as will be seen below, Edwards' conception of the relationship of the attributes of God is such that God would not be God if any one of His perfections were compromised.

In the following chapters we will observe Edwards' understanding of the violation of God's unchanging rule of righteousness as the ground of mankind's need for redemption, and the absolute necessity of Christ meeting the standard of God's unchanging rule of righteousness in order that sinners might be redeemed and God's ultimate purpose be accomplished. In the present chapter, the former of these two considerations will be examined as follows. First, Adam was required to give honor to God's authority and law

---

[1] "Justification By Faith Alone," *Works* 19:188.

by perfect obedience, as perfect obedience is the minimum God requires of His creatures. Second, Adam stood as the representative for all mankind in his trial of obedience. Third, all commands, including the specific command of Adam's trial of obedience, are comprehended in the one great law of God (to which angels are even subject), God's unchanging rule of righteousness. And last, God's unchanging rule of righteousness reflects the nature of God. As Creator, His creatures owe Him perfect obedience, and as the moral head of the universe, He must uphold the honor of His authority and law.

Adam Was to Honor God's Authority and Law by Perfect Obedience to God's Rule of Righteousness

The circumstances of God's trial of Adam's obedience in the Garden of Eden make apparent that a mere absence of sin was not sufficient for eternal life, for so Adam was created. Rather, God would require of Adam a "positive" act of righteousness for Adam to pass from his created state into the state of eternal life. He was "not immediately invited" to eat of the tree of life when he was created, "he was first to obey."[2]

> If Adam had finished his course of perfect obedience, he would have been justified; and certainly his justification would have implied something more than what is merely negative; he would have been approved of, as having fulfilled the righteousness of the law, and accordingly would have been adjudged to the reward of it.[3]

That righteousness required by the law included a "positive" righteousness, the perfect obedience required by God's unchanging rule of righteousness. "The rule of righteousness, which God never altered, which shall never pass away—the heaven and earth passes away [*sic*], which is the law—fixes death as the wages of sin

---

[2] M 498, *Works* 13:540.
[3] "Justification by Faith Alone," *Works* 19:150.

and perfect obedience as the only price of eternal life."[4] The words of Genesis 2:17, wherein Adam was commanded not to eat of the tree, "signify that perfect obedience was the condition of God's covenant that was made with Adam, as they signify that for one act of disobedience he should die."[5]

> God saw meet to place man first in a state of trial…that he should first give honor to his authority, by fully submitting to it, in will and act, and perfectly obeying his law. God insisted upon it that his holy majesty and law should have their due acknowledgement, and honor from man, such as became the relation he stood in to that Being that created him, before he would bestow the reward of confirmed and everlasting happiness upon him; and therefore God gave him a law when he created him, that he might have opportunity, by giving due honor to his authority in obeying it, to obtain this happiness.[6]

By God's design, His creatures would not be confirmed to eternal life apart from "the exercise and manifestation of the creature's respect to God and his authority."[7]

---

[4] "None Are Saved by Their Own Righteousness," *Works* 14:336.
[5] "Genesis 2:17," *Works* 24:134. See also M 786, *Works* 18:472.
[6] "Justification by Faith Alone," *Works* 19:188. In M 1127, *Works* 20:497-500, Edwards lists eleven reasons why God required that "intelligent creatures should first be in a STATE OF PROBATION before they are in a state of confirmed happiness." God requiring honor to His authority and law is the primary reason, as will be seen repeatedly in the discussion with regard to Christ's obedience as surety in fulfillment of God's unchanging rule of righteousness in chapters four and five. An adequate discussion of the oftentimes speculative and sometimes potentially problematic reasons for Adam's trial given in M 1127 would take the present discussion far beyond its scope and purpose. Nonetheless, an analysis of whether or not Edwards improperly deduces pre-temporal and pre-Fall purposes for what God ultimately accomplishes from the fall of Adam, and in so doing makes God's glory ultimately dependent upon evil, would be a worthwhile contribution to Edwards scholarship.
[7] M 664b, *Works* 18:202.

Adam Stood as Surety for All Mankind

God appointed Adam to stand for all mankind in his trial of obedience.[8] He stood as a "surety," as "a public head for himself and his posterity."[9] In speaking to Adam, God spoke to his posterity also.[10] Had he stood the test, his posterity would have come into being with a "title to eternal life,"[11] for just as all received the penalty of his disobedience, so by his obedience he would have been given to eat of the tree of life and "tasted of that as our head, and therein confirmed holiness and life would have been sealed to him and all his posterity."[12] And as it was God's will that Adam stand for mankind in his trial of obedience and honor to God's law, so it remains God's will "that man should not have eternal life without this honor to his authority being done."[13] This will be discussed further in chapters four and five below.

---

[8] M 997, *Works* 20:325-6.

[9] M 1091, *Works* 20:476.

[10] "Romans 5:13-14," *Works* 24:998-9. "There are two things the Apostle would prove in these words, one of which establishes the other. First, he would prove that all mankind were under the law God gave to Adam that revealed death to be the wages of sin. This is evident because that sin, as bringing death, was in the world before there was any other legislation or solemn giving of law to mankind besides what was to Adam, viz. in that space of time that was from Adam to Moses. There being sin therefore in the world as bringing death, in that space of time before the giving of the law by Moses, shows that there was a law given of God before that time, threatening death, that they were under, but this could be no other than the law God gave to Adam. This proves that Adam was the legal head of mankind, that mankind were under the law given to him, wherein God threatened death for transgression, and that God in that law given to Adam, saying, 'When thou sinnest, thou shalt die,' did not only speak to him, though he spake in the singular number, but in him spake to his posterity also."

[11] M 1091, *Works* 20:476.

[12] M 695, *Works* 18:279.

[13] M 483, *Works* 13:526. The eternal life promised to Adam did not include heaven, for that "inheritance…is alone by the purchase of Christ." As noted in chapter one, heaven is the prepared abode for Christ and His bride, given to Him by the Father, and purchased by his fulfillment of the terms of the covenant of redemption. "Adam, our first head, was a native of this world; he was of the earth, earthly. And if he had stood he would have obtained eternal happiness here in his own country for himself [and] all his earthly posterity. But Christ, our second head, is one that properly belongs to heaven; he is the Lord from heaven, and the

All Commands Are Comprehended in the One Great Law of God

Though Edwards often uses different terms to describe it, such as the "grand rule," "moral law," "law of nature," or "covenant of works," the command given to Adam was but an expression of that "one great law of God" in which all the laws and commands of God are comprehended.

> There is indeed but one great law of God, and that is the same law that says, "If thou sinnest, thou shalt die," and "Cursed is everyone that continues not in all things contained in this law to do them": all duties of positive institution, are virtually comprehended in this law.[14]

"The moral law virtually includes all right acts, on all possible occasions, even occasions that the law itself allows not."[15] All acts of disobedience to God are breaches of God's "unalterable rule of righteousness," as all acts of disobedience are subject to the threat to Adam, "'Thou shalt surely die."

> The law is the eternal and unalterable rule of righteousness, between God and man, and therefore is the rule of judgment, by which all that a man does shall be either

---

happiness he obtains by his obedience for himself and his spiritual posterity is eternal blessedness in his country, even heaven." M 809, *Works* 18:512-3. In the Genesis account "there is not a word tending to lead Adam to a thought of another unseen world. And if God did not by anything he said lead him to expect it, then it is certain that he did not promise it and make it over to him by covenant." M 809, *Works* 18:513. In M 884 Edwards notes "there was a promise of glorious life to obedience, is further evident from Rom. 3:23, 'For all have sinned, and come short of the glory of God,' which implies that there was a glory that God offered." *Works* 20:140-1. Though an apparent discrepancy in Edwards' view, it is more likely that the latter reference to glory is an earthly glory consistent with M 809. In any case, Christ's perfect obedience would purchase far greater glory for the elect than Adam's obedience would have purchased for his posterity, as will be discussed in chapter five. With respect to the promise of glory to Adam, he cites Matthew 19:17, Leviticus 18:5, Ezekiel 20:11, Romans 6:23.

[14] "Justification by Faith Alone," *Works* 19:197.
[15] "Justification by Faith Alone," *Works* 19:197.

justified or condemned; and no sin exposes to damnation, but by the law....all sins whatsoever, are breaches of the law or covenant of works, because all sins, even breaches of the positive precepts, as well as others, have atonement by the death of Christ: but what Christ died for, was to satisfy the law, or to bear the curse of the law.[16]

All God's laws, be they the verbal command to Adam, the "great rule of righteousness written in his heart,"[17] the Jewish "ceremonial law,"[18] the Ten Commandments,[19] or others, are all comprehended in "the supreme and everlasting, unalterable rule of righteousness between God and man that must some way or other be fulfilled."[20] The covenant of works requires obedience to "all God's positive commands,"[21] and the threats of Deuteronomy 27:26, "'Cursed is everyone that continues [not] in all things contained in the law to do them,' was in force before it was written in the law of Moses, even from the beginning of the world."[22] To God's covenant with the nation Israel there were added "a great number of positive precepts" to the "covenant of works"[23] that was "still in force."

> Indeed, the covenant of works was not merely proposed as an antiquated thing, which the people were fond of, for their trial and conviction, but as a thing still in force and of the greatest importance, in several respects. It was, indeed, wherein was the supreme and everlasting, unalterable rule of righteousness between God and man that must some way or other be fulfilled; in some sense the rule of God's proceeding with them all, the rule of his

---

[16] "Justification by Faith Alone," *Works* 19:197-8.
[17] M 884, *Works* 20:143.
[18] "Justification by Faith Alone," *Works* 19:197.
[19] M 884, *Works* 20:144.
[20] M 1353, *Works* 23:497.
[21] M 1353, *Works* 23:500-1. Edwards cites Hosea 6:7 as support for calling the command and "promise" of God to Adam a "covenant." "But they like men have transgressed the covenant: there have they dealt treacherously against me." M 884, *Works* 20:140.
[22] M 884, *Works* 20:143.
[23] M 1353, *Works* 23:500.

94   *The Infinite Merit of Christ*

proceeding with the righteous and faithful among them mediately and through a Mediator, but immediate with all such of them as should continue in sin. And in these respects it was not only proposed but established, or re-established, with the children of Israel at Mt. Sinai in the Ten Commandments.[24]

With respect to Adam, the law had already been written on His heart when he was given the specific command concerning the fruit of the tree.

His main rule was that great rule of righteousness written in his heart, when God first made him, which it must be supposed that he knew sufficiently, before God gave the positive precept. Otherwise, when God did give that precept, Adam would have been at a loss whether he ought to submit to it or not, for this could be known only by the law of nature, the sum of which is that God is to be fervently regarded and loved, and his will to be universally complied with. And this was the grand rule given

---

[24] M 1353, *Works* 23:496-7. The covenant God instituted with the nation Israel was nonetheless a "mixed covenant." The covenant "resembled" the covenant of works as it was "delivered and proposed to them for the trial of their obedience," and that it also partook "partly of the nature of the covenant of grace." "Therefore, this covenant was like a shell enveloping the gospel two ways: first, as an appendage [to] the covenant of works delivered to the children of Israel...and secondly, as all things appertaining to it were typical of gospel things, shadows of good things to come, and so exhibited them under a veil.

Thus we see that under the old testament the kernel of the gospel was delivered under a twofold shell: viz. *1.* the law, or covenant of works, containing the moral with the ceremonial and judicial laws; *2.* the symbolical cortex, and which also in Scripture language may be called the carnal covenant, which is the thing the Scripture calls the 'veil.'...

Both these things may be signified by 'the letter' and 'the spirit.' The symbols themselves, which are expressed by the letters of the institution, are well expressed by 'the letter,' as well as the covenant of works in the Ten Commandments. And the spiritual thing typified, which was the substance and end of the type aimed at by the Spirit of God in the institution, is the 'spirit.'" M 1353, *Works* 23:500-1. M 1353 is an excellent and detailed discussion on the relationship between the Old and New Testament, beyond the scope of this present work.

to Adam; and the command of not eating the forbidden fruit was only given to try whether he would keep God's commands or no, to try whether he would be obedient to the law of nature, or moral law.[25]

Thus, "the positive precept of not eating the forbidden fruit *was added* to the covenant [of] works as delivered to our first parents" [my italics].[26] Adam possessed the revelation of the "rule of righteousness" in his heart "with great clearness," for he was "created in knowledge," in God's image, "without one deceitful lust to blind his reason and conscience, and [with] the Spirit of God dwelling in him, as a principle of perfect holiness, to enlighten him."[27] Such may be why God did not give the "precepts of the moral law" to Adam, as there was no "need of God's expressly and particularly forbidding these and those immoralities to one that is perfectly righteous in his nature, either for the making known his obligation, or for enforcing it."[28] Accordingly, Adam had "sufficient reason to expect" he would be punished as a rebel should he sin in a manner other than the prescribed prohibition of eating of the forbidden fruit.[29] Such was the case with respect to Adam's immediate posterity, for the "law of nature" or "rule of righteousness" was "written in the hearts of men, both in its precepts and penalties… from Adam to Moses, without an express revealed law."[30]

---

[25] M 884, *Works* 20:143-4.

[26] M 1353, *Works* 23:500.

[27] M 884, *Works* 20:142-3.

[28] "1 Timothy 1:9," *Works* 24:1125.

[29] M 884, *Works* 20:140-1.

[30] M 884, *Works* 20:142. "Indeed, the world had their rule of obedience from Adam to Moses, not merely by the light of nature, as it was in them, but had it partly by tradition from Adam, which they might have well delivered for a time, by reason of the long lives of Adam and the other Patriarchs." See also the text of "Romans 5:13-14," *Works* 24:998-9, noted above.

Perfect Obedience Is Required of Angels for Eternal Life

Not only is the covenant of works a universal principle to which all mankind is subject, both as to its requirement of perfect obedience and its penalty of death for disobedience, but angels also are subject to its requirements. A "sweet harmony" exists between God's transactions with angels and mankind. Angels were tried concerning their "respect and honor to God's authority," whether or not they would acquiesce to God's command "to attend upon and minister to a race of beings by nature far inferior in nature to them," and to obey, serve, and worship one of human nature, namely, Christ as God-man. In persevering in obedience to this arrangement, the angels would be confirmed in eternal life by "their adherence and voluntary submission and self-dedication to Christ crucified." Thus the angels that did not participate in Satan's rebellion "had eternal life by a covenant of works upon condition of perfect obedience."[31] Mankind had eternal life by virtue of Christ's "humiliation and sufferings." "Both have eternal life, though different ways, by their adherence and voluntary submission and self-dedication to Christ crucified." For our present purpose, it is important to see that Edwards viewed God's unchanging rule of righteousness as the foundation of God's dealings with all of His creatures. For as will be seen in the next section, His rule of righteousness is a reflection of His perfect and unchanging justice, by which He judges all things in righteousness.[32]

---

[31] "None Are Saved by Their Own Righteousness," *Works* 14:338.
[32] Edwards has an elaborate explanation of the fall of Satan and the angels with respect to God's ultimate purpose of redeeming sinful creatures and the submissive and subordinate roles that angels would be given in accomplishing that purpose. By his own admission, his views are not original, as esoteric sounding they may be. See 1057, *Works* 20:395 where he references Charles Owen and John Glas, saying, "How 'tis agreeable to the opinions of many divines, that their refusing to be ministering spirits to beings of inferior rank, and to be subject to Jesus Christ in our nature, when the design of his incarnation was first revealed in heaven, and how that, as man, he was to be the head of the angels." Unfortunately, an adequate discussion of his view of the fall and salvation of angels would take us too far afield, but in my opinion, despite the sometimes speculative nature of his explanation, he makes a plausible case that appears consistent with the biblical account. See M 320, *Works* 13:401-2; M 664b, *Works* 18:202-211; M

God's Unalterable Rule of Righteousness Reflects the Nature of God

In the following section, Edwards' understanding of the nature of God's unchanging rule of righteousness with respect to His attribute of righteousness will be examined, while a more in-depth treatment of the nature and necessity of God's justice will follow in chapter four. First, God must always uphold the honor of His authority and law, for it is a reflection of His very character. Second, God as Creator is owed perfect obedience by all His creatures. And last, as God's righteousness is unchanging, so also His rule of righteousness is unchanging.

God Must Always Uphold the Honor of His Authority and Law

"God is supreme judge of the world," and possesses "power sufficient to vindicate his own right" as that judge. "He has omnipotence wherewith to maintain his dominion over the world, and he maintains his government in the moral as well as the natural world." His right to rule and judge "cannot be disputed," while His power "cannot be controlled," and by no rebellion can sinful creatures avoid Him as their judge.[33]

God's moral government consists in His perfect execution in "giving laws" and "judging," to which all mankind is subject.[34]

> God orders all things in the moral and rational world according to that beautiful and harmonious equity and proportion which we call justice so the laws that God makes are most harmonious and equal and God distributes re-

---

744, *Works* 18:387-90; M 833, *Works* 20:45-6; M 935, M 936, M 937, M 938, M 939, M 940, M 942, *Works* 20:189-201; "Approaching the End of God's Grand Design," *Works* 25:118.
[33] "The Day of Judgment," *Works* 14:512.
[34] "The Day of Judgment," *Works* 14:511.

wards and punishments in an exact proportion to their fitness and preparedness for them.[35]

He is "necessarily and unalterably" just "to every particular person," and could "as soon cease to be" than "not render unto every one his own." To do a single unjust act is "a contradiction to the very nature and being of God."[36] Indeed, God is not required by His nature to be merciful to all, but He must always be just.

> When we say justice and holiness and a disposition or inclination of the nature of God, it is not to be distinguished from the will of God. Justice is God's constant will of giving to every one what is according to a regular equality. Yet in some things we in our way of conceiving are forced to distinguish between the free will of God and the unalterable inclination of his nature. God is merciful and gracious infinitely and yet he is not necessarily merciful to every one, but he is necessarily just to all. He can't be otherwise than just to every particular person, he is so necessarily and unalterably.[37]

Edwards may have in mind here God's gracious choice of particular persons to be redeemed according to the free choice of His benevolent will. Though a merciful act, it is nonetheless in strict accordance with His justice. For the elect were chosen in Christ, who had set His love upon them from eternity, and were united to Christ, by whom God's perfect justice was fulfilled on their behalf. As will be seen in chapters four and five, none can be redeemed apart from possessing the perfect righteousness of Christ, while any other redemption would not be "according to equality" and thus contrary to God's justice. As we have seen, the very terms of the covenant were conceived by God as a means to show goodness and mercy without injury to His justice. Christ would pay an infinite price, at infinite cost, that God's authority be honored

---

[35] "Deuteronomy 32:4," *WJEO*, L. 2v.
[36] "Deuteronomy 32:4," *WJEO*, L. 2v.
[37] "Deuteronomy 32:4," *WJEO*, L. 2r.

and justice maintained. His very majesty would be obscured if He were ever unjust.

> We have been guilty of sin, whereby we have affronted and despised God's infinite majesty. We have violated the law and despised the authority of an infinite God. Now if this contempt of divine authority and majesty may be allowed of, if he that governs the world tolerates [it] without some suitable manifestation of the evil of it by his opposition to it, and in his providence showing how dreadful a thing it is to affront such a majesty by punishing of it, it would be an obscuring of God's majesty, and it would not appear such a dreadful thing to cast contempt upon it as it is. There would be no proper manifestation of the evil of the contempt of his majesty, and consequently no proper vindication or defense of God's majesty itself.[38]

Furthermore, God's justice is both consistent and necessarily implied in God's perfections. God is creator of all things, upholds all things, and knows all things, and as He is infinite and perfect in knowledge, He knows what is the "fittest" in all things.[39] His perfect knowledge precludes His ever being deceived, and He cannot be tempted to receive any more than He already has, "for it is impossible that he should want any addition to his happiness or pleasure," for He is "self-existent" and "independent as to his happiness."[40] Should He need anything, "with infinite power he can procure it," while He cannot be tempted to procure it unjustly.[41] Injustice in God contradicts His all-sufficiency, self-existence, infinity, holiness, mercy, immutability, omniscience, and goodness.[42] Indeed, "to suppose that God is unjust contradicts all the

---

[38] "None Are Saved by Their Own Righteousness," *Works* 14:334-5.
[39] "Deuteronomy 32:4," *WJEO*, L. 4r.
[40] "Deuteronomy 32:4," *WJEO*, L. 4v.
[41] "Deuteronomy 32:4," *WJEO*, L. 5r.
[42] "Deuteronomy 32:4," *WJEO*, L. 5r. – 6r.

attributes and so the very being of God."[43] For God to be unjust is to no longer be God.[44]

Perfect Obedience Is Owed to God as Creator

God, by virtue of His "infinite greatness and excellency," is "infinitely worthy of the highest respect of the creature," such "that it would be injustice to deny it him." "He has a right in everything to be harkened to and to have his determinations attended and subjected to" by virtue of who He is as God.[45] What is more,

> All creatures…are wholly derived from and are wholly dependent on him every moment for being and all good, so that they are properly his possession. And as he has right by virtue of that to give what rules of action soever he pleases, what rules soever are agreeable to his own wisdom, [so] the mind and will of the creature ought to be entirely conformed to the nature and will of the Creator and to those rules he gives that are expressive of it.[46]

He therefore has the "absolute right himself to judge of their actions and to fulfill the sanctions of His law. He that has an absolute and independent right to give laws, has evermore the same right to judge those that he gives laws to." His rule as "supreme judge" is absolute, for "none has any right to reverse his judgment, or to receive appeals from him, or to say to him, 'Why judgest thou thus?'"[47]

Further, beings created and dependent upon God for all things have no claim on God for the blessing of eternal life. The offer of eternal life to Adam and his posterity as a reward for obedience

---

[43] "Deuteronomy 32:4," *WJEO*, L. 5r.
[44] "Deuteronomy 32:4," *WJEO*, L. 12r.
[45] "The Day of Judgment," *Works* 14:512.
[46] "The Day of Judgment," *Works* 14:512.
[47] "The Day of Judgment," *Works* 14:512.

was gracious and not required by God's justice.[48] The offer was unmerited, for there was no "proper merit in their obedience," for "their perfect obedience was a debt that they owed God." Moreover, the reward was not "bestowed for any proportion between the dignity of their obedience, and the value of the reward."[49] Rather, "God was not obliged to reward Adam for his perfect obedience any otherwise than by covenant, for Adam by standing would not have merited happiness."[50] God's offer of eternal life on the condition of "justification by works" by Adam's perfect obedience was of grace.[51] The penalty of death was pure justice, while the offer of eternal life was gracious, though consistent with God's justice as covenanted with Adam, and as all Adam's posterity would have participated in the reward had Adam obeyed.

Summary

God created Adam innocent and sinless, yet without eternal life. By God's design, or "covenant of works," Adam, as the representative and surety for all his posterity, would be required by God to give honor to His authority and law by perfect obedience to obtain eternal life. This specific command to Adam, however, was representative of the one great law of God to which all mankind in every age are subject. That law, or God's unchanging rule of righteousness, requires perfect obedience as the just requirement for eternal life and death as the penalty for sin. As the moral head and judge of the universe, God must judge sin to maintain His perfect justice or He would not be a righteous judge. Moreover, as His perfections are mutually interdependent and reflective of each other, God could not perform a single unrighteous or unjust

---

[48] Briefly defined, God's grace is "free love and kindness to his creatures," an "unmerited" love and kindness that cannot be "demanded." Moreover, it is "disinterested" and "done only from a mere inclination to beneficence and kindness," "from mere good will and not for self interest." "Romans 6:14," *WJEO*, L. 2r. – 2v.
[49] "Justification by Faith Alone," *Works* 19:238.
[50] "Glorious Grace," *Works* 10:391-2.
[51] "Romans 4:16," *WJEO*, L. 2r.

act and remain God. He must always and in every way maintain a proper honor to His authority and law according to His standard of perfect righteousness. With respect to beings created by God and dependent upon Him for all things, they necessarily owe God perfect obedience for which God is under no obligation to offer a reward, for perfect obedience is their just due to their Creator. Nonetheless, He graciously offered the reward of eternal life for Adam's obedience.

This brief chapter set out Edwards' understanding of the terms of eternal life according to God's unchanging rule of righteousness. We turn now to his understanding of the result of Adam's disobedience and failure to meet the terms of eternal life for himself and his posterity.

CHAPTER FOUR

Adam's Sin Makes Christ's Perfect Obedience the Only Basis of Salvation

In the present chapter, the following aspects of Edwards' theology of Adam's sin necessitating Christ's perfect obedience for the salvation of sinners will be examined. First, as Adam stood in the garden as the representative and surety for all mankind in his trial of obedience to God's rule of righteousness, he rendered his entire posterity guilty of sin and subject to the penalty of God's wrath for disobedience. Moreover, the inflexible and exacting nature of God's law renders all people guilty of sin in every act, while making no provision for deliverance from sin and guilt. Second, all sinners possess infinite guilt and cannot obtain eternal life by obedience to God's rule of righteousness. Every sin creates infinite guilt, while the best works of saints and sinners are infinitely sinful in light of the honor due to an infinitely holy and benevolent God. Third, Adam's sin neither altered nor abrogated God's rule of righteousness, as it is inalterable and eternal. Fourth, justification in accordance with God's rule of righteousness requires perfect positive obedience as well as pardon of sin, as mere freedom from punishment does not achieve the believer's title to glory and exaltation in heaven. Fifth, God as a righteous judge cannot judge without a rule and cannot justify without perfect righteousness. Sixth, if God's strict rule of righteousness has been replaced with a milder law that requires imperfect obedience only, then imperfect obedience meets the terms of the law and no atonement is needed, rendering Christ's death needless. Seventh, God's rule of righteousness precludes justification by any virtue or righteousness inherent in faith itself. Rather, faith unites to Christ who alone possesses the perfect righteousness required by God's rule of righteousness. And lastly, justification by the virtue or righteousness of mankind insults the glory of the Trinity, making the glory of the heavenly arrangement among the persons of the Trinity for the redemption of sinners superfluous and foolish.

Adam's Sin Makes All Mankind Guilty Sinners Under God's Wrath According to the Strict Nature of God's Rule of Righteousness

Fundamental to Edwards' understanding of the necessity of Christ's perfect obedience to God's rule of righteousness to redeem sinners is that "all men are guilty of Adam's first sin."[1] Adam stood for himself and his posterity in his trial of obedience, as the covenant God made with Adam was made with all mankind.

---

[1] "True Repentance Required," *Works* 10:512. For Edwards, the denial of both original sin and the imputation of Adam's sin to his posterity was an attack on the foundation of the gospel. For what is likely the most compelling work ever written in defense of the doctrine of original sin, see Jonathan Edwards, *Original Sin*, ed. Clyde A. Holbrook, vol. 3 of *The Works of Jonathan Edwards* (New Haven: Yale University Press, 1970), 107-437. Edwards argues from the evidence of "facts and events," as well as from an extensive array of Scriptural support, in addition to answering common objections to the doctrine. With the exception of a few instances of uncritical acceptance of Perry Miller's explanation of the nature of Covenant Theology (pp. 4-7), Holbrook's excellent introduction to *Original Sin* provides helpful context and background to the controversy and how Edwards viewed the denial of original sin as destructive to Christianity, *Works* 3:4-85. See also *Works* 3:432-458 for an excellent and concise account of Edwards' motive for writing the treatise.

Therefore, when Adam sinned, "all mankind sinned and fell in Adam."

> This is evident by Adam's being the legal head of mankind, which is the first thing insinuated. For if God, when he spake to Adam in the singular number, giving him a precept, spake to him as representing his posterity, so it will follow that he spake to him as representing his posterity in the threatening. And this is further evident by this, that death did not only reign from Adam to Moses, but also reigned over them that had not violated Adam's law themselves by their actual personal transgression, as Adam had done.[2]

Moreover, "Adam was our common father and representative who stood in our room: we were all in his loins."[3] Thus, when

---

[2] "Romans 5:13-14," *Works* 24:999. In supporting the doctrine of original sin from Romans 5:12-14, Edwards writes, "and this is further evident by this, that death did not only reign from Adam to Moses, but also reigned over them that had not violated Adam's law themselves by their actual personal transgression, as Adam had done." In other words, as death is the penalty for sin, the meaning of "because all sinned" in v. 12 must be by their participation in Adam's sin, as evidenced by the fact that those who did not sin by their "actual transgression" still die. Additionally, in the sermon "True Repentance Required," he argues from the fact that all have suffered the effect of Adam's sin: "The covenant which he broke was made with us all, and for us all in him; it cannot be supposed that the covenant that God made with Adam, He made only for his single person. That is ridiculous, for at that rate there must be a particular covenant made with every particular person, in all nations and ages. We might know that we are guilty of Adam's sin because we see that the effects of it are transmitted down to all his posterity; which if it were not so, there would be no more reason for than that all the world should feel the effect of every particular man's sin in these days." *Works* 10:512.

[3] Edwards' understanding of Adam as both the natural and covenantal head of the human race is consistent with the traditional federal or covenantal view. Turretin writes: "The bond between Adam and his posterity is twofold: (1) natural, as he is the father, and we are his children; (2) political and forensic, as he was the prince and representative head of the whole human race. Therefore the foundation of imputation is not only the natural connection which exists between us and Adam (since, in that case, all his sins might be imputed to us), but mainly the moral and federal (in virtue of which God entered into covenant with him as

Adam disobeyed God's rule of righteousness as surety for mankind, the necessary condition of man's entrance into eternal life went unfulfilled, and remained to be fulfilled if any of mankind were to obtain eternal life. Further, as all sinned in Adam and are thereby guilty of disobeying God's rule of righteousness, no one of Adam's posterity could fulfill it, as perfect obedience was and remains the requirement.

The Law Is Exceedingly Strict

The exceedingly strict nature of the law is seen in that every violation or falling short of its requirements, "however light," is sin, and that all violations of the law are punishable by death.

> The Law of God not only requires holiness in our disposition and actions, but it requires it to the utmost capacity of our natures. It don't answer the Law for us to love God unless we love him with all our hearts and with all our soul and with all our strength and with all our minds.... The Law is so strict that it allows not of any unholiness in any case whatsoever. The Law don't only bind at ordinary times and in ordinary cases but in all cases. Whatever our circumstances are, whatever our temptations are, yet the Law allows of no unholiness....The Law is so strict that it binds men in every action they do. Men are never at liberty from the obligation of the Law in any act that

---

our head). Hence Adam stood in that sin not as a private person, but as a public and representative person- representing all his posterity in that action and whose demerit equally pertains to all." Francis Turretin, *Institutes of Elenctic Theology*, vol. 1, trans. George Musgrave Giger, ed. James T. Dennison, Jr. (Phillipsburg, N.J.: Presbyterian and Reformed Publishing, 1994), 1:9:11. Also, see Murray for an excellent discussion and clarification of the misunderstanding that Edwards taught "mediate" imputation of Adam's sin to his posterity (that Adam's sin is imputed to Adam's posterity by virtue of their hereditary corruption and is the result of corruption) in contrast to "immediate" imputation where the imputation of Adam's sin precedes corruption and is the cause of inherited corruption, the latter being Edwards view. John Murray, *The Imputation of Adam's Sin* (Grand Rapids: W. B. Eerdmans, 1959), 42-70.

they perform in their whole lives, in every voluntary action they perform.[4]

The penalty for disobedience to any command of the law is death, without exception, as "it binds over to the suffering of eternal death for every transgression."[5]

> We are told, Rom. 6:23, that "the wages of sin is death," and Ezek. 18:20, [that] "the soul that sinneth, it shall die," by which is undoubtedly meant eternal destruction. The Scripture has sufficiently explained itself in that matter. When it is said, 'tis its wages, the meaning of it is that it is the recompense it deserves, and the recompense that is appointed or stated. And [that] 'tis not only intended that this is the wages of a wicked life or sinful course, but of one sin, of any one thing that is a sin or a breach of the divine law.[6]

"There is no particular sin but what deserves death...even those that were committed through ignorance," as evidenced by the fact that all sin required an animal sacrifice, signifying that the sin was worthy of death.[7] All manner of sins deserve death, including sins great or small, or the omission of prescribed duties, where the mere "tendency" or "inclination" to neglect such duties is condemnable sin. Indeed, all actions or thoughts that fall short in degree, such as the command to love God with *all* our heart, or sins of positive disobedience to any command of God, are worthy of death.[8]

---

[4] "Matthew 5:27-28," *YMSS*, L. 4r. - 5r.

[5] "Matthew 5:27-28," *YMSS*, L. 9r. - 9v.

[6] M 646, *Works* 18:179. That a single sin brings death "is evident by these texts: Genesis 2:17, 'In the day that thou eatest thereof, thou shalt surely die'; James 2:10, 'He that offends in one point, is guilty of all'; Galatians 3:10, 'Cursed is every one that continueth not in all things which are written in the book of the law to do them.'"

[7] M 646, *Works* 18:182.

[8] M 646, *Works* 18:179-85. Edward provides a comprehensive list of the various types of sins that are damnable by death, with Scripture references in support, including "one idle word," Matthew 12:36; "an ill spirit towards an enemy," Proverbs 24:17-18; "inordinate desire," "not only total omissions of what should be

> Everything in the heart of life of men that is contrary to any rule of the gospel or anything in the whole Word of God, must merit the curse and must be implied when it is said, "Cursed is every one that continues not in all things that are found written in the book of the law to do them" [Gal. 3:11].[9]

In fact, the law is so strict that not only does it "forbid the exercises of corruption, but the very being of corruption." As all are born into the world with a corrupt heart, all are therefore born "under sin" according to the law before the corruption of the heart is exercised in thought or deed. The law "requires…a perfectly holy nature."[10]

Further, not only is the law strict in its rendering of sin, the penalty of the law is exceedingly strict in that it allows for no exceptions. The threat "'thou shalt surely die'" is "so positive and absolute" that it "binds the sinner to this punishment as it were with chains of brass that cannot be broken." Indeed, "so firm is the connection between sin and death that no repentance, no tears, no cries or moans, will avail for a release."[11]

> God shows his justice in…that all that die unbelieving sinners shall by no means escape this punishment of hell. Whatever shrieks and cries and moans the punished may make there is no escaping because God is strictly just and will by no means depart from the strict rule of justice.[12]

Thus, all are condemned by the law to a "terrible," "eternal,"[13] and "exceeding great and intolerable misery as all sin deserves."[14] The judgment of God's strict rule of justice is sure, for with respect to

---

in us in heart of life, but the failure of it in any degree wherein it ought to be," Deuteronomy 6:5, 10:12, 11:13, and several others.
[9] M 646, *Works* 18:184-5.
[10] "Matthew 5:27-28," *YMSS*, L. 8r.
[11] "Matthew 5:27-28," *YMSS*, L. 6v.
[12] "Deuteronomy 32:4," *WJEO*, L. 8r.
[13] "Matthew 5:27-28," *YMSS*, L. 6r. – L. 6v.
[14] "Deuteronomy 32:4," *WJEO*, L. 8r.

the promised penalties of the law, "what God has once said, you may assuredly expect he will fulfill."[15]

Moreover, not only are all mankind sinners all the time, with all sins subject to the penalty of death by the "fixed and eternal rule of righteousness," "the Law condemns them to be entirely and only the objects of wrath without any favour or acceptance in any wise."[16] With respect to fallen creatures considered apart from Christ, "it is contrary to the Law that any thing should be accepted from them."[17] In other words (as will be discussed below), no work of fallen creatures considered apart from Christ, however positive, is acceptable to God according to the strict requirements of the law. "Our guilt and pollution is such that we can't come to God by our selves," for "our guilt is such that the glory and honour of God suffers not our coming in our own names." "God is a holy, sin-hating God, is of purer eyes than to behold evil," for "evil shall not dwell with him."[18] Man has made himself an enemy of God by his sin.

> But man has broken this friendship. He has broken the covenant that was made between God and man and broken the command of God and departed from his allegiance with heaven. Departed from his subjection to him as his sovereign, hereby man became an enemy of God.[19]

"Where sin is, there God's displeasure and hatred will be."[20] Adam, by his sin as surety for mankind, plunged all mankind into a state of enmity with God, with no hope of reconciliation apart from Christ.

---

[15] "Deuteronomy 32:4," *WJEO*, L. 11r. – 11v.
[16] "1 Peter 2:5," *YMSS*, L. 5r.
[17] "1 Peter 2:5," *YMSS*, L. 4v.
[18] "Job 33:6-7," *WJEO*, L. 4r. Edwards here quotes and cites Habakkuk 1:13.
[19] "A Glorious Foundation for Peace," *MDM*, 176. Notice Edwards' reference to the sin of Adam as the sin of "man," and the covenant with Adam as the covenant with "man." Seeing Adam as representative and surety for all mankind, Edwards often speaks in this manner.
[20] "A Glorious Foundation for Peace," *MDM*, 176-7.

> God can't be reconciled unto sin, though he may be reconciled unto sinners. Wrath must be executed upon sin till that be done. God never will be reconciled to them that committed it. Now the wrath of God is diverted from the head of the sinners and is executed upon the head of his beloved Son, who interposes himself and stands in the gap and bears all upon his own body and soul.[21]

Thus, all mankind is bound to the strict and comprehensive stipulations of the law and the unforgiving and unalterable requirement of its penalty. Further, as will be discussed below, the strict nature of God's law is founded upon the infinite excellence, goodness, and unchanging righteousness of God as the moral governor of the universe. As such, the law is a reflection of the very standard of God's own holiness and immutability, requiring the unqualified subjection of the creature to its requirements.

The Law Has No Provision for Deliverance from Sin and Guilt

Fallen sinners are under the "dominion of sin" as "it governs their hearts and behaviour" and holds them "bound to punishment."[22]

> The Law indeed strictly forbids sin, and not only so, but very severely threatens the commission of it, but yet administers no other principle to preserve from it but only a servile fear, the spirit of bondage, which principle can never deliver the heart from the love and so the power of sin or make them sincere and hearty in their obedience, and therefore is called a dead Letter.[23]

---

[21] "A Glorious Foundation for Peace," *MDM*, 176-7.
[22] "Romans 6:14," *WJEO*, L. 1r.
[23] "Romans 6:14," *WJEO*, L. 1r. – 1v. See also Edwards' commentary on Galatians 4:9, in *Works* 24:1084, wherein he writes, "the law is here called 'weak,' because it could not give righteousness and life. See Romans 8:3 and Galatians 2:21. And it is called 'beggarly,' because it kept men in the poor estate of pupils from the possession of the inheritance. See vv. 1-3."

What's more, rather than diminishing the power of sin, the law excites and intensifies it to a "more violently raging in the heart."[24]

Furthermore, the Ten Commandments and "other passages of the Law of Moses" were given to highlight mankind's inability to meet the strict standard of God's rule of righteousness and the corresponding need of a mediator.

> Nothing is more apparent by the Scripture than that the terms of the covenant of works, or terms of that kind, were often proposed in the Old Testament to men as though God insisted on their being fulfilled, and as though God expected that they should fulfill 'em, and in that way obtain life, because the fulfillment of those terms was indeed their duty, and because God would put 'em on trial for their conviction and humiliation, to fit them for the proper exercise of faith in a Mediator.[25]

Both the Old and New Testaments testify that the law was given "as though" it should be perfectly fulfilled to obtain eternal life.[26] "Christ, after He appeared in the flesh, still went on to treat men after the same manner. He proposed legal terms to the rich young man for his conviction."[27] In commenting on Christ's encounter with the rich young ruler in Matthew 19:17-18, Edwards writes,

> And so doth God still in the law of Moses promise life upon condition of perfect obedience, that men, by trial and experience of themselves, might be convinced of the impossibility of their being justified by the law. God

---

[24] "Romans 6:14," *WJEO*, L. 1r. – 1v.
[25] M 1354, *Works* 23:511.
[26] "It is out of all dispute that the Ten Commandments were delivered at Mt. Sinai as a covenant of works, in this manner and for these ends, by what the Apostle says, Gal. 3:17-25, Rom. 7:1-13, Rom. 3:19-21 with ch. 5:13-14, II Cor. 3:7-9.

The same is no less manifest concerning other passages in the Law of Moses, as particularly that in Lev. 18:5, 'Ye shall therefore keep my statutes, and my judgments: which if a man do, he shall live in them,' and other passages of the same tenor." M 1354, *Works* 23:511.
[27] M 1354, *Works* 23:512.

> promises life for future obedience, for though if a man should perfectly obey for the future, he could not be justified according to the tenor of the law, because he is guilty of Adam's sin and of original sin.[28]

Accordingly, Moses and Christ offer "a thing impossible" in proposing life by obedience to the law for another purpose, for "it could not be God's design to leave the matter so, having only revealed to the people a way for them to obtain righteousness that is impossible." The purpose, therefore, of "the former revelation of an impossible way was only to make way for this," that "'Christ is the end of the law for righteousness to everyone that believeth.'"[29] The giving of the law, in light of the unforgiving strict nature of the law, reveals the impossibility of salvation by human effort and the need of salvation by faith in Christ alone. The strict nature of the law precludes the obtaining of eternal life any other way. Even Abraham was not justified by works of the law, because "the promise that he should be the heir of the [world] was not to Abraham or to his seed through the Law but through the righteousness of faith." If the promise to Abraham was "made through the law the promise would be of no effect because the Law worketh wrath. There are none of the seed of Abraham that ever perfectly kept the Law."[30]

The greatest evidence of the strict nature of the law is the extent to which God went to fulfill it.

> There is in some respects the most glorious discovery of God's vindictive justice in the work of redemption by Jesus in his punishing of sin when imputed to his own and only son intimately near and dear to him…rather than justice should not have its course. He would bring such sore and dreadful pain, misery distress and wrath upon the son of his eternal and infinite delight. This shows the se-

---

[28] "Matthew 19:17-18," *Works* 24:859.
[29] "Romans 10:4-8," *Works* 24:1026.
[30] "Romans 4:16," *WJEO*, L. 1v.

verity and inflexibleness of God's justice beyond any thing else and so as nothing else can do.[31]

The nature of Christ's redemptive work in meeting the requirements of God's justice will be examined in chapter five.

All Sinners Possess Infinite Guilt and Cannot Obtain Eternal Life by Obedience

All Sin Bears Infinite Guilt Requiring Infinite Satisfaction

The infinite demerit of sin in light of the infinite holiness of God is foundational to Edwards' understanding of the necessity of Christ's perfect obedience.[32] The principle that renders sin against God an infinite demerit is this: the greater the excellence of the being to be loved and honored, the greater the obligation to love and honor that being. Therefore, "if a being be infinitely excellent and lovely, our obligations to love him are therein infinitely great."[33]

Further, "the sin of the creature against God is ill-deserving in proportion to the distance there is between God and the creature, the greatness of the object, and the meanness of the subject that aggravates it."[34] Thus, in consideration of the excellent worthiness of God as compared to the creature, "all sin is infinitely heinous," and the sinner, "before he is justified, is under infinite guilt

---

[31] "Deuteronomy 32:4," *WJEO*, L. 9r.
[32] Edwards' *Quæstio*, in *Works*, 14:55-64, delivered at Yale in September of 1723, represents his early understanding of the absolute inadequacy of "sincere obedience" for the salvation of sinners, and the absolute necessity of Christ's perfect obedience for the same in light of God's infinite holiness and the corresponding infinite demerit of sin. It is not apparent that Edwards ever deviated from this view, though over the years of his ministry he further developed and expounded it.
[33] "Justification by Faith Alone," *Works* 19:161. See also M 713, *Works* 18:343.
[34] "Justification by Faith Alone," *Works* 19:162.

in God's sight."[35] And despite the fact that everything is "infinitely easy" to God by virtue of His omnipotence, we are by sin "so deeply plunged into a most miserable and sinful condition," that "with respect to God's holiness and justice, God himself could not redeem us without...infinite costs."[36] "God is a God of infinite justice and it is impossible there should be any breach made in it."[37] Sin is of "infinite demerit" and therefore requires something of "infinite worth and value" to purge it away.[38] There can be no alternative, for the infinite demerit of sin can only be paid by an infinite price. It is "requisite that God should punish all sin with infinite punishment; because all sin, as it is against God, is infinitely heinous, and has infinite demerit," and "is justly infinitely hateful to him, and so stirs up infinite abhorrence and indignation in him."[39] "It would not be a prudent, decent and beautiful thing for a being of infinite glory and majesty, and the sovereign of the world, to let an infinite evil go unpunished."[40] "The honor of the greatness, excellency, and majesty of God's being requires that sin be punished with an infinite punishment."[41] Indeed, God's glory requires that He take vengeance on sin.

> If it be to God's glory that he is in his nature infinitely holy and opposite to sin, then it is to his glory to be infinitely displeased with sin; and if it be to God's glory to be infinitely displeased with sin, then it must be to God's glory to exercise and manifest that displeasure, and act according to it. But the proper exercise and testimony of displeasure against sin, in the supreme being and absolute governor of the world, is taking vengeance.[42]

---

[35] "Justification by Faith Alone," *Works* 19:163. Also, "Deuteronomy 32:4," *WJEO*, L. 11v: "The justice of God obliges Him to punish every one of your sins. The least of your sins you deserve eternal burnings for."
[36] "Glorious Grace," *Works* 10:393.
[37] "Christ's Sacrifice," *Works* 10:601.
[38] "Christ's Sacrifice," *Works* 10:599.
[39] M 779, *Works* 18:435. See also "Glorious Grace," *Works* 10:601.
[40] M 306, *Works* 13:391.
[41] M 779, *Works* 18:439.
[42] M 779, *Works* 18:438.

It would not be "becoming" of "the sovereign of the world," of "infinite glory, purity, and beauty," to make no opposition or display "of his infinite abhorrence" in the world to such "an infinitely detestable pollution" as sin. Such "would be countenancing of it, which God cannot do: For 'he is of purer eyes than to behold evil, and cannot look on iniquity.'"[43]

Further, "it is not consistent with the perfections of the divine to justify on account of…repentance, which is so slight that it bears absolutely no proportion to the offense," and is "infinitely inadequate to the fault, and hence is a repentance utterly worthless if it is compared to the sin."[44] Indeed, "it would be as dishonorable for God to pardon the injury upon repentance that did not bear the least proportion to the injury, as for him to pardon without any repentance at all."[45] "There can be no repentance of it, or sorrow for it, in any measure answerable, or proportionable, to the heinousness of the demerit of the crime."[46] "The greatest finite repentance bears no proportion at all" to "infinite wickedness," while "the same thing can be said of all good works, namely that they are infinitely inadequate for sin." Thus, "it is contradictory to the divine attributes that a sinner should somehow in the least degree be justified because of sincere repentance or obedience."[47]

> Sin, of which he [fallen man] is guilty, is an evil of infinite badness….So that let him do what good works he will, yet if they are put in the scale with the evil, they bear absolutely no proportion at all; the scale of evil is not at all raised by it: the man taken together is every whit as bad in the sight of God as if he had no good works at all, because his evil infinitely outweighs it, and the good is perfectly adequate to nothing in comparison of it.[48]

---

[43] M 779, *Works* 18:438. Edwards cites Habakkuk 1:13.
[44] "Quæstio," *Works* 14:61-2.
[45] M oo, *Works* 13:188.
[46] M 779, *Works* 18:435.
[47] "Quæstio," *Works* 14:62.
[48] M 40, *Works* 13:223.

Apart from Christ, God views man "as he is in himself; and so his goodness can't be beheld by God, but as taken with his guilt and hatefulness, and as put in the scales with it," thus "his goodness is nothing; because there is a finite on the balance against an infinite, whose proportion to it is nothing."[49] "There is no merit in the goodness that is in them, or gracious works that they perform, but there is infinite demerit in the sins that they have been guilty of."[50] If good works are "considered separately and by themselves, they are infinitely abominable" and cannot compensate for the "infinite evil and demerit of sin."[51]

All said, sin is an infinite evil and demerit against an infinitely holy God, who as a righteous judge must judge sin according to its desert. Therefore, an infinite price must be paid if sin is to be adequately punished. Indeed, it requires the blood of Christ, the "least drop" of which renders "all created beings" as "nothing" to God by comparison.[52]

> When we were fallen, it was come to this: either we must die eternally, or the Son of God must spill his blood; either we, or God's own Son must suffer God's wrath, one of the two; either miserable worms of the dust that had deserved it, or the glorious, amiable, beautiful, and innocent Son of God. The fall of man brought it to this; it must be determined one way or t'other.[53]

In view of this, the infinite demerit of sin is most clearly manifest in the sufferings of Christ for sin, in the "sufferings of a person of infinite glory."[54]

---

[49] "Justification by Faith Alone," *Works* 19:164. See also "None Are Saved by Their Own Righteousness," *Works* 14:341.
[50] "1 Peter 2:5," *YMSS*, L. 4r.
[51] "1 Peter 2:5," *YMSS*, L. 3v.
[52] "Christ's Sacrifice," *Works* 10:599.
[53] "Glorious Grace," *Works* 10:393.
[54] M 941, *Works* 20:199-0.

All Good Works Are Corrupt and Infinitely Hateful

In the previous section we have seen that good works possess infinite demerit, since they can never compensate for the infinite demerit of sin. In this section we see that the good works themselves are infinitely sinful, apart from consideration of the infinite demerit of other sins that may accompany, precede, or follow. In other words, "the virtuous acts themselves," viewed apart from Christ and the consideration of any accompanying sin, are "corrupt."[55] The best acts are defective, and "that defect is properly sin, and expression of a vile sinfulness of heart, and what tends to provoke the just anger of God."[56] It is impossible that any human or angelic work of "love" or "grace" can be equal to the loveliness of God.

> The act is so very disproportionate to the occasion given for love or other grace, considering God's loveliness, and the manifestation that is made of it, and the exercises of kindness, and the capacity of human nature, and our advantages (and the like) together. A negative expression of corruption may be as truly sin, and as just cause of provocation, as a positive....And so it is with respect to our exercise of love, and gratitude, and other graces towards God, they are defectively corrupt and sinful.[57]

Accordingly, "this defect is sin, it is infinitely hateful." And as our best response to the infinite goodness of God toward us is so out of proportion to the goodness received, it constitutes "an act of ingratitude, or positive exercise of a base unworthy spirit."[58] In fact, should someone live an entirely perfect life according to the law with the exception of a single sin, he or she would become

---

[55] "Justification by Faith Alone," *Works* 19:212-3.
[56] "Justification by Faith Alone," *Works* 19:212.
[57] "Justification by Faith Alone," *Works* 19:212-3.
[58] "Justification by Faith Alone," *Works* 19:213. See also "1 Peter 2:5," *YMSS*, L. 7v.

118   *The Infinite Merit of Christ*

an object of God's infinite displeasure.[59] And while the works themselves corrupt in this manner, they are also "mixed" with large amounts of corruption.[60] So, in both respects, all that we do is corrupt.

Further, even the best works and most "gracious exercises" of the saints are corrupt, and would be abhorrent to God if their sin and corruption were not concealed by Christ.[61] "God…accepts them for Christ's sake, which but of him would be worthy of his detestation."[62] Thus the "freeness and sovereignty of the grace of God in saving sinners" is seen by the fact that our good works or personal righteousness cannot be a positive influence in the matter. "Surely all that they do before they love God can have no influence to draw God's love," for *all* human works of themselves are odious to God and only made acceptable for Christ's sake alone. Therefore:

> How unreasonable is it to think that God's love should be drawn by what they do from no sort of respect to him at all. And what they do after they love God don't draw the love of God, and don't at all the more incline God to be gracious to them, to forgive their sins and show and bestow any outward or spiritual mercy upon them, for that

---

[59] M 627, *Works* 18:156. "If we had never committed but one sin and at all other times had exercised perfect holiness and performed perfect obedience, yet looking upon us as we are by ourselves, with all that belongs to us, we should be in no degree lovely persons but hateful, though we had performed many lovely acts; and no one act of holiness is a lovely act in itself and with consideration of any relation to Christ, unless it be a perfect act."

[60] "1 Peter 2:5," *YMSS*, L. 5v. Also, in commenting on Romans 3:10 and following, Edwards writes: "The passages here quoted out of the Old Testament are to prove three things. 1. That mankind are universally sinful; that everyone is corrupt. That is what is aimed at in the tenth, eleventh, and twelfth verses. 2. That everyone is not only corrupt, but everyone totally corrupt in every part. That is aimed at by the quotations in the thirteenth, fourteenth, fifteenth verses, where the several parts of the body are mentioned. And 3. That everyone is not only corrupt in every part, but corrupt throughout in an exceeding degree, in the sixteenth, seventeenth, eighteenth verses." "Romans 3:13ff.," *Works* 24:991.

[61] "Colossians 3:17," *Works* 24:1117.

[62] "Colossians 3:17," *Works* 24:1117-8.

love is a fruit of God's love to them. All their good works be not the cause of God's love, but the effect of it. God in his infinite love gives them grace to love him and enables them to do things of love to him. Their good works are God's gift to them and not their Gift to God.[63]

In the same way, the good works of the saints are only rewarded in Christ, for the sake of His righteousness alone (to be discussed further in chapter five).

Adam's Sin Does Not Cancel or Alter God's Rule of Righteousness

The Nature of God and His Law Will Not Allow It

Much of what has been said thus far gives evidence that God's rule of righteousness is unalterable. And as will be seen in chapter five, the fact that it was necessary for Christ to fulfill God's rule of righteousness clearly shows that Adam's sin did not alter its requirements, but necessitated that Christ fulfill the requirements on behalf of sinners if any sinners were to obtain eternal life. Additionally, however, Edwards provides a concise list of five reasons why "the law of God should be maintained and executed, and not dispensed with or abrogated for the sake of the sinner," answering the question of why God would not reduce the requirements of the law in light of the impossibility of the sinner to meet its standards.[64] He gives the following reasons.

First, a law that is not fixed with respect to those subject to its requirements is without authority and is no longer a law. "It fails of being a rule of the supreme Judge."[65]

> The law is the great rule of righteousness and decorum, that the supreme and universal Rector has established and

---

[63] "1 John 4:19," *WJEO*, L. 8r.
[64] M 779, *Works* 18:442-5.
[65] M 779, *Works* 18:442.

published, for the regulation of things in the commonwealth of the universality of intelligent beings and moral agents, in all that relates to them as concerned one with another; a rule by which things are not only to be regulated between one subject and another, but between the King and [his] subjects, that it may be a rule of judgment to the one, as well as a rule of duty to the other.[66]

"'Tis needful that this great rule of regulation of things in this universal commonwealth, should be fixed and settled, and not vague and uncertain," for if it is not fixed, "it ceases to be of a nature of a rule."[67]

Second, the design of the law is to regulate the sinner, not to be regulated by the sinner. The law is made "that [it] might prevent sin, and cause that not to be, and not that sin should disannul that, and cause it not to be." "It would be very indecent for the supreme Rector to cause this great rule to give place to the rebellion of the sinner."[68]

Third, "the perfection of the law" is "an expression of the perfection of the Lawgiver."

The holiness and rectitude and goodness of this great rule, that the supreme Lawgiver has established for the regulation of the commonwealth of moral agents, and its universal fitness and wisdom and absolute perfection, render a partial abrogation for the sake of them that dislike it, and won't submit to it, needless and unseemly. If the great rule should be set aside for the sake of the rebel, it would carry too much of the face of an acknowledgement in the Lawgiver, of want of wisdom and foresight, or of some defect in point of holiness or righteousness in his law.[69]

---

[66] M 779, *Works* 18:442.
[67] M 779, *Works* 18:443.
[68] M 779, *Works* 18:443.
[69] M 779, *Works* 18:443.

To "set aside" even a part of the law would be "unfit" and "a dishonor to the excellency of the law and Lawgiver." Moreover, "if the rule be perfect, perfectly right and just and holy, and with infinite wisdom adapted to the good of the whole, then the public good require that it be strongly established." Accordingly, "the more strongly it is guarded and defended, the better, and the more is it for the public benefit," while "everything by which it is weakened, is a damage and loss" to the same.[70]

Fourth, "the authority of a ruler should be sacred proportionably to the greatness of that authority," of "his worthiness of honor and obedience, the height of his exaltation above us, and the absoluteness of his dominion over us, and the strength of his right to our submission and obedience." Thus, the "sacredness of the authority and majesty of the Lawgiver" must "maintain and fulfill his law, when it is violated by a rebellious subject."[71]

> It is not becoming the sacredness of the majesty and authority of the great παντοκράτωρ[72] that that perfectly holy, just, and infinitely wise and good law that he has established, as the great rule for the regulation of all things in the universal commonwealth of beings, should be set aside to give place to the infinitely unreasonable and vile opposition that sinners make to it, and their horrid and daring rebellion against it.[73]

Fifth, "the truth of the Lawgiver" requires "that the threatenings of the law should be fulfilled in every punctilio. The threatening of the law is absolute: 'Thou shalt surely die' [Gen. 2:17]"[74]

The laws of "weak and fallible and very imperfect" lawgivers may be discarded, but not so the laws of "the great, infinitely wise, omniscient, holy, and absolutely perfect Rector of all, to whom it

---

[70] M 779, *Works* 18:444.
[71] M 779, *Works* 18:444.
[72] Almighty, omnipotent.
[73] M 779, *Works* 18:445.
[74] M 779, *Works* 18:445.

belongs to establish a rule for the regulation of the whole universality of beings, throughout all eternity," of one who rules "in the exercise of an infinitely strong right of supreme, absolute dominion and sovereignty." The more wise and good a law, and "the nearer any law approaches to the supreme in perfection and in extent of jurisdiction, the more care should be taken of its execution."[75]

God's Rule of Righteousness Is Eternal and Unaltered by Salvation by Grace

Connected to Edwards' understanding of the nature of God and the law prohibiting its abrogation by the sinfulness of its subjects is that the law is eternal, "a fixed and eternal rule of righteousness."[76] As noted in chapter three, the command to Adam was an expression of God's unchanging rule of righteousness. Moreover, as Adam stood as representative and surety for all mankind in his trial of obedience to God's rule of righteousness, the covenant made with Adam was made with all mankind. Thus, with respect to "the condition of eternal life,"

> God never made but one with man, to wit, the covenant of works; which never yet was abrogated, but is a covenant stands in full force to all eternity without the failing of one tittle. The covenant of grace is not another covenant made with man upon the abrogation of this, but a covenant made with Christ to fulfill it.[77]

Accordingly, "for this end came Christ into the world, to fulfill the law, or covenant of works, for all that receive him."[78] In other words,

> The covenant of grace or redemption (which we have shown to be the same) cannot be called a new covenant,

---

[75] M 779, *Works* 18:448.
[76] "1 Peter 2:5," *YMSS*, L. 4v.
[77] M 30, *Works* 13:217.
[78] M 30, *Works* 13:217.

or the second covenant, with respect to the covenant of works; for that is not grown old yet but is an eternal immutable covenant, of which one jot nor tittle will never fail.[79]

Though Edwards often speaks of the covenant of grace in distinction from the covenant of works, "there have never been two covenants, in strictness of speech," rather, "only two ways constituted of performing of this covenant" (the covenant of works). The first was with Adam as "the representative and federal head," and the second was with Christ as "the federal head;" the former a "dead way," the latter "a living way and an everlasting" way.[80] In either case, perfect obedience is the required condition of the covenant.

We noted earlier that Israel was under the covenant of works and made "to understand that none of those promises he had made could be challenged without perfect obedience," that they might be driven by their inability to meet its terms to trust only in the "mere underserved mercy of God" and be "saved by grace."[81] Indeed, the Old Testament sacrifices "were necessary…for the maintaining the honor of God's law and authority."

> If they had only been taught that upon their repentance and flying to God's mercy they should be pardoned by mercy, without giving any hints wherefore, it would lead them into this thought, that howsoever wicked men were and how much soever they had provoked and affronted God, yet he was ready at any time to forgive them; which would tend to their despising and making little of God's commanding authority, and to lessen their thoughts of his holy majesty.[82]

God was "careful to instruct them that he was a jealous God and would in no wise clear the guilty; and by requiring these sacrifices

---
[79] M 35, *Works* 13:219.
[80] M 35, *Works* 13:219.
[81] M 250, *Works* 13:362.
[82] M 326, *Works* 13:405.

intimated to them that he would not pardon without satisfaction." Moreover, "the sufferings of the slain beast intimated that sin must be suffered for, hereby showing his holy hatred and discountenancing of sin and trespasses against his authority."[83]

The same principle applies to the present day, though the nature of its presentation may differ.

> We are indeed now under the covenant of works so, that if we are perfectly righteous we can challenge salvation. But herein is the difference betwixt us and them: to us God has plainly declared the impossibility of obtaining life by that covenant, and lets us know that no mortal can be saved but only of mere grace, and lets us know clearly how we are made partakers of grace. All ever since the fall were equally under the covenant of grace so far, that they were saved by it all alike, but the difference is in the revelation: the covenant of works was most clearly revealed to the Israelites, to us the covenant of grace.[84]

Thus, the way of salvation and the underlying requirement of perfect obedience remain the same in both the New and Old Testaments. And as the Old Testament saints received grace with the understanding of God's "holy hatred and discountenancing of sin and trespasses against his authority," and that pardon could not be without satisfaction, as He "would in no wise clear the guilty," so also New Testament saints, in trusting "the mere mercy of God," God's holiness and "sovereign authority" are understood as upheld by Christ crucified.[85]

---

[83] M 326, *Works* 13:405.
[84] M 250, *Works* 13:362.
[85] M 326, *Works* 13:405-6.

God's Unalterable Rule of Righteousness Requires Perfect Positive Righteousness for Justification

In introducing the present section concerning the requirement of perfect positive righteousness for justification, a review of the main points of chapter three will help explain how Edwards defines justification as consistent with and founded upon the unchanging nature of God and the rule of righteousness by which God regulates His relationship to His creatures. Additionally, this will further clarify the many facets of his overall understanding of the doctrine.

First, the justification of sinners relates to Adam's original trial of obedience as substitute and surety for mankind. Mankind, in Adam, was to obey and give honor to God's authority and law by perfect and positive obedience in order to obtain eternal life. As a result of Adam's sin, however, mankind did not and could not meet the standard of perfect positive obedience for the obtaining of eternal life.

Second, all God's commands are comprehended in that one great law that demands perfect obedience and fixes death as the penalty for any and all disobedience. The command to Adam was a manifestation of God's unchanging rule of righteousness, to which all mankind in all ages is subject. Moreover, the requirement of positive and perfect obedience for the obtaining of eternal life and the penalty of death for any and all acts of disobedience to God's rule of righteousness has never been abrogated. Thus, when mankind sinned in Adam, the requirement for mankind to obtain eternal life went unmet.

Third, God's rule of righteousness reflects the righteousness of God's own nature. Perfect righteousness characterizes God's justice. To act in any one instance in a manner inconsistent with righteousness is impossible, for God would not be God. Moreover, as the sovereign moral ruler of the universe, He must at all times uphold His authority and law. And as Creator, perfect obedience is owed Him by the creature.

Thus, Edwards' understanding of the nature of justification is founded upon and consistent with the nature of God in His unchangeable and righteous authority as the moral creator and sovereign ruler over the universe. God's requirement of perfect obedience from Adam for the obtaining of eternal life was neither arbitrary nor alterable, as it reflected an eternal principle rooted in the very nature of God Himself. This will be explained further in the present discussion and in chapter five.

Pardon Gives Freedom from Punishment Only, Justification Requires Perfect Positive Righteousness

Edwards' two-fold definition of justification as requiring a "negative" and "positive" righteousness further reveals how Adam's sin made Christ's perfect obedience the only possible basis for the salvation of sinners. He defines justification as follows:

> A person is said to be justified when he is approved of God as free from the guilt of sin, and its deserved punishment, and as having that righteousness belonging to him that entitles to the reward of life.[86]

Further, to be justified or "approved" requires a "law or rule" by which one is judged.

> To justify a person in a particular case, is to approve of him as standing right, as subject to the law or rule in that case; and to justify in general, is to pass him in judgment, as standing right, in a state correspondent to the law or rule in general.[87]

To be justified by God, therefore, is to be judged by God as "standing right" with respect to God's rule or law. So, if conformity to God's law requires more than the "negative" righteousness of the absence of the guilt of sin, requiring also that the "positive" re-

---
[86] "Justification by Faith Alone," *Works* 19:150.
[87] "Justification by Faith Alone," *Works* 19:150.

quirement of the law be met, then justification requires more than the absence of guilt.[88]

> We are no more justified by the voice of the law, or of him that judges according to it, by a mere pardon of sin, than Adam our first surety, was justified by the law, at the first point of his existence, before he had done the work, or fulfilled the obedience of the law, or had had so much as any trial whether he would fulfill it or no.[89]

In other words, if the mere absence of guilt met the requirement of God's law by which Adam and all mankind were judged, then Adam would have been justified and fit for eternal life prior to his trial of obedience, for he was created without sin. Nonetheless, despite his sinless status prior to his fall, Adam was to be tried for his obedience to God's authority and law for the obtaining of eternal life.

As we have seen above, all mankind are sinners bearing infinite guilt that can only be remedied by an infinite satisfaction. Additionally, none have met the standard of perfect positive obedience as required by God's unchanging rule of righteousness for the obtaining of eternal life. Both would need to be satisfied, however, for the obtaining of eternal life according to God's eternal rule of righteousness, of which the command to Adam was representative. To be pardoned apart from possessing righteousness, therefore, would not meet God's standard of righteousness.

Edwards defines pardon as that which "signifies forgiving one freely, though he is not innocent, or has no right to be looked on as such." Though guilty, the sinner is "freed from punishment." When Christ acquits people from the penalty of sin, however, He

---

[88] "Justification by Faith Alone," *Works* 19:150. See also "The Threefold Work of the Holy Ghost," *Works* 14:394: "Justification consists in these two things, viz. in removing guilt in the pardon of sin and reconciliation, which is only a negative righteousness and a mere removal of God's anger; and then second, a looking upon the sinner as positively righteous and receiving him as the object of favor, not only as merely not the object of anger."

[89] "Justification by Faith Alone," *Works* 19:150.

acts according to justice, for He views and accepts them as possessing satisfaction for sin, the "equivalent to innocence."[90]

> 'Tis called pardon because, though in itself it be an act of justice, and strictly speaking the person pardoned has no sin or guilt to be pardoned, yet considered with those preceding free and sovereign acts of God that are its foundation, viz. the free gift of Christ, and the free establishment of the covenant of grace, the free giving us repentance and faith in Christ for remission, I say, considered with these things, 'tis a most free and wonderfully gracious act, and may well be called pardon.[91]

Thus, insofar as "pardon" signifies a gracious sovereign act of God as judge, Christians are "pardoned," though not according to the common meaning of the guilty released from punishment. For justification is more than pardon of sin, and strictly speaking, is not equivalent to pardon of sin, but a "sentence approving" the sinner "as innocent and positively righteous, and so having a right to freedom from punishment, and to the reward of positive righteousness."[92] The believer's freedom from punishment, or "pardon," is founded on innocence and satisfaction. Accordingly, justification entails the imputation of righteousness as the basis of the believer's pardon.

> To pardon sin is to cease to be angry for sin. But imputing righteousness and ceasing to be angry for sin are two

---

[90] M 812, *Works* 18:522.

[91] M 812, *Works* 18:522.

[92] M 812, *Works* 18:522. See also "Romans 5:1-2," *Works* 24:995: "There is a threefold benefit of justification mentioned in these two verses. 1. Peace with God, which consists in deliverance from God's displeasure and wrath. 2. The present free and rich bounty of God that we are admitted to, those spiritual enjoyments, and that spiritual good and blessedness, which is bestowed upon us in this life, as in the beginning of the next verse, 'By whom also we have access by faith to this grace wherein we stand.' 3. Our hope of future blessedness, or those fruits of God's grace that are to be given hereafter, in these words, 'And rejoice in the hope of the glory of God.'" The latter two blessings are the reward for Christ's positive righteousness.

> things; one is the foundation of the other. God ceases to be angry with the sinner for his sin because righteousness is imputed to him.
>
> Mere pardon can in no propriety be called justification. If one that is called before a judge, and is tried—whether he be guilty of such a crime, and so whether he be bound to the punishment of it—be acquitted in judgment as being found innocent, and so under no obligation to punishment, then he may properly be said to be justified. But if he be found guilty, and is condemned, but afterward, as a justly condemned malefactor, is freely pardoned, whoever calls that justifying of him?[93]

Therefore, "persons cannot be justified without a righteousness consistent with God's truth, for it would be a false sentence."[94] "To suppose a sinner pardoned without a righteousness implies no contradiction, but to justify without a righteousness is self-contradictory."[95] God justifies the sinner in pronouncing him "perfectly righteous" with respect to "the rule that he is under," and this, "according to the established rule of nature, reason, and divine appointment, is a positive perfect righteousness."[96]

The declaration of the believer's righteousness is no fiction, no proclamation contrary to the facts of the case.

> Now in order to a sinner's being thus accepted with God, there must be some real righteousness that must be the sinner's. God don't look upon sinners as righteous for

---

[93] M 812, *Works* 18:522-3.
[94] M 812, *Works* 18:523.
[95] M 812, *Works* 18:522-3.
[96] "Justification by Faith Alone," *Works* 19:190-1. See also, "The Threefold Work of the Holy Ghost," *Works* 14:395: "All that is needed therefore in order to a sinner's reconciliation and acceptance {with God} is a righteousness. And then the righteousness must be perfect, that is, righteousness fully and completely answerable to God's commandments, because one sin brings guilt and a desert of punishment incurs displeasure and hatred. And then it is necessary according to the law, the eternal, invariable rule {of God}."

nothing, when they have no righteousness properly theirs; he don't look upon them to be or to have what they are or have not. 'Tis not a notion, but a reality.[97]

Indeed, to be "entitled to happiness in God's favour," one must have a "positive" and "perfect" righteousness that "must some way or other be ours."[98]

> Either we our selves must perform such a righteousness, or such a righteousness performed by some other must be imputed to us and we must some way or other become entitled to it so that it should be ours in the sight of God.[99]

Having no righteousness of our own, "we have a necessity that some other person worthy to be accepted of God on our account should perform that righteousness for us."[100] God will have "no regard" for an imperfect righteousness, "but will reject it and cast it as dung in our faces if we pretend to bring it and offer it to him. He is so righteous and holy a being that he will not accept such an offering."[101] The righteousness accepted by God must be "a reality."[102]

---

[97] "The Threefold Work of the Holy Ghost," *Works* 14:395.
[98] "Deuteronomy 32:4," *WJEO*, L. 10r.
[99] "Deuteronomy 32:4," *WJEO*, L. 10r. That "some way or other" by which one is "entitled" to the righteousness performed by another is union with Christ by faith, whereby Christ's perfect righteousness becomes the believer's righteousness. An adequate discussion of Edwards' understanding of the application of redemption is well beyond the scope of this work, as the present topic concerns the accomplishment of redemption, primarily. Nonetheless, the nature of faith as the believer's part of union with Christ, and the nature of the union will be discussed briefly in chapter five. Such is Edwards' answer to how the perfect righteousness of Christ becomes the believer's righteousness in a manner that God, in truth and according to reality, justifies a sinner in declaring him or her to be perfectly righteous, as having met the strict requirement of His unchanging rule of righteousness.
[100] "Deuteronomy 32:4," *WJEO*, L. 10v.
[101] "Deuteronomy 32:4," *WJEO*, L. 10r. Edwards here alludes to the requirement of unblemished animals to be used in the animal sacrifices of the Old Testament.
[102] "The Threefold Work of the Holy Ghost," *Works* 14:395.

Therefore, for the sinner to be justified according to the "negative" and "positive" righteousness required by God's rule of righteousness is to be judged as having fulfilled its requirements, "such as Adam would have had if he had withstood the temptation and had persevered in obedience."[103] Granted, the exaltation earned for the believer by the infinite merit of Christ's obedience will greatly exceed that which Adam would have gained by his obedience (as will be explained in chapter five). Nonetheless, the principle for obtaining eternal life is exactly the same for Adam as for his posterity, as it is according to the same requirements of the same rule of righteousness.

Therefore, to be forgiven one's sins only, without having performed the positive righteousness required by the law, would render one's status with respect to eternal life as equal to that of Adam's status before his fall.[104] "Supposing…that the sinner himself could by suffering pay the debt, and afterwards be in the same state that he was in before his probation," namely, "negatively righteous, or merely without guilt," and "should have eternal life bestowed upon him, without performing that condition of obedience, then God would recede from his law" and "never have respect and honor shown to it."[105]

> Christ by suffering the penalty, and so making atonement for us, only removes the guilt of our sins and so sets us in the same state that Adam was in the first moment of his creation: and it is no more fit, that we should obtain eternal life, only on that account, than that Adam should have the reward of eternal life, or of a confirmed and unalterable state of happiness, the first moment of his existence, without any obedience at all.[106]

---

[103] "Romans 4:16," *WJEO*, L. 2v.
[104] "The Threefold Work of the Holy Ghost," *Works* 14:396-7. "Christ, by suffering in our stead and removing guilt, only places us in the state Adam was in the first moment {he was created}, without any probation at all."
[105] "Justification by Faith Alone," *Works* 19:188. See also M 322, *Works* 13:403, from which Edwards apparently quoted in "Justification by Faith Alone."
[106] "Justification by Faith Alone," *Works* 19:187.

If Adam were to be rewarded with eternal life for his innocence, "he would have had it fixed upon him at once, as soon as ever he was created; for he was as innocent then as he could be."[107] "There would have been no occasion to make any covenant at all with our first parents: for they were free from guilt the first moment they were created."[108] On the contrary, "he was to have the reward on account of his activeness in obedience; not on the account merely of his not having done ill, but on account of his doing well." In the same way, believers do not possess eternal life "merely on the account of being void of guilt," but also "on the account of Christ's activeness in obedience, and doing well."[109]

> Christ is our second federal head, and is called the second Adam (I Cor. 15:22), because he acted the part for us, that the first Adam should have done: when he had undertaken to stand in our stead, he was looked upon, and treated as though he were guilty with our guilt; and by his satisfying, or bearing the penalty, he did as it were free himself from this guilt. But by this, the second Adam did only bring himself into the state that the first Adam was in on the first moment of his existence, viz. a state of mere freedom from guilt; and hereby indeed was free from any obligation to suffer punishment: but this being supposed, there was need of something further, even a positive obedience, in order to his obtaining, as our second Adam, the reward of eternal life.[110]

---

[107] "Justification by Faith Alone," *Works* 19:187. See also M 1220, *Works* 23:154.
[108] "The Threefold Work of the Holy Ghost," *Works* 14:397.
[109] "Justification by Faith Alone," *Works* 19:187. See also M s, *Works* 13:173, from which Edwards apparently quoted in "Justification by Faith Alone."
[110] "Justification by Faith Alone," *Works* 19:187. See also "Justification by Faith Alone," *Works* 19:151, and M 711, *Works* 18:340-1: "And again, that a believer's justification implies not only deliverance from the wrath of God, but a title to glory, is evident by Rom. 5:1-2, where the Apostle mentions both these as joint benefits implied in justification. 'Therefore being justified by faith, we *have peace with God* through our Lord Jesus Christ: by whom also we have access into this grace wherein we stand, and *rejoice in hope of the glory of God*.' So remission of sins, and inheritance among them that are sanctified, are mentioned together as what are jointly obtained by faith in Christ. Acts 26:18, 'That they may receive

Thus, as the requirement of perfect obedience went unanswered by Adam's disobedience on behalf of all mankind, the requirement of God's unchanging rule of righteousness remains to be answered by mankind to obtain eternal life. This was answered on behalf of the elect through Christ's perfect obedience.

God's Law and Authority are Not Honored Without the Righteousness of Christ's Perfect Obedience

Edwards' understanding of Adam's trial of obedience was that the honor of God's authority and law could only be upheld by Adam's perfect obedience to God's unchanging rule of righteousness. As the sin of Adam and mankind did not alter or abrogate God's rule of righteousness, so the requirement of perfect obedience to honor God's authority and law remained to be fulfilled. And given that all mankind were made sinners in Adam's disobedience, the

---

forgiveness of sins, and inheritance among them that are sanctified through faith that is in me.' Both these are without any doubt implied in that passing from death to life, which Christ speaks of as the fruit of faith, and which he opposes to condemnation. John 5:24, 'Verily, I say unto you, He that heareth my word, and believeth on him that sent me, hath everlasting life, and shall not come into condemnation; but is passed from death to life.'" See also "Quaestio," *Works* 14:60: "But there can be no doubt that justification is a certain act of *positive* favor that not only frees a person from sin but is also understood in fact as the approval of him as righteous through the righteousness of Christ, both active and passive in both obedience and satisfaction. For in all respects the reason why positive righteousness is now required from us by God so that we may be received into eternal life is the same reason such righteousness was required of Adam and why he was not immediately secured into immutable happiness at the first moment of creation without any testing at all." Edwards early understood Christ's death as "active" obedience and employed the "active" and "passive" obedience language in his earlier writings, the traditional Reformed distinction between the suffering and death of Christ ("passive" obedience) and His life of obedience ("active" obedience). He later rejected the "active" and "passive" obedience terminology as confusing, while maintaining and emphasizing the traditional Reformed understanding of Christ's death as both meritorious active obedience *and* propitiatory, and His entire life of active obedience in His state of humiliation as both meritorious *and* propitiatory. See "Justification by Faith Alone," *Works*, 19:194-5. Edwards' rejection of the "active/passive" terminology will be discussed further in chapter five.

requirement of perfect positive righteousness for eternal life could only be met by the perfect obedience of Christ on their behalf, for "if sinners should be saved without the active righteousness of Christ, God's authority would not be sufficiently honored."[111]

> There is the very same need of Christ's obeying the law in our stead, in order to the reward, as of his suffering the penalty of the law, in our stead, in order to our escaping the penalty; and the same reason why one should be accepted on our account, as the other, there is the same need of one as the other, that the law of God might be answered: one was as requisite to answer the law as the other.[112]

"Christ's active obedience was as necessary to retrieve the honor of God's law and authority as his suffering," for if eternal life is given "without active righteousness, this would not be honorable to that rule which God had fixed, because now God recedes from it." God's law would "never have respect and honor shown to it in that way of being obeyed."[113]

> But God in wisdom saw it meet that he should not only be free from guilt, but should be required to perform an active righteousness before he should have eternal life confirmed to him. This was the price that God fixed—perfect active obedience to his law—and he never altered that price. If

---

[111] "The Threefold Work of the Holy Ghost," *Works* 14:397.

[112] "Justification by Faith Alone," *Works* 19:186. Edwards cites Galatians 3:10-13 as support, "for this the Scripture plainly teaches: this is given as the reason why Christ was made a curse for us, that the law threatened a curse to us (Gal. 3:10, 13). But the same law that fixes the curse of God, as the consequent of not continuing in all things written in the law to do them (v. 10), has as much fixed doing those things as an antecedent of living in them (as v. 12, the next verse but one): there is as much of a connection established in one case as in the other. There is therefore exactly the same need from the law of perfect obedience being fulfilled, in order to our obtaining the reward, as there is of death's being suffered, in order to our escaping the punishment, or the same necessity by the law, of perfect obedience preceding life, as there is of disobedience being succeed by death: the law is without doubt, as much of an established rule in one case as in the other," 186-7.

[113] "The Threefold Work of the Holy Ghost," *Works* 14:398.

he has, the law is dispensed with, and we need trouble ourselves no more about answering the law.[114]

Additionally, if the positive requirement could be so easily altered or abrogated, why then the threat of death for disobedience and the "dreadful consequences," the "dreadful havoc" of death, and its "universal reign" and "dismal calamities, which overspread the nations of the earth through all generations?" Or, how is it consistent with God's wisdom to insist on the trial of obedience, to require the honor of His authority and law as the prerequisite for eternal life, if only to later forego the requirement and bestow heaven for mere freedom of guilt, the state of Adam before his trial? Why not confirm Adam without the trial?[115] Though Edwards does not give the rhetorical answer in the passage quoted here, the apparent conclusion is that the trial of Adam's obedience would be neither reasonable nor according to God's wisdom should the requirement of perfect obedience be altered or abrogated on account of Adam's sin.

God as a Righteous Judge Cannot Falsely Justify Imperfect Righteousness

The historical backdrop and impetus for much of Edwards' discussion regarding the inadequacy and absurdity of imperfect righteousness to meet the perfection required by God's law was the threat of "Arminianism."[116] For Edwards, the Arminian doctrines with respect to justification "exceedingly derogate from the glory of the gospel or new covenant" and are "very displeasing to

---

[114] "The Threefold Work of the Holy Ghost," *Works* 14:397.
[115] M 1220, *Works* 23:154.
[116] For basic historical context of the Arminian controversy in New England see Marsden, *Jonathan Edwards: A Life*, 137-41, 175-82. For a more specific analysis of Arminianism with respect to justification, and Edwards' specific target in "Justification by Faith Alone," see Michael McClenahan, "Jonathan Edwards' Doctrine of Justification in the Period up to the First Great Awakening," unpublished Ph.D. dissertation, University of Oxford (2006).

136   *The Infinite Merit of Christ*

God."[117] Increasingly popular in Edwards' lifetime, the "Arminian" and "modern" doctrine posited that the "old law given to Adam, which requires perfect obedience is entirely repealed" and replaced with a "new law" that "requires no more than imperfect, sincere obedience." Because of the "poor, infirm, impotent circumstances since the fall…we are unable to perform that perfect obedience that was required by the first law."[118] According to this view, "it would be unjust in God to require anything of us that is beyond our present power and ability to perform."[119] Christ only "purchases heaven for us, in this sense, that he satisfies for the imperfections of our obedience, and so purchases that our sincere imperfect obedience might be accepted as the condition of eternal life."[120] He "purchases an opportunity for us to obtain heaven by our own obedience."[121] To the contrary, Edwards argues that justi-

---

[117] "Romans 4:16," *WJEO*, L. 8v. – 9r.

[118] "Justification by Faith Alone," *Works*, 19:166. See also "Romans 4:16," *WJEO*, L. 8r. – 9r., where Edwards describes Arminianism, with respect to justification, as follows: "Arminians…maintain justification upon the account of sincere obedience. They hold that seeing we have broken the first covenant that proposed perfect obedience as the condition of justification, that now God has given us another covenant wherein sincere obedience is proposed in the room, and herein they suppose the grace of the new covenant appears, that seeing we have made ourselves unable to perform perfect obedience, that God will take up with sincere [obedience], though imperfect obedience, in the room of it. They suppose that Christ has satisfied for the imperfections of our obedience and purchased an abatement of the strictness of the terms of justification, viz., the perfection of obedience for us, and made God willing to accept of imperfect [obedience] in the room of it. They hold indeed that faith has something to do in the affair of justification, but 'tis as a good work, as a principal part of evangelical obedience and not merely as a reception of Christ."

[119] "Justification by Faith Alone," *Works* 19:166.

[120] "Justification by Faith Alone," *Works* 19:192-3.

[121] "Justification by Faith Alone," *Works* 19:192-3. This "Arminian" doctrine is problematic to Edwards in that it posits a justification by works. Though the defects of imperfect obedience are paid for, heaven is earned by the righteousness of the believer's acts. He writes: "But to purchase heaven for us, only in this sense, is to purchase it in no sense at all; for all of it comes to no more than a satisfaction for our sins, or removing the penalty by suffering in our stead: for all the purchasing they speak of, that our imperfect obedience should be accepted, is only his satisfying for the sinful imperfection of our obedience, or (which is the same thing) making atonement for the sin that our obedience is attended

fication concerns law, and a law that requires imperfect obedience is not a law, but a contradiction, while justification without perfect righteousness would be a "false sentence."

Righteousness and Justification Concern Judgment According to Law

In addition to the inflexible and strict nature of God's law that requires perfect obedience as the price of eternal life, God as a righteous judge must uphold His law in accord with His own righteousness and justice. "God is inflexibly and unalterably a righteous Judge and therefore is inflexibly determined to punish sin according to its deserts,"[122] and will "never accept of any person except it be for a perfect righteousness." God is righteous and can never depart from His "eternal rule" that neither men nor angels be accepted without "perfect righteousness."[123]

As noted above, Edwards' two-fold definition of justification includes both a "negative" and "positive" righteousness, corresponding to freedom from guilt and punishment and a righteousness that entitles to eternal life, respectively. The standard for God's judgment in each case is His rule of righteousness, by which He must judge rightly, consistent with His own nature as a righteous judge. In justification, therefore, God acts as a judge, and judges according to a fixed rule. Without a "rule" or "law," there is no basis of judgment or standard by which the creature can be deemed in conformity or violation of the requirement of eternal life. Without a rule, there can be no justification.

---

with. But that is not purchasing heaven, merely to set us at liberty again, that we may go, and get heaven by what we do ourselves: all that Christ does is only to pay a debt for us; there is no positive purchase of any good. We are taught in Scripture that heaven is purchased for us, 'tis called 'the purchased possession' (Eph. 1:14). The gospel proposes the eternal inheritance, not to be acquired, as the first covenant did, but as already acquired and purchased: but he that pays a man's debt for him, and so delivers him from slavery, can't be said to purchase an estate for him, merely because he sets him at liberty, so that henceforward he has an opportunity to get an estate by his own hand labor."

[122] "Deuteronomy 32:4," *WJEO*, L. 10v.
[123] "Deuteronomy 32:4," *WJEO*, L. 9v.

> The judge's work is two-fold: it is to determine first what is fact, and then whether what is in fact be according to rule, or according to the law. If a judge has no rule or law established beforehand, by which he should proceed in judging, he has no foundation to go upon in judging, he has no opportunity to be a judge; nor is it possible that he should do the part of a judge. To judge without a law or rule by which to judge, is impossible, for the very notion of judging is to determine whether the object of judgment be according to rule.[124]

Additionally, the nature of a law is to require perfect obedience, for it is "a contradiction to suppose otherwise; for…a law that don't require perfect obedience to itself…is a law that don't require all that it requires." The introduction of a "new law" that only requires imperfect obedience "won't help" the difficulty. Whether an old or new law, "an imperfect righteousness cannot answer the law of God we are under…for every law requires perfect obedience to itself: every rule whatsoever requires perfect conformity to itself."[125] In reducing the Arminian view to a logical absurdity, Edwards writes:

> That law that now forbids sin, is certainly the law that we are now under (let that be an old one, or a new one); or else it is not sin: that which is not forbidden, and is the breach of no law, is no sin: but if we are now forbidden to commit sin, then 'tis by a law that we are now under, for surely we are neither under the forbiddings, nor commandings of a law that we are not under. Therefore if all sin is now forbidden, then we are now under a law that requires perfect obedience; and therefore nothing can be accepted as a righteousness in the sight of our Judge, but perfect righteousness.[126]

---

[124] "Justification by Faith Alone," *Works* 19:190.
[125] "Justification by Faith Alone," *Works* 19:190.
[126] "Justification by Faith Alone," *Works* 19:190. No doubt this was a simple statement of the obvious for Edwards.

In other words, we are under a law that forbids all sin, and that which is not sin, the law does not forbid. Therefore, all commands of the law must be obeyed, or we sin. As all sin is forbidden, the law requires perfect obedience.

Further, "a law without sanctions, that is, without being enforced with threatenings of punishment and promises of rewards, is no law at all." If violations "pass unregarded and without any compensation," God's authority appears without authority.[127]

Justification Would Be a "False Sentence" Without Perfect Righteousness

God will always judge according to truth and "reality" according to the requirement of His rule of righteousness.

> Justification is manifestly a *forensic* term, as the word is used in Scripture, and the thing a judicial thing, or the act of a judge: so that if a person should be justified without a righteousness, the judgment would not be according to truth: the sentence of justification would be a false sentence, unless there be a righteousness performed that is by the judge properly looked upon as his.[128]

"When he acts as a judge he will not justify the wicked, and cannot clear the guilty" and "cannot justify without righteousness."[129] "God's judgment will be a true judgment; he will judge things as they be, or that his judgment will be conformed to the nature of things." If "sin was not punished according to its desert, God's judgment would not be according to truth."[130] And for God "to accept of something that falls short of the rule, instead of some-

---

[127] "None Are Saved by Their Own Righteousness," *Works* 14:335.
[128] "Justification by Faith Alone," *Works* 19:188-9.
[129] "Justification by Faith Alone," *Works* 19:189-90.
[130] "Romans 2:2," *Works* 24:987.

thing else that answers the rule, is no judicial act, or act of a judge, but a pure act of sovereignty."[131]

The Purpose of God's Judgment is to "Glorify God's Righteousness"

As noted in chapter one, the final result of the accomplishment of God's ultimate purpose to display and communicate His glory is that the holy bride of Christ will spend eternity in intimate fellowship with God in heaven, the holy abode prepared by God for the enjoyment of Christ and the elect. The saints will forever be happy in enjoying a view of the excellent perfections of the Father and the Son. However, the salvation of sinners by an incomplete righteousness is incompatible with God's purpose to display and communicate His glory.

With respect to the *display* of God's glory in the ultimate purpose of God, the admittance into heaven of a single sinner with imperfect righteousness would be a breach of God's law and authority, a compromise of His righteousness and justice, and thus contrary to God's excellent perfections.[132] The glory of God's perfections could not be displayed in such circumstances, for as noted earlier, God could not be God if He ever committed an act of unrighteousness. In fact, "at the day of judgment there will be the most glorious discovery of the justice of God that ever was made," for "God will appear to all to be universally righteous towards everyone; the justice of all God's moral government will at that day at once be discovered."[133]

---

[131] "Justification by Faith Alone," *Works* 19:189.
[132] "Christ's Sacrifice," *Works* 10:601.
[133] "The Day of Judgment," *Works* 14:515-516. See also "Deuteronomy 32:4," *WJEO*, L. 8v: "There will be a more remarkable discovery of the justice of God at the day of judgment when all shall be judged in the most open and solemn manner possible, all the inhabitants of heaven and earth being present. Then God will wonderfully display his justice in acquitting of believers who are legally innocent and in rewarding of holy men according to his promise in fulfilling and completing all those good things to them which he so often spoke of to them. He will then remarkably display his vindictive justice in so open and solemn a manner, condemning and punishing men and devils, in punishing the princes of darkness

> All objections will be removed; the consciences of every man shall be satisfied; the blasphemous cavils of the ungodly will be forever put to silence; and there will be argument given for the saints and angels to praise. Rev. 19:1-2, "And after these things I heard a great voice of much people in heaven, saying, Alleluia; Salvation, and glory, and honor, and power be to the Lord our God; for true and righteous are his judgments."[134]

If God were to allow a single person into heaven without perfect righteousness, the Day of Judgment could neither be a display of the glory of God's righteous justice, nor a vindication of His righteous judgments.

With respect to the *communication* of God's glory in the ultimate purpose of God, no sinner could be admitted to heaven apart from a perfect righteousness. The communication of His glory to the redeemed would be impossible without perfect righteousness, as God's justice would require their condemnation, while His holiness could not suffer their presence in heaven. It is "contrary to God's justice, to make a wicked man eternally happy."[135]

> 'Tis impossible by reason of God's holiness, that anything should be united to God and brought to the enjoyment of him which is not holy. Now is it possible that a God of infinite holiness, that is perfect and hates sin with perfect hatred, that is infinitely lovely and excellent, should embrace in his arms a filthy, abominable creature, a hideous, detestable monster, more hateful than a toad and more poisonous than a viper?[136]

---

and the great men of this world, wicked proud kings and emperors, princes and noblemen, in punishing those rulers who gathered themselves against him when he was on earth. God's justice in many things now lies hid, as it were, but then it came forth into the light and will be wonderfully discovered."

[134] "The Day of Judgment," *Works* 14:515-516.
[135] "The Way of Holiness," *Works* 10:474.
[136] "The Way of Holiness," *Works* 10:475.

Thus, the smallest compromise of God's justice in the redemption of a single sinner, apart from perfect righteousness, has monumental implications in the theology of Edwards, as the very accomplishment of redemption in fulfilling God's ultimate purpose of displaying and communicating His glory to His creatures is precluded, rendering Christ's redemptive work useless.

Christ Died Needlessly If Believers Are Under a Law That Only Requires Imperfect Obedience

In responding further to the Arminian contention that the strict law requiring perfection has been abolished and that imperfect and sincere obedience is the new requirement for eternal life, Edwards identifies the unintended implication that Christ's death is thereby rendered needless.

To begin, if sinners are put under a "more mild constitution" in the cancelling of the strict law that required perfection, "there is no need of supposing that the condemnation of it remains, to stand in the way of the acceptance of our virtue."[137]

> There is no other way of avoiding this difficulty; the condemnation of the law must stand in force against a man till he is actually interested in the Savior, that has satisfied and answered the law, effectually to prevent any acceptance of his virtue, before, or in order to such an interest, unless the law or constitution itself be abolished.[138]

Accordingly, "this doctrine of the imputation of Christ's righteousness is utterly inconsistent with the doctrine of our being justified by our own virtue, or sincere obedience."[139] Eternal life cannot be given for our obedience and Christ's obedience.

---

[137] "Justification by Faith Alone," *Works* 19:165.
[138] "Justification by Faith Alone," *Works* 19:165-6.
[139] "Justification by Faith Alone," *Works* 19:199.

> If acceptance to God's favor, and a title to life, be given to believers, as the reward of Christ's obedience, then it is not given as the reward of our own obedience. In what respect soever, Christ is our Savior, that doubtless excludes our being our own saviors, in that same respect. If we can be our own saviors in the same respect Christ is, it will thence follow that the salvation of Christ is needless, in that respect; according to the Apostle's reasoning. Gal. 5:4, "Christ is rendered of no effect unto you, whosoever of you are justified by the law."[140]

Furthermore, if the law is abolished, and nothing more than imperfect obedience is required, then imperfect obedience is no longer sin as it meets the requirement of the new law.

> I would ask what law these imperfections of our obedience are a breach of? if they are a breach of no law, then they ben't sins; and if they ben't sins, what need of Christ's dying to satisfy for them? but if they are sins, and so the breach of some law, what law is it? they can't be a breach of their new law, for that requires no other than imperfect obedience or obedience with imperfections; and they can't be a breach of the old law, for that they say is entirely abolished, and we never were under it; and we can't break a law that we never were under.[141]

The Arminian "mild law" is founded upon the principle that sinners are unable to meet the strict requirement of the "old law," for "they [Arminians] strenuously maintain that it would be unjust in God to require anything of us that is beyond our present power and ability to perform." But, if God would be unjust to require perfect obedience, God would be unjust to punish imperfect obedience. Why, then, did Christ die for what did not deserve

---

[140] "Justification by Faith Alone," *Works* 19:199. Edwards devotes 16 pages of detailed and convincing Scriptural arguments to show that the "law" by which no one can be justified, as cited here in Galatians 5:4, as well as elsewhere in the Pauline corpus, is the moral law, not the ceremonial law.

[141] "Justification by Faith Alone," *Works* 19:166.

punishment?[142] Also, if "Christ died to satisfy that law for us, that so we might not be under that law," but "under a more mild law," did Christ have to die to bring sinners out from under an unjust law of God? Or, "is there any need of Christ's dying to persuade God not to do unjustly?"[143] In other words, if God sent Christ to die to remove sinners from under God's "unjust" requirement, God and His law are made the problem to be remedied, not the sin and guilt of the sinner. For Edwards, this is both contrary to God's perfections and absurd.

God's Rule of Righteousness Precludes Justification by Any Virtue or Merit in Faith

As noted earlier, all the works of a sinner are of infinite demerit and worthy of an infinite penalty, including the best works of the saints when viewed by themselves apart from Christ. We have seen that Adam's sin did not cancel or alter God's rule of righteousness, and that perfect positive obedience and pardon of sins is required for justification. Moreover, God as a righteous judge must judge in righteousness and according to reality. Accordingly, no virtue or sincere obedience can avail anyone of justification, including imperfect faith, for nothing but the perfect righteousness of Christ can meet the strict standard of God's rule of righteousness for the obtaining of eternal life. The requirement of perfect positive righteousness remains, and nothing of sinful mankind can meet it.

Concerning Romans 4:5, wherein the Apostle Paul writes that Abraham's faith "is counted for righteousness," Edwards writes:

> There is no need to understand the Apostle that his faith, though in itself an imperfect righteousness, is accepted instead of a perfect righteousness, as that God had respect to any goodness or righteousness at all in faith; but only

---

[142] "Justification by Faith Alone," *Works* 19:166.
[143] "Justification by Faith Alone," *Works* 19:166-7.

that God by reason of his faith in God, accepted of him and dealt with him as though he had been righteous in himself.[144]

How then can Abraham's imperfect faith meet God's strict unchanging rule of righteousness?

Faith Unites to Christ That Salvation Might Be by Grace

As the focus of this work is Edwards' understanding of the accomplishment of redemption by Christ, an adequate treatment of the nature of the application of redemption by faith and union is beyond the present scope. Nonetheless, it is important to note that Edwards' understanding of the nature of faith as union with Christ, who alone met the standard of God's rule of righteousness, is not only consistent with the justice of God in the salvation of sinners according to His righteous rule, but highlights and sustains it.[145] Indeed, there can be no other way by which a sinner can be justified according to God's standard of justice.[146] As we have seen, God cannot accept an imperfect righteousness, and must in

---

[144] "Romans 4:5," *Works* 24:993.

[145] An adequate treatment of the nature of faith, faith as the condition of the covenant of grace, or union with Christ is beyond the scope of this work. For a helpful discussion of Edwards' understanding of the nature of faith and justification, see Bogue, *Jonathan Edwards and the Covenant of Grace*, 253-78; Cherry, *The Theology of Jonathan Edwards: A Reappraisal*, 90-106. For a treatment of the Holy Spirit as the bond of union in Edwards' theology, see Caldwell, *The Holy Spirit as the Bond of Union in the Theology of Jonathan Edwards*.

[146] See also "Justification by Faith Alone," *Works* 19:188: "'Tis absolutely necessary that in order to a sinner's being justified, the righteousness of some other should be reckoned to his account; for 'tis declared that the person justified is looked upon as (in himself) ungodly; but God neither will nor can justify a person without a righteousness." Also, "Matthew 5:27-28," *YMSS*, L. 10r. -10v: "This should stir us all up to labour to get an interest in him who has perfectly answered this strict Law of God. We cannot do it [and] it is in vain for us to aim at any such thing, and yet we are all naturally under the Law. The Law takes hold of us and exacts perfect obedience, upon pain of eternal death. We are held bound by it as with chains of brass. There is therefore no other way for us, but to get into Christ, who alone has answered and fulfilled this Law. Though it be so strict, yet Christ answered exactly and perfectly in every point. He perfectly

perfect righteousness judge according to reality. In light of this, faith itself cannot be the righteousness that justifies, as it neither meets the standard of righteousness required, nor pays the infinite debt of sin. Faith as a work of righteousness is as infinitely inadequate and sinful as all human works. Faith, therefore, cannot be that in the believer that meets the perfection required by God's rule of righteousness, for that is impossible and contrary to God's righteous and perfect justice.

> This is plainly what our divines intend when they say that faith don't justify as a work, or a righteousness, viz. that it don't justify as a part of our moral goodness or excellency, or that it don't justify as a work, in the sense that man was to have been justified by his works by the covenant of works, which was to have a title to eternal life, given him of God in testimony of his pleasedness with his works, or his regard to the inherent excellency and beauty of his obedience. And this is certainly what the apostle Paul means, when he so much insists upon it that we are not justified by works, viz. that we are not justified by them as good works, or by any goodness, value, or excellency of our works.[147]

Rather, faith is the human act of union with Christ, the union of God to the elect having taken place in the Father and Son setting their benevolent love upon the elect in eternity past. Faith allows for the believer, with no merit of his or her own, to obtain eternal life in a manner consistent with God's unchanging justice, while the merit that earned it completely resides in the perfect righteousness of Christ.[148] In union with Christ by faith the sinner is

---

fulfilled the commands of the Law, and has answered the demands of it for our sins, its demands of suffering eternal death."
[147] "Justification by Faith Alone," *Works* 19:160.
[148] "Grace so greatly appears in the manner of justification proposed by it. We that have justification offered to us only for our acceptance of Christ, notwithstanding all our unworthiness and provocations, that God is willing freely to pardon us and accept us into favour and bestow eternal life upon us, upon the account of the righteousness of another that we were at no pains to work out,

justified, for the fulfillment of God's standard of righteousness by the bridegroom becomes the possession of the bride. To see faith any other way is contrary to the gospel of Christ.

> Neither salvation itself, nor Christ the Savior, are given as a reward of anything in man: they are not given as a reward of faith, nor anything else of ours: we are not united to Christ as a reward of our faith, but have union with him by faith, only as faith is the very act of uniting, or closing on our part....By these things it appears how contrary to the scheme of the gospel of Christ, their scheme is, who say that faith justifies as a principal of obedience, or as a leading act of obedience; or (as others) the sum, and comprehension of all evangelical obedience: for by this 'tis the obedience or virtue that is in faith, that is the thing, that gives it its justifying influence; and that is the same thing as to say, that we are justified by our own obedience, virtue or goodness.[149]

Moreover, the idea that one is accepted into God's favor prior to possessing Christ's righteousness and satisfaction is self-contradictory, for "if our interest in God be the fruit of God's favor, then it can't be the ground of it."

> Such a scheme destroys itself, for it supposes that Christ's satisfaction and righteousness are necessary for us to recommend us to the favor of God; and yet supposes that we have God's favor and acceptance before we have Christ's satisfaction and righteousness, and have these given as a fruit of God's favor.[150]

In other words, if God cannot accept sinners into His favor apart from a perfect righteousness, the sinner must possess that righteousness before he or she is accepted into God's favor. As dis-

---

and upon the account of sufferings that we had no share in." "Romans 4:16," *WJEO*, L. 9v.
[149] "Justification by Faith Alone," *Works* 19:200-1.
[150] "Justification by Faith Alone," *Works* 19:200.

cussed in chapter two, God's benevolent love to sinners precedes any worth in the sinner and is despite the infinite unworthiness of the sinner, whereas God's love of complacence, the love of any excellence in the sinner, is purchased by Christ and consists of God's love of Christ's righteousness possessed by the believer. With respect to John 16:27, "'the Father loves you, because ye have loved me, and have believed,'" God's "love of favor and acceptance…is consequent on believing," for the believer's love to Christ is the fruit of union with Christ, for "love to Christ is included in faith in Christ."[151]

> But if you answer, That though God loves us because we love Christ, but 'tis not in the same sense that he loves us, because we believe on him, the words of the verse don't allow of that, for 'tis said, "the Father loves you, because ye have loved me, and have believed," etc. Loving and believing would not thus have been coupled together, if it was not because of one in the same sense as the other. But this, in general, is what Christ would signify to them, viz. that the Father loved them because of their union to him, and so he loved them for his sake.[152]

Sinners cannot be accepted into God's favor and then given the righteousness and satisfaction of Christ as the fruit of that favor. The sinner must possess righteousness and satisfaction in order to be accepted into God's favor in the first place. If the sinner's acceptance precedes the possession of Christ's merit and satisfaction,

---

[151] "John 16:27," *Works* 24:957.

[152] "John 16:27," *Works* 24:957. Edwards also cites John 14:20-21, 23, and 1 Timothy 1:14 in this regard. In commenting upon the latter, he writes: "'But the grace of our Lord Jesus Christ was exceeding abundant with faith and love which is in Christ Jesus.' This seems to be by the figure which is called hendiadys, and by faith and love are not meant two proper distinct things. But 'tis as much as to say, a loving faith, or that faith whose life and spirit is love, or that faith which works by love, as when it is said, 'He shall baptize you with the Holy Ghost and with fire' [Luke 3:16], i.e., with a fiery Spirit, or a Spirit that shall be like fire." Editor Stephen Stein, footnote 6, notes that hendiadys is "a grammatical term referring to the expression of an idea by two nouns connected by 'and,' instead of by a noun and an adjunct."

the sinner is thereby justified on account of some virtue of his or her own, be it faith or otherwise.

> For a rewarding anyone's excellency, evermore supposes favor and acceptance on the account of that excellency: it is the very notion of a reward, that it is a good thing, bestowed in testimony of respect and favor for the virtue or excellency rewarded. So that it is not by virtue of our interest in Christ and his merits, that we first come into favor with God, according to this scheme; for we are in God's favor before we have any interest in those merits; in that we have an interest in those merits given as a fruit of God's favor for our own virtue.[153]

But as we have seen, no virtue in a sinner could merit God's favor. To the contrary, the best work of a sinner or saint falls infinitely short of God's rule of righteousness and deserves the penalty of death.

Further, there can be no difference between earning an interest in the merits of Christ and earning heaven directly. In either case, the redeeming work of Christ is not needed.

> If God gives us Christ, or an interest in him, properly in reward of our obedience, he does really give us salvation in reward for our obedience; for the former implies the latter; yea it implies it as the greater implies the less. So that indeed it exalts our virtue and obedience more, to suppose that God gives us Christ in reward of that virtue and obedience, than if he should give salvation without Christ.[154]

To give us "an interest in Christ in reward for our virtue, is as great an argument that it instates us in God's favor, as if he bestowed a title to eternal life, as its direct reward," in which case Christ's righteousness is not needed. But to imagine that it is "our own goodness, virtue, or excellency, that instates us in God's acceptance

---

[153] "Justification by Faith Alone," *Works* 19:200.
[154] "Justification by Faith Alone," *Works* 19:200.

and favor," is "the thing that the Scripture guards, and militates against."[155]

> God don't give those that believe, an union *with*, or an interest *in* the Savior, in reward for faith, but only because faith is the soul's active uniting with Christ, or is itself the very act of unition [uniting], on their part.[156]

Moreover, faith cannot be earned, or God cannot be made favorably disposed to give sinners saving faith by their acts of righteousness, for "thus is the same, in effect, as trusting in their own righteousness for justification."[157] Such will "keep men from embracing the righteousness of Christ."[158]

Justification by Man's Righteousness Insults the Glory of the Trinity

The sin of Adam and mankind made salvation by the sinner's own works impossible by virtue of the perfection required by God's rule of righteousness. God, however, in His ultimate purpose of displaying and communicating His glory in accord with His perfect justice, conceived and initiated the covenant of redemption, the terms of which would accomplish redemption for elect sinners. As will be seen in chapter five, the infinite extent to which Christ went in bearing infinite humiliation and suffering that He might communicate God's happiness to the elect in the giving of the Holy Spirit accomplishes God's ultimate purpose in the display and communication of His glory. The Trinity is thereby glorified in the salvation of unworthy sinners. But to posit salvation by the righteousness of the sinner, however small, is to render God's eternal plan of salvation, via the covenant of redemption, "to no purpose" and "altogether needless."[159] In speaking to the hypo-

---

[155] "Justification by Faith Alone," *Works* 19:200.
[156] "Justification by Faith Alone," *Works* 19:158.
[157] "Romans 9:31-32," *YMSS*, L. 5v.
[158] "Romans 9:31-32," *YMSS*, L. 7r.
[159] "The Threefold Work of the Holy Ghost," *Works* 14:410.

thetical proponent of a redemption based on righteousness in the sinner, Edwards writes:

> And what a reflection do you cast upon them as the contrivers of this wonderful way. The persons of the Trinity, they consulted from all eternity about it as being the main work of divine wisdom. The Father entered into a covenant of redemption with the Son before the foundation of the world, and if your way be true, it was all for nothing; it was only for a frivolous notion.
>
> The Father, Son [and] Holy Ghost, they busied themselves about it needlessly. You, by your practice, reflect upon them as though they made a great ado and consulted to do some great and strange thing to no purpose, but only to surprise and amuse the world.
>
> Is not this the plain language of your practice? And what a horrid reflection is it upon the wisdom and majesty of the glorious Trinity, as though they were only mere triflers.[160]

With respect to the Father, those that trust in their own worthiness "do as much say that God the Father was unreasonable in his demands to go to require so hard a thing," and imply that God is "cruel, and delighted in the pain and disgrace of his own Son." Moreover, they "rob God of all the glory of his mercy in sending his Son" and make the act of sending His Son "as much to his dishonor as it is indeed to his honor." The act by which God would be most glorified, they "would make the greatest reproach to God that can be."[161]

With respect to the Son, the opinion that one's own righteousness is sufficient for salvation "robs the Son of God of all the glo-

---

[160] "The Threefold Work of the Holy Ghost," *Works* 14:410-11.
[161] "The Threefold Work of the Holy Ghost," *Works* 14:411.

ry of his love" in His suffering and death.[162] Scripture speaks of Christ's work as "a wonderful act of love and grace," and "Christ counts it his glory, and would have men admire him for it." On the other hand, in speaking to those viewing their righteousness as sufficient, Edwards writes:

> You don't see that there is any such glory in it: you don't thank him for his love, for he only did this to give you that that you have already without his giving; he did [this] that you might be partakers of his righteousness, and you want none of his righteousness: you have righteousness enough of your own.[163]

Christ saw sinners as "poor" and in need of help, "but you think he was mistaken," and "he might have kept his gifts to himself, for all you [care]."[164]

> According to your opinion of your own righteousness, he was guilty of the most egregious folly in running himself into such a miserable case for nothing. Self-righteousness blasphemes Christ as though he were the greatest fool in the world to leave heaven, where he had perfect happiness. Christ stands high in reputation in the gospel for his {sacrifice}, but in your account, he was the greatest fool in the world for his pains.[165]

---

[162] "The Threefold Work of the Holy Ghost," *Works* 14:411. In commenting on Exodus 20:25, Edwards writes: "Their being forbidden to lift up their tool on the stones of the altar seems to signify to us these two things, viz. 1. That we must not add anything of our own works to Christ, because Christ is sufficient alone without our righteousness. If we go to add our works to make up his deficiencies, instead of making the altar of the foundation of our acceptance with God better, we shall utterly spoil it. We must depend on Christ as he is....

The altar was that which sanctified the gift, and added worth or merit to the sacrifice. We must not add our works to that by which acceptance is merited, must not join our works to Christ to make the merit greater or better in order to the acceptance of the offering. Hewn stone seem to be used as a type of our own righteousness in Is. 9:10." "Exodus 20:25," *Works* 24:236-7.

[163] "The Threefold Work of the Holy Ghost," *Works* 14:411.
[164] "The Threefold Work of the Holy Ghost," *Works* 14:411-12.
[165] "The Threefold Work of the Holy Ghost," *Works* 14:411-12.

"To suppose a man is justified by his own virtue or obedience, derogates from the honor of the Mediator, and ascribes that to man's virtue, that belongs only to the righteousness of Christ."[166]

With respect to the Holy Spirit, "you rob him of all the glory of convincing men of righteousness, or of convincing men of the way of justification." The Holy Spirit is glorified in the "application of Christ's redemption," in giving people the knowledge of the way of justification, in His effects on the soul, but "is robbed of all this glory by men's opinion of their own righteousness." If people are justified by their own righteousness, "this work of the Holy Ghost is altogether needless; 'tis no glorious work." The Holy Spirit's work is to convince mankind "that the righteousness of Christ is that alone by which we can have acceptance. But this is a lie, if men's own righteousness be sufficient."[167] In qualifying his language somewhat, Edwards writes:

> Perhaps self-righteous [men] don't distinctly think of all [this]; but yet so, these are the direct and plain consequences of a self-righteous opinion. They rob God of all his glory in this glorious work or redemption, by which he designed such peculiar glory to himself....[They] rob every person [in the Trinity] of their special glory.[168]

Thus, according to the requirement of God's unchanging rule of righteousness and the perfections of God's nature which it reflects, no amount of human righteousness can be attributed to the justification of a sinner without injury to the Trinity in His ultimate purpose to display and communicate His glory through Christ. The following quotation is lengthy, but is an excellent summary of

---

[166] "Justification by Faith Alone," *Works* 19:185. Edwards continues, "it puts man in Christ's stead, and makes him his own savior, in a respect, in which Christ only is his Savior: and so 'tis a doctrine contrary to the nature, and design of the gospel which is to abase man, and to ascribe all the glory of our salvation to Christ the Redeemer. It is inconsistent with the doctrine of the imputation of Christ's righteousness, which is a gospel doctrine."
[167] "The Threefold Work of the Holy Ghost," *Works* 14:412.
[168] "The Threefold Work of the Holy Ghost," *Works* 14:412.

Edwards' understanding of the relationship of a works righteousness to the glory of the Trinity.

> He that is entrusted with the rights and honor of the majesty and authority of the whole Trinity, surely will not forgive sin without a perfect satisfaction [and] a perfect obedience. Therefore, [we] presume not to go to him in our own righteousness. If he should bestow salvation upon you in any other way, he would not only injure the honor of his majesty and justice, but he would disparage his own wisdom [and] oppose all that he has done in the great things he has contrived and approved and brought to pass to reproach [sin and evil]. But if you come to him in the way that he has appointed, then his regard to the honor of his own wisdom, and his regard to the honor of his Son, and his regard to his own eternal promise and oath made to him and through him to believers, all will engage to receive you and make you happy. And Christ, the second person, he will be engaged: he will present you to the Father, yea, [to] all the persons [of the heavenly society]: not only the Father and the Son, but the Holy Spirit and the glorious angels, yea, all creatures. For all things shall be yours whatever they be, whether the world or life or death, or things past or things to come: all will be yours in that you are Christ's and Christ is God's.[169]

Summary

In the present chapter we examined Edwards' understanding of the result of Adam's sin with respect to the nature of God's rule of righteousness and the accomplishment of God's ultimate purpose in the redemption of sinners. As a result of Adam's sin as surety and representative of all mankind, all were made guilty sinners under God's wrath according to the strict and unchanging nature of God's rule of righteousness. The strict and exacting terms

---

[169] "Of God the Father," *Works* 25:154.

of that law render everyone sinners at all times, with no provision for deliverance from sin and guilt. Moreover, the guilt of every sin is infinite as an affront to the infinite majesty of God. Even the best acts of saints are mingled with sin, or, considered by themselves apart from intermingled sin, fall infinitely short of the standard required by the nature of God and His goodness. As God's rule of righteousness is reflective of His perfect righteousness and justice, Adam's sin neither altered nor abrogated its requirements. Justification of sinners, therefore, requires both freedom from the penalty of sin *and* the perfect positive righteousness required by the rule of righteousness. Apart from perfect obedience to God's law, God's authority is not properly honored and the requirement for eternal life is not met. Therefore, apart from the perfect obedience of Christ, the salvation of sinners is impossible, for the honor of God's authority and law and the requirement for the obtaining of eternal life would go unanswered. The nature of God as judge demands this, for in righteousness He must judge according to rule or law, or He cannot judge. Indeed, a law by definition requires perfect obedience to its requirements or it is not a law, for it "does not require all that it requires." In judging according to His rule of righteousness, justification apart from perfect righteousness would be a false judgment, contrary to God's nature as a righteous judge. If God were to make a single unjust judgment, He would no longer be God, for God is perfectly righteous in all His ways.

In light of the nature of God and His law, any scheme of justification that posits a new law that requires imperfect obedience only renders Christ's perfect obedience and death needless. If imperfect obedience meets the demands of such a law, then no satisfaction or perfect obedience is required, for all sinners meet its requirements. Additionally, the strict nature of God's law precludes justification by any virtue or merit in faith. Rather, faith is union with Christ, in whom the perfect righteousness of Christ's obedience becomes the possession of the believer. Indeed, the favor of God to the believer is consequent upon his or her possession of Christ's righteousness, and does not precede it on the basis of any virtue or righteousness in the believer, including any virtue or righteousness in faith.

Lastly, as all persons of the Trinity are equally involved and equally glorified by the salvation of elect sinners, so the justification of a sinner by any supposed virtue or merit in the sinner is an insult to the Trinity in His ultimate purpose to display and communicate His glory by the perfect obedience of Christ to God's unchanging rule of righteousness. Thus, we see that Christ's perfect obedience to God's rule of righteousness is the only possible basis of the justification of sinners, and the only means by which God's ultimate purpose to display and communicate His glory to sinful creatures can be accomplished.

We turn now to an examination of Edwards' understanding of the basis and nature of the merits of Christ's perfect obedience in fulfillment of God's ultimate purpose.

CHAPTER FIVE

Christ Infinitely Satisfies God's Unalterable Rule of Righteousness on Behalf of the Elect

In the nature and circumstances of Christ's perfect obedience, He not only satisfied the "positive" and "negative" demands of God's rule of righteousness, but *infinitely exceeded them.* He accomplished a display and communication of God's glory that infinitely surpassed what Adam would have accomplished for his posterity had he obeyed in his relatively easy trial of obedience. Accordingly, the merit and benefits of this exceeding glory would be displayed and communicated to the elect for whom Christ accomplished this great work. What, then, rendered the nature of Christ's perfect obedience such an infinitely glorious display and communication of God's glory? Or put another way, what constitutes the infinite merit of Christ's perfect obedience that both meets and infinitely exceeds the requirement of God's unchanging rule of righteousness? We turn now to an examination of Edwards' understanding of the nature of Christ's merit in His perfect obedience to God's rule of righteousness in the salvation of sinners.

The following aspects of Edwards' theology concerning the infinite merit of Christ's obedience will be examined. First, having freely bound Himself to the terms of the covenant of redemption, Christ as mediator was subject to God's rule of righteousness, as was Adam. Second, Christ justifies unworthy sinners by the meritorious righteousness of His perfect obedience as their surety and representative. As both perfect and voluntary, Christ's obedience was meritorious, while sinners are justified by possessing the meritorious righteousness of Christ. Third, Christ's obedience unto death was not only propitiatory, but the "most exalted part of Christ's positive righteousness." As a voluntary and infinite condescension of one of infinite glory to infinite humiliation and suffering on behalf of the infinitely undeserving, Christ's obedience was an infinitely meritorious act of love to the Father and the elect. Fourth, all of Christ's works as mediator were propitiatory in their suffering and humiliation, and meritorious in their obedience and righteousness. Fifth, the infinite merit of Christ's obedience, as the surety and representative of His bride, earned the exaltation promised by the Father in the covenant of redemption. And last, Christ accomplished, *to an infinite degree*, the ultimate Trinitarian purpose of God to display and communicate His glory to His creatures.

Christ as Second Adam Was Under God's Unalterable Rule of Righteousness, as Was Adam

As we have seen, in Adam's sin as the surety and representative of his posterity, the strict requirement of God's rule of righteousness for eternal life went unfulfilled and, as a result, could not be fulfilled by Adam's posterity. Nonetheless, the Father conceived and initiated the covenant of redemption between Himself and the Son, requiring that the strict requirement of God's rule of righteousness be met by the Son as the surety and representative of sinners. Christ would accomplish by His perfect obedience as the Second Adam what the first Adam failed to accomplish in his trial of obedience. From love to the Father and the elect, the Son would freely obligate himself to the role of a servant in condescending to take upon Himself a human nature and body, and in freely binding Himself to keep the terms of the covenant perfectly. In so doing, Christ would be subject to the penalties of the law for disobedience and the rewards of the covenant for perfect obedience. In His mediatory work, therefore, Christ was under the same rule of righteousness as was Adam.[1]

Christ Was Bound to Perfect Obedience Regardless of Specific Commands, as Was Adam

As the command to Adam in his trial of obedience was representative of God's unchanging rule of righteousness that promised life for perfect obedience and death for disobedience, so "the law that Christ was subject to and obeyed was the same that Adam was subject to and was to have obeyed, notwithstanding that the positive precepts…were not the same."[2]

> There is no need that the law that Christ obeys should be precisely the same that Adam was to have obeyed, in that sense that there should be no positive precepts wanting, nor any added: there was wanting the precept about the forbidden fruit, and there was added the ceremonial law. The thing required was perfect obedience: it is no matter whether the positive precepts were the same, if they were equivalent.[3]

Christ did not receive the command to abstain from the tree, as did Adam, while Adam did not receive the command to lay down His life, as did Christ. "It was needful that Christ should be subject to the same moral law, but it was not necessary there should be the same positive precepts exactly."[4] Yet, both Adam and Christ were subject to the same law, as the law given to Adam is an eternal, unchanging law.

---

[1] See chapter two for the discussion of Christ freely obligating Himself to the terms of the covenant of redemption.
[2] M 399, *Works* 13:464.
[3] "Justification by Faith Alone," *Works* 19:196.
[4] "The Threefold Work of the Holy Ghost," *Works* 14:399.

> The moral law, or the law of nature, is an eternal, unalterable rule, always the same. But positive precepts, such as was that of not eating the forbidden fruit, and the precepts of the ceremonial law, such as circumcision, etc. is temporary and alterable. And with respect to these latter, the law that Christ obeyed need not be the same that Adam was to have obeyed.[5]

In either case, however, "the thing required was perfect obedience,"[6] though the conditions and terms of obedience were significantly more difficult in Christ's trial of obedience.[7]

> The positive precepts that Christ was to obey, were much more than equivalent to what was wanting, because infinitely more difficult, particularly the command that he had received to lay down his life, which was his principal act of obedience, and which above all others, is concerned in our justification.[8]

As will be seen below, the extent of the merit accrued to Christ's specific tasks is directly related to their difficulty, though the underlying principle of perfect obedience in the case of Adam and Christ is the same.

As the command to Adam in his trial of obedience represented God's rule of righteousness or covenant of works, so also the laws to which Christ was subject in His humiliation as Mediator represented the same, including the following:

> (1) the moral law; and the law that he was subject to as a Jew, which includes (2) the ceremonial law, and all the positive precepts that were peculiar to that nation. (3) The mediatorial law, which contained those commands of God that he was subject to purely as he was mediator, to

---

[5] "The Threefold Work of the Holy Ghost," *Works* 14:399.
[6] M 381, *Works* 13:450-1.
[7] "Justification by Faith Alone," *Works* 19:196.
[8] "Justification by Faith Alone," *Works* 19:196.

which belong all those commands that the Father gave him to work such miracles, and teach such doctrines, and so to labor in the works of his public ministry, and to yield himself to such sufferings.[9]

Christ alone was subject to the "mediatorial law," or those commands of God that constitute the stipulations of the covenant of redemption for the salvation of sinners. Nonetheless, all the commands Christ obeyed in His state of humiliation "may be reduced to one law, and that is that which the Apostle calls the law of works, to which indeed all laws of God properly so called may be reduced."[10]

> Every command that Christ obeyed may be reduced to that great and everlasting law of God that is contained in the covenant of works, that eternal rule of righteousness that God has established between himself and mankind. Christ came into the world to fulfill and answer the covenant of works, that is the covenant that is to stand forever as a rule of judgment, and that is the covenant that we had broken, and that was the covenant that must be fulfilled.[11]

As "'tis a general rule of the law of works, and indeed of the law of nature, that God is to be obeyed and that he must be submitted to in whatever positive precept he is pleased to give us," so "this law of works indeed includes all laws of God that ever have been given to mankind."[12] Both Adam and Christ were tried with respect to the honor of God's authority and law on behalf of those for whom they stood as representative. And in each case it was "suitable" that they should be tried by a "positive precept."

> It was suitable that it should be a positive precept that should try both Adam's and Christ's obedience: such pre-

---

[9] M 794, *Works* 18:496.
[10] M 794, *Works* 18:496.
[11] *Works* 9:308-9. Edwards cites Romans 3:27 in support.
[12] *Works* 9:309.

cepts are the greatest and most proper trial of obedience, because in them, the mere authority and will of the Legislator is the sole ground of the obligation (and nothing in the nature of the things themselves); and therefore they are the greatest trial of any person's respect to that authority and will.[13]

Thus, Christ obeyed the specific positive precepts of the Father as Adam was to have obeyed the specific command given him. In either case, perfect obedience would meet the requirement of perfect positive righteousness for the obtaining of eternal life. Had Adam obeyed, "his justification would have implied something more than what is merely negative; he would have been approved of, as having fulfilled the righteousness of the law."[14] So Christ, "our second surety... was not justified till he had done the work the Father had appointed him, and kept the Father's commandments, through all trials." Having perfectly obeyed, He was justified in His resurrection.[15]

The Perseverance of Christ Remedies the Defect of the First Covenant with Adam

Adam failed to persevere in obedience to the authority and command of God. The circumstances of the first covenant, however, allowed for such an outcome, as the "righteousness of the covenant, and man's perseverance, was betrusted with man himself, with nothing better to secure it than his own strength." In this way the first covenant was "deficient," as it depended upon the weakness of man for its fulfillment.[16] God, however, would offer a remedy to the weakness of the first covenant in the provision of "a better surety to supply the defects of the first surety, a surety that might stand and persevere, and one that has actually persevered

---

[13] "Justification by Faith Alone," *Works* 19:196. See also M 381, *Works* 13:451.
[14] "Justification by Faith Alone," *Works* 19:150.
[15] "Justification by Faith Alone," *Works* 19:150-1.
[16] M 695, *Works* 18:277.

through the greatest imaginable trials." In the better covenant, fulfilled by a better surety, "eternal life won't be suspended on our perseverance by our own poor, feeble, broken strength."[17] Thus, "God in his providence made void the first covenant to make way for a better covenant; one that was better for man."[18] In His mercy toward man He made a second covenant, "that in the way of this covenant he might be brought to the glory of God."[19]

> God introduces a better covenant that should be an everlasting covenant, a new and living way, wherein that which was wanting in the first covenant would be supplied, and a remedy should be provided against that which under the first covenant proved man's undoing, viz. man's own weakness and instability, by a mediator's being given, who is the same yesterday, today and forever, who cannot fail, who would undertake for them, who should take the care of them, that is able to save to the uttermost all that come unto God through him, and who ever lives to make intercession for them.[20]

The weakness of the first covenant is remedied by the perseverance of the Second Adam in the better covenant.

> The second Adam has persevered not only for himself, but for us; and has been sealed to confirmed, persevering and eternal life as our head. So that all those that are his, and that are his spiritual posterity, are sealed in him to persevering life.[21]

"If Christ had not kept the Father's commandments, he could not have continued in his love. He would have been cast out of favor."[22]

---

[17] M 695, *Works* 18:279.
[18] M 695, *Works* 18:277.
[19] M 774, *Works* 18:424.
[20] M 695, *Works* 18:277.
[21] M 695, *Works* 18:279.
[22] M 1188, *Works* 23:108. Edwards references Romans 11:22, Colossians 1:21-23, 1 Timothy 2:15, 2 Timothy 4:7-8, Romans 4:3, as "compared with" Genesis 15:6, 1 John 2:24-28.

Nevertheless, "it was impossible that Christ should not continue in His Father's love, "for He was entitled to such help and support from him as should be effectual to uphold him in obedience to his Father."[23] Therefore, through the perfect obedience of Christ, God remedied the weakness of the first covenant and guaranteed the success of the second covenant. "What the law failed of, being weak through the flesh, Christ performed."[24]

Christ Justifies Sinners by the Meritorious Righteousness of His Obedience on Their Behalf

In chapter four we noted Edwards' understanding of justification as requiring a "negative" righteousness of freedom from guilt and punishment, and a "positive" righteousness that gives title to the reward of eternal life. Had Adam obeyed God in his trial of obedience, he would have been justified as having both a "positive" and "negative" righteousness. Nonetheless, his obedience, considered of itself and apart from the covenant arrangement of God, would not have been meritorious in the sense of deserving a reward, as perfect obedience was the minimum required of Adam as a creature subject to God's rule of righteousness. According to the terms of God's gracious covenant, however, Adam's perfect obedience would have merited eternal life for himself and his posterity.[25]

Similarly, Christ's justification as the surety and representative of His people would consist of His perfect "negative" and "positive righteousness." Having bound Himself to the terms of the covenant of redemption, Christ became subject to God's strict rule of righteousness and could only be justified by the righteousness

---

[23] M 1188, *Works* 23:108.
[24] M 774, *Works* 18:425. Edwards cites Romans 8:34, "For what the law could not do, in that it was weak through the flesh, God sending his own Son in the likeness of sinful flesh, and for sin, condemned sin in the flesh: that the righteousness of the law might be fulfilled in us, that walk not after the flesh. [sic] but after the Spirit."
[25] As noted in chapter three.

of perfect obedience. Should He disobey in the least, He would disqualify Himself and His people from justification and become subject to the condemnation of God's rule of righteousness. As with the terms of the covenant with Adam, the reward of eternal life for the elect was gracious, while the reward to Christ was according to the merit of Christ's obedience. Whereas Adam's obedience was meritorious by virtue of God's gracious terms alone, Christ's obedience was infinitely meritorious of itself by virtue of Christ's voluntarily undertaking the role of mediator, as perfectly fulfilling all laws, as performed by one of infinite dignity and worth, and as an infinite condescension to infinite suffering on behalf of infinitely unworthy sinners.

The *basis* of the merit of Christ's obedience, in the freeness of the undertaking and perfection of its fulfillment of God's laws, will be examined in the present discussion concerning Christ's perfect obedience as constituting the righteousness by which sinners are justified. The infinite *extent* of the merit of Christ's obedience, as performed by one of infinite dignity and worth, and as an infinite condescension to infinite suffering on behalf of infinitely unworthy sinners, will be examined in the following section concerning the death of Christ as the "most exalted part of Christ's positive righteousness."

Christ's Obedience Is Meritorious as Voluntary

In chapter two we saw that Christ's obligating Himself to the terms of the covenant of redemption was consistent with the order of the persons of the Trinity, though not required by that order. As equal with the Father in divinity and glory, the Son was not required to subordinate Himself to the Father according to the terms of the covenant other than by voluntary agreement. Moreover, the Son possessed all the authority of God and had no need of the promised rewards of the covenant and, as perfectly righteous, had no need of meeting the demands of God's unchanging rule of righteousness for His own account. But in freely agreeing to the terms of the covenant of redemption, He bound himself to the perfect obedience required by the covenant, subject to the penalty of death for disobedience. Nevertheless, though bound to perfect obedience under penalty of death, all of Christ's acts in His humiliation, in fulfillment of the covenant terms, were meritorious in that He subjected Himself to the terms of the covenant voluntarily. "He voluntarily put himself in subjection and into the state of a servant, as the servant that had his ear bored, and therefore his obedience was properly meritorious."[26] Christ did not become the Father's servant by virtue of the humiliation of the incarnation, but by freely submitting to the terms of the covenant that required the incarnation for the Son to be a fitting mediator between God and mankind.[27] Accordingly, Christ's voluntary undertaking of the task of mediator according to the terms of the covenant of redemption is the basis of the merit of Christ's obedience.

> The whole tenor of the gospel holds this forth: that the Son acts altogether freely, and as in his own right, in undertaking the great and difficult and self-abasing work of our redemption, and that he becomes obliged to the Father with respect to it by voluntary covenant engagements, and not by any establishment prior thereto; so that he merits infinitely of the Father in entering into and fulfilling these engagements.[28]

Therefore, that perfect obedience required of Christ in His state of humiliation is no argument against the merits of the obedience accruing to those for whom Christ died, as the entire transaction was voluntarily undertaken by Christ on behalf of the elect and not for His own account (to be discussed further below).[29]

---

[26] M 454, *Works* 13:499.
[27] M 454, *Works* 13:499 and "Galatians 2:20," *WJEO*, L. 8r. – 8v. See also chapter two above.
[28] M 1062, *Works* 20:436.
[29] "Justification by Faith Alone," *Works* 19:192.

Christ's Obedience Is Meritorious as Perfectly Fulfilling All Laws

Having bound Himself to perfectly obey God's rule of righteousness according to the requirements of the covenant of redemption, Christ bound Himself to obey all laws, as all laws reflect God's one great rule of righteousness. And having voluntarily bound Himself to obey all laws, Christ's perfect obedience was thereby meritorious on account of the freeness and perfection of it. If Christ's obedience was imperfect in any respect, "it could not have been meritorious; for imperfect obedience is not accepted as any obedience at all in the sight of the law of works, which was that law that Christ was subject to."[30]

Christ's obedience was perfect in every respect, including sins to be avoided, positive commands to be obeyed, particulars of specific commands, the purity of His heart and motives, in perseverance, in any and every trial, *et al.*[31] He was perfectly obedient in His private life, including his childhood and the last years of His life during His public ministry.[32] Christ perfectly kept "the commands of the moral law, which was the same with that given at Mount Sinai, written in two tables of stone, which are of obligation to mankind of all nations and all ages of the world."[33] He also perfectly kept the ceremonial "Jewish" law.

> That Christ might the more fully honor God's authority, he was made under and obeyed the ceremonial law also. Christ's obedience to positive laws of God, [such] as the ceremonial laws, was equivalent to Adam's obedience to the positive precept of not eating the forbidden fruit. As that precept was given for the trial of Adam's obedience, so the ceremonial law was given for the trial of the second Adam's obedience.[34]

---

[30] *HWR, Works* 9:312.
[31] *HWR, Works* 9:311-2.
[32] *HWR, Works* 9:313.
[33] *HWR, Works* 9:309.
[34] M 322, *Works* 13:403. See also "Even As I Have Kept My Father's Commandments," *MDM*, 216, 219.

In addition to the moral and ceremonial law, Christ perfectly kept the "mediatorial law" given Him by the Father for "the execution of His mediatorial office."[35] Such commands include "coming into the world and taking upon him the human nature and dwelling amongst us,"[36] "deliver[ing] God's message to the world," and "working those miracles for the confirmation of his doctrine."[37] The most important of the "mediatorial" commands was to "lay down his life,"[38] "the greatest act of his obedience by which he purchased heaven for believers."[39]

> The greatest thing that Christ did in the execution of his office, and the greatest thing that ever he did, and the greatest thing that ever was done, was the offering up [himself a sacrifice to God]. Herein he was the antitype of all that had been done, by all the priests, and in all their sacrifices and offerings, from the beginning of the world.[40]

The "principle command that he had received of the Father was, that he should lay down his life, that he should voluntarily yield up himself to those terrible sufferings on the cross." This was Christ's "principal errand into the world; and doubtless the principal command that he received" from the Father, and the most difficult trial of His obedience.[41]

> It was the greatest trial of his obedience, because it was by far the most difficult command: all the rest were easy in comparison of this. And the main trial that Christ had, whether he would obey this command, was in the time of his agony; for that was within an hour before he was ap-

---

[35] *HWR, Works* 9:310.
[36] "Even As I Have Kept My Father's Commandments," *MDM*, 213.
[37] "Even As I Have Kept My Father's Commandments," *MDM*, 215. See also *Works* 9:315-7.
[38] *HWR, Works* 9:310.
[39] *HWR, Works* 9:318.
[40] *HWR, Works* 9:318.
[41] "Luke 22:44," *Works* (Hickman), 2:871.

prehended in order to his sufferings, when he must either yield himself up to them, or fly from them.[42]

As the most difficult and greatest trial of His obedience, Christ's obedience to death was therefore the most meritorious. Moreover, "Christ's righteousness, by which he merited heaven for himself and all that believe in him, consists principally in his obedience to this mediatorial law," for this was Christ's "chief work and business in the world."[43]

The mediatorial commands were to Christ alone, and were not given to others as were the moral and ceremonial laws, "but they were commands that he had received of the Father that purely respected the work he was to do in the world in his mediatorial office."[44] Nonetheless, the unique mediatorial commands given to Christ as the Second Adam parallel the unique command given to the first Adam, as they both constitute the specific standard for the righteousness required for the obtaining of eternal life.

> As the obedience of the first Adam, wherein his righteousness would have mainly consisted if he had stood, would not have been in his obedience to the moral law that he was subject to merely as man, or as one possessed of the human nature, but in his obedience to that special law that he was subject to as a moral head and surety; so the righteousness of the second Adam consists mainly in his obedience to the special law that he was subject to, in his office of mediator and surety.[45]

Christ speaks of the mediatorial commands when He speaks of doing the Father's will, as in John 15:19, when He says: "'Verily, verily I say unto you, the Son can do nothing of himself but what he seeth the Father do.'" Or in verse 30, "'I can of mine own self do

---

[42] "Luke 22:44," *Works* (Hickman), 2:871. See also "Even As I Have Kept My Father's Commandments," *MDM*, 216-19.
[43] *HWR, Works* 9:310. See also M 794, *Works* 18:496.
[44] *HWR, Works* 9:310.
[45] M 794, *Works* 18:496.

nothing. I seek not mine own will but the will of the Father that sent me.'"[46] In accomplishing the mediatorial commands, Christ fulfilled the terms of the covenant to which He voluntarily bound Himself on behalf of His bride.

> By making intercession, Christ did all upon earth that God required and fully accomplished the terms of the covenant of redemption and finished all by his death and continuance in the grave. He went into heaven to make representation of what he had done and suffered before the throne of God. He enters with his blood and shows his wounds and has this plea to make for those who believe in him—that he had done all that God required. John 17:4 says, "I have finished the work which thou gavest me to do."[47]

Christ's obedience, therefore, was meritorious in His perfect fulfillment of all laws, of which the mediatorial law is the most important and meritorious.

Christ's Perfect Obedience to God's Rule of Righteousness Constitutes His Justifying Righteousness

Edwards poses the question of how fallen sinners can be justified before a righteous God as follows:

> Now the question after man had sinned was how the sinner should properly be [a] partaker of perfect righteousness, i.e., how his guilt could be removed so that, consistent with God's nature and with his law, he might notwithstanding be looked upon without any offense or displeasure by God; and then, how a complete, positive righteousness should become properly his, that is, should be so his that, consistent with the same divine nature and rule of righteousness, he might be accepted with the same favor and to the same reward as if he had perfectly, with-

---

[46] "Even As I Have Kept My Father's Commandments," *MDM*, 215.
[47] "A Glorious Foundation for Peace," *MDM*, 177.

out ever sinning himself, performed. This righteousness we have through Jesus Christ.[48]

As noted in chapter four, the sin of mankind made salvation impossible apart from Christ fulfilling the requirement of perfect obedience to God's rule of righteousness on behalf of sinners. "We are so much saved on the account of [Christ's] righteousness, that if he had not been righteous, as well as if he had not died, we should unavoidably [have] been damned."[49] As Christ voluntarily bound himself to the terms of the covenant of redemption as the surety and representative of unworthy sinners, so also the righteousness of Christ's perfect obedience in fulfillment of God's rule of righteousness is the righteousness by which sinners are justified. The righteousness Christ performed according to the covenant terms consists of "his negative righteousness, or his removing guilt by suffering," and "his positive righteousness in his perfect obedience."[50] By this righteousness of Christ the sinner is made righteous and justified.

> This righteousness of Christ that consisted in his obedience to all God's commands is offered to us. God is willing to look on us as righteous on the account of it if we will receive Jesus Christ by faith. Romans 5:19 says, "For as by one man's disobedience many were made sinners, even so by the righteousness of one many are made righteous." However sinful we have been in how many instances so ever, we have not obeyed God's commands and broken them, yet Christ has obeyed and we may safely trust in his obedience.[51]

The righteousness of Christ received by faith is an "infinitely more glorious righteousness than that that many other men trust in, even their own righteousness, which is as filthy rags; 'tis a righteousness that will justify 'em." He "perfectly fulfilled the law, be-

---

[48] "The Threefold Work of the Holy Ghost," *Works* 14:395.
[49] M s, *Works* 13:173.
[50] "The Threefold Work of the Holy Ghost," *Works* 14:395.
[51] "Even As I Have Kept My Father's Commandments," *MDM*, 220.

ing obedient unto death, and by his sufferings has fully satisfied divine justice and answered the law."[52] Thus, Christ's righteousness is a "better righteousness," a "glorious righteousness" performed on behalf of His people. And as Christ's obedience to the mediatorial commands of God were by far the most difficult, important, and meritorious, so also this obedience comprises Christ's justifying righteousness.

> 'Tis true he obeyed the law of nature as he was a man and a reasonable creature, and he observed the law of Moses as he was a Jew and of the seed of Abraham; but that was by virtue of the mediatorial law, and as a part and branch of it: so that all he did in this world, and what he is now doing in heaven, in obedience to his Father's will and for the salvation of men, is properly his righteousness.[53]

We have seen Edwards' understanding that every command of God, including the commands of the moral, ceremonial, and mediatorial law, are representative of God's one great rule of righteousness to which perfect obedience is required. Christ would not be righteous if He disobeyed any command of God, having bound Himself to do so by the terms of the covenant. "All the virtue that Christ exercised in the human nature in any respect belongs to that righteousness which is imputed to believers for their justification."[54]

> Every [act] that Christ performed in obedience to the Father, after he once put himself into a state of subjection, was part of his righteousness imputed to us, and performed in obedience to the same law that Adam was made under.[55]

---

[52] "Glorying in the Savior," *Works* 14:466-7.
[53] M 278, *Works* 13:377-8. See also "Proverbs 16:6," *Works* 24:562: "Legal sacrifices in themselves are of no efficacy to atone for sin, and that nothing can avail to this but spiritual sacrifices, Christ's righteousness consisting in his obedience and faithfulness to God, and mercy to men."
[54] M 791, *Works* 18:494.
[55] M 399, *Works* 13:465. See also M 794, *Works* 18:496.

Though Christ's justifying righteousness includes His perfect obedience to all of God's laws, His perfect obedience to the mediatorial law is the specific means by which God determined that Christ would save sinners.[56] Accordingly, Christ's merit is only by the positive holiness and righteousness of His acts, and the righteousness by which sinners are justified. "We are justified by Christ's active obedience thus: his active obedience was one thing that God saw to be needful in order to retrieve the honor of his law, as well as his suffering for the breach of it."[57] Indeed, "Christ came into the world to render the honor of God's authority and his law consistent with the salvation and eternal life of sinners." Should eternal life be given "without active righteousness, the honor of His law would not be sufficiently vindicated."[58]

Additionally, it cannot be that Christ's redemptive work on behalf of the elect as their surety and representative for their justification was meritorious by virtue of the righteousness of it, yet that same righteousness and merit accomplished on behalf of the elect for their justification not be imputed to them.

> One would wonder what Arminians mean by Christ's merits: they talk of Christ's merits as much as anybody, and yet deny the imputation of Christ's positive righteousness: what should there be that anyone should merit or deserve anything by, besides righteousness or goodness? If anything that Christ did or suffered, merited or deserved anything, it was by virtue of the goodness, or righteousness, or holiness of it: if Christ's sufferings and

---

[56] See "John 16:8-11," *Works* 24:955, wherein Edwards favorably quotes Doddridge with respect to John 16:10: "'He will convince the world of my righteousness and innocence, because it will evidently appear, that I go to my Father, and am accepted of him, when I send the Spirit from him in so glorious a manner (Compare Acts 2:33 and Rom. 1:4.), and that my righteousness may therefore be relied on for the justification and acceptance of my people, since you see me no more appearing among you in the form of a servant, but are assured that having finished what I was to do on the earth, I am taken up to heaven, and received into glory.'"
[57] M 261, *Works* 13:368.
[58] M 322, *Works* 13:403. See also M 161, *Works* 13:319.

> death merited heaven, it must be because there was an excellent righteousness, and transcendent moral goodness in that act of laying down his life: and if by that excellent righteousness he merited heaven for us, then surely that righteousness is reckoned to our account, that we have the benefit of it, or which is the same thing, it is imputed to us.[59]

The foundation of Edwards' understanding of Christ's redemptive work is that it was all freely performed on behalf of the elect, as Christ was in no need to submit Himself to the requirements of the covenant of redemption to perfectly obey God's rule of righteousness, nor was He in any need of any of the benefits that would be rewarded for His obedience, as He possessed all the privileges of His divinity eternally. All that He did and accomplished was done for the elect as their surety and representative. And as He accrued infinite merit for the entirety of His redemptive work, it does not follow that this merit would not become the possession of those for whom it was earned.

> It seems strange to me, that those that hold that Christ's merits are imputed to us, or, which is the same thing, that he merited for us, or that we have the benefit of his merit, should deny that his active righteousness is imputed to us. For what was it that Christ merited by, if it was not by his righteousness; or what should there be that ever anyone should merit or deserve anything by, besides their righteousness or goodness?[60]

Notice Edwards' understanding of that which Christ "merited for us" is "the same thing" as Christ's merits "imputed to us." The righteousness of Christ accomplished the merit for which He was exalted to the right hand of God. He purchased heaven for those whom He undertook the task of obedience, earning the reward of heaven on their behalf. If believers receive the reward for Christ's

---

[59] "Justification by Faith Alone," *Works* 19:199.
[60] M 532, *Works* 18:76–77.

obedience, why not the merits of the obedience by which the reward was earned on their behalf? To receive the reward of Christ's obedience without the imputation of the merits by which the reward was earned is "strange" to Edwards. To be united to Christ, or members of His mystical body, is to have the perfect righteousness of Christ imputed to you.

> 'Tis most agreeable to the tenor of the Scripture that believers shall partake with Christ in that exaltation and glory which the Father gives him in reward for his obedience, his doing the work which he did in the world by the Father's appointment. The whole mystical Christ shall be rewarded for this, which is the same thing as having Christ's righteousness imputed to them.[61]

Granted, theologians often use the term "imputation" with respect to the imputation of both Christ's satisfaction for sin and obedience. Nonetheless, with respect to the imputation of righteousness, imputation is of the obedience of Christ to the covenant terms and God's unchanging rule of righteousness.[62]

> By that righteousness being imputed to us, is meant no other than this, that that righteousness of Christ is accepted for us, and admitted instead of that perfect inher-

---

[61] M 502, *Works* 18:51.
[62] Edwards distinguishes the imputed righteousness of Christ from the "inherent righteousness communicated" to believers in salvation. Justification is by imputed righteousness only, though imputation is never apart from the communication of righteousness by the giving of the Holy Spirit. He writes: "There is a two-fold righteousness that the saints have: an imputed righteousness, and 'tis this only that avails anything to justification; and an inherent righteousness, that is, that holiness and grace which is in the hearts and lives of the saints. This is Christ's righteousness as well as imputed righteousness: imputed righteousness is Christ's righteousness accepted for them, inherent holiness is Christ's righteousness communicated to them. They derive their holiness from Christ as the fountain of it. He gives it by his Spirit, so that 'tis Christ's holiness communicated, 'tis the light of the sun reflected. Now God takes delight in the saints for both these: both for Christ's righteousness imputed and for Christ's holiness communicated, though 'tis the former only that avails anything to justification. "None Are Saved by Their Own Righteousness," *Works* 14:340-1.

ent righteousness that ought to be in ourselves: Christ's perfect obedience shall be reckoned to our account, so that we shall have the benefit of it, as though we had performed it ourselves: and so we suppose that a title to eternal life is given us as the reward of this righteousness.[63]

With respect to those who see such an imputation as "absurd," the concept is no more absurd than a debt or credit transfer between accounts, or the acceptance of payment for a purchase by one person for another. Would such payment not be accepted on behalf of the one for whom the purchase was made?[64] Further, if Christ's satisfaction is imputed to the believer, why not His obedience?

Why is there any more absurdity in supposing that Christ's obedience is imputed to us, than that his satisfaction is imputed? If Christ has suffered the penalty of the law for us, and in our stead, then it will follow, that his suffering that penalty is imputed to us, i.e. that it is accepted for us, and in our stead, and is reckoned to our account, as though we had suffered it. But why mayn't his obeying the law of God be as rationally reckoned to our account, as his suffering the penalty of the law?[65]

"Justification by the righteousness and obedience of Christ, is a doctrine that the Scripture teaches in very full terms," as in Romans 5:18-19: "'By the righteousness of one, the free gift came upon all men unto justification of life. For as by one man's disobedience many were made sinners, so by the obedience of one shall many be made righteous.'"[66]

---

[63] "Justification by Faith Alone," *Works* 19:185-6. With respect to the definition of "impute," Edwards cites Philemon 18; Romans 4:6, 5:13.
[64] "Justification by Faith Alone," *Works* 19:186.
[65] "Justification by Faith Alone," *Works* 19:186.
[66] "Justification by Faith Alone," *Works* 19:193. "Here in one verse we are told that we have justification by Christ's righteousness, and that there might be no room to understand the righteousness spoken of merely of Christ's atonement, by his suffering the penalty. In the next verse, 'tis put in other terms, and asserted that 'tis by Christ's obedience that we are made righteous. 'Tis scarce possible anything should be more full and determined: the terms, taken singly, are such as

Concerning the Holy Spirit's use of the term "righteousness of God" in Scripture to denote the righteousness of Christ imputed to believers,[67] such conveys "the principal and most proper distinction between the righteousness by which men are justified under this covenant from that by which mankind would have been justified by the first covenant if Adam had stood in his integrity." If Adam had obeyed, "we should have been justified by the righteousness of man, of mere man; it would have been properly an human righteousness."[68] Indeed, in justification by the righteousness of Christ as God, as well as the manner by which this righteousness becomes the believer's righteousness, the ultimate purpose of God in the display and communication of His glory is advanced.

> The glory of God in our justification is greatly secured and advanced by these two things: 1. that our justifying righteousness is the righteousness of God, the righteousness not of an human but a divine person, so that a divine person is the author of it and the value of it arises from the dignity of the divine nature; and 2. as the very bond of union, by which we are united to this divine person so as to be interested in his righteousness, is that principle and act of the soul by which we know that the righteousness is thus the righteousness, and by which we cordially and with all our hearts ascribe it wholly to him and give him all the glory of it.[69]

In this way the creature is "abased and annihilated" and thrown into complete dependence upon God for his happiness, that all of justification "should be of God and in God; that the righteousness should not be the righteousness performed by man, as an human

---

to fix their own meaning, and taken together, they fix the meaning of each other: the words show that we are justified by that righteousness of Christ, that consists in his obedience, and that we are made righteous or justified by that obedience of his, that is his righteousness, or moral goodness before God."

[67] According to Edwards' understanding of the inspiration of Scripture, terms used in Scripture are terms used by the Holy Spirit.

[68] M 1177, *Works* 23:93. See also "Romans 10:3," *Works* 24:1024-5.

[69] M 1177, *Works* 23:94.

person by himself." The value of mankind's justification "should arise from the infinite dignity of the divinity to which the man Christ Jesus was personally united."[70] "This principally shows the infinite value and excellency and merit of that righteousness, viz. that it was the righteousness of a divine person."[71] This divine righteousness "is fit to succeed in the room of the human righteousness which we have failed of."[72] God by Christ accomplishes what human righteousness did not and cannot accomplish.

> That this is the reason why Christ's righteousness is called "God's righteousness," viz. to set it in a more clear opposition to the righteousness of men, is confirmed from the antithesis in Rom. 1:17-18. "For therein is the *righteousness of God* revealed from faith to faith; as it is written, the just shall live by faith. For the wrath of God is revealed from heaven against all ungodliness and *unrighteousness of men*"[73] [Edwards' emphasis].

---

[70] M 1177, *Works* 23:93-4.
[71] M 893, *Works* 20:153.
[72] "Romans 10:3," *Works* 24:1025-6.
[73] "Romans 10:3," *Works* 24:1024-5. Further, with respect to Hebrews 4:5: "The Apostle by 'God's righteousness' means the righteousness that a divine person hath, or is the subject of, and is given to believers; as by God's 'rest,' the same Apostle means the rest which God or Christ hath, and is also given to believers," 1026. Also, "THE RIGHTEOUSNESS by which believers are justified is called GOD'S RIGHTEOUSNESS, not merely because 'tis a righteousness of God's providing, nor is thereby meant only that 'tis a fruit of God's wonderful contrivance and extraordinary dispensation, but because 'tis a righteousness of God's working and inherent in God, i.e. in a divine person. This is agreeable to the style of the gospel. Thus the rest that remains for the people of God, the rest which God has provided for them and which they enter into, is called God's rest, in that sense, that 'tis Christ's own rest, the rest which he himself enters into (compare Heb. 3:11, 14, and ch. 4:5, 9-10). So it is said in God's light we shall see light [Ps. 36:9], and that the saints shall drink of the river of God's pleasures [Ps. 36:8], and shall enter into the joy of their Lord [Matt. 25:21, 23], and the glory of the saints, which is the fruit of righteousness, is [the] glory of God [Phil. 1:11]. Rom. 3[:23], we 'have sinned, and come short of the glory.' So the kingdom of God is promised to them, and the inheritance which is reserved for the saints in heaven (or in the holy places) is called Christ's inheritance (Eph. 1:18)." M 1271, *Works* 23:216.

The righteousness of Christ, the "righteousness of God" in distinction from the righteousness of man, becomes the possession of the believer through the "spiritual" and "active union" of faith. The righteousness by which the believer is justified is the divine "righteousness of another," of "our surety."[74]

Christ's Obedience as Surety Achieves the Two-Fold Righteousness Required for Justification of the Elect

As defined in chapter four, justification requires both pardon from guilt and the positive righteousness of obedience. And as we have just seen above, the righteousness by which believers are justified is the righteousness of Christ in His perfect obedience to the Father, fulfilling the terms of the covenant of redemption in perfect obedience to God's rule of righteousness. By His perfect obedience, "Christ obeyed to the degree that the law required," hence "his righteousness is the righteousness of the law, so that if we trust in this righteousness, the law will not oppose our justification and acceptance of God."[75] In His obedience unto death, Christ stood in the place of those for whom He came to redeem and accomplished justification on their behalf. "Christ came into the world not only to free us from guilt, but to do that work which Adam failed of. This is implied in Christ being called 'the second Adam.'"[76]

> By the same law that Christ, when he had once put himself in our stead, was obliged to suffer, by the same was he obliged to obey. After he was become our surety, he could not be acquitted till he had suffered, nor can be rewarded till he has obeyed; and as he is not acquitted as a private person, so neither is he rewarded as a private person. But we are partakers as well of the reward of his obedience,

---

[74] "Romans 10:3," *Works* 24:1024.
[75] "Even As I Have Kept My Father's Commandments," *MDM*, 220.
[76] "The Threefold Work of the Holy Ghost," *Works* 14:397. Edwards cites 1 Corinthians 15:45.

as of his acquaintance upon his sufferings; for in both, he appears as our head.[77]

Christ as the Second Adam, acting as a public person and not out of private interest, obeyed and accomplished what Adam failed to accomplish by his disobedience. Romans 5:17-19 "plainly shows that as what Adam did brought death, as it had the nature of disobedience, so what Christ did brought life, not only as a sacrifice, but as it had the nature of meriting obedience," "'for as by one man's disobedience many were made sinners, so by the obedience of one shall many be made righteous.'"[78] 1 John 2:1 implies the same, "'and if any man sin, we have an advocate with the Father, Jesus Christ the righteous.'" Christ's righteousness "is mentioned as that which makes us acceptable to God, as sin makes us unacceptable and offensive."[79] With respect to Galatians 4:4-5, "'God sent forth his Son, made under the law, to redeem them that are under the law, that we might receive the adoption of sons,'" Edwards comments: "By his [being] made under the law, it is fair to understand all manner of subjection, both as requiring his passive and active subjection, and that both were to redeem us, that we might be made partakers of the adoption of sons."[80] As surety and representative, He bore the imputed guilt of those for whom He suffered and was "acquitted and justified of the Father in his resurrection."[81] Those for whom Christ suffered are justified in His justification.[82]

---

[77] "The Threefold Work of the Holy Ghost," *Works* 14:397.
[78] "The Threefold Work of the Holy Ghost," *Works* 14:398. "For if by one man's offense death reigned by one; much more they which receive abundance of grace and of the gift of righteousness shall reign in life by one, Jesus Christ. Therefore as by the offense of one judgment came upon all men to condemnation; even so by the righteousness of one the free gift came upon all men unto justification of life. For as by one man's disobedience many were made sinners, so by the obedience of one shall many be made righteous." Romans 5:17-19.
[79] "The Threefold Work of the Holy Ghost," *Works* 14:398.
[80] "The Threefold Work of the Holy Ghost," *Works* 14:398-9.
[81] "The Peace Which Christ Gives His True Followers," *Works* 25:544.
[82] Edwards did not hold to eternal justification, for though both the Father and Son set their love on particular individuals in eternity past, the union whereby the believer's justification is realized is the union with Christ when the believer

After Christ had once placed himself in man's stead, or stood forth as man's representative, all which he did by taking upon himself the character of mediator, all the excellency that was seen in him in that character, or all his mediatorial excellency, was properly and fitly accepted for man; or rather, was fitly accepted for Christ mystical, that is, for Christ himself and for all his: whatever he did as mediator, he did as representing the whole body, head and members. Christ's excellency as mediator was his excellency as head of this body, and was rewarded in both head and members.[83]

Thus, Christ is the "forerunner" that goes "before his church to heaven to prepare a place for them. He is entered into his rest as their forerunner; he is entered for them, and to take possession in their name."[84] With respect to Ephesians 1:18, "'of his inheritance in the saints,'" Christ's inheritance is the saints' inheritance, as the "saints and he are one."[85] As one, the saints are identified with Christ's exaltation as they are identified with His suffering and glory.[86] What belongs to Christ as mediator belongs to the saints.

Concerning John 10:17, "'Therefore doth my Father love me, because I lay down my life, that I might take it again,'" the love of the Father to Christ is said to be consequent on the righteousness of Christ in "that great act of obedience, his laying down his

---

exercises faith in Christ. Faith is the believer's part of what constitutes union with Christ. See "Justification by Faith Alone," *Works*, 19:155.
[83] M 496, *Works* 13:539.
[84] "Numbers 10:33," *Works* 24:263.
[85] "Ephesians 1:18," *Works* 24:1093.
[86] "They are raised up with him, and set with him 'in heavenly places' [v. 20], as it follows in the next words and next chapter, fifth and sixth verses. 'Tis called the inheritance of Christ in his saints, as the sufferings of the saints are called the sufferings of Christ in the saints (Col. 1:24). As here the Apostle speaks of the glory of Christ's inheritance in his saints, so in II Thess. 1:10 he says that at the day of judgment Christ 'will come to be glorified in his saints.' See note *in loc*. The saints' future reward is called Christ's glory (II Thess. 2:14)." "Ephesians 1:18," *Works* 24:1093-4.

life." The apparent difficulty of the Father's love for His Son as contingent upon Christ's obedience is eliminated in that Christ acted as surety for those for whom He was purchasing God's love. "Christ purchased the love of God for himself, and therefore for all that are in him. God loves Christ for his own righteousness, and therefore He loves all to whom his righteousness is imputed for the same righteousness."[87]

In the same way, *the justification of Christ* is with respect to His obedience as surety for the elect. In commenting on 1 Timothy 3:16, "'God manifest in the flesh, justified in the Spirit,'" Edwards comments:

> But what need had Christ of any justification, that had never sinned, was never guilty? Why, he had this need of it because he voluntarily took on him our guilt and as it were became guilty, became a debtor to justice; and therefore when he paid the debt by suffering, then he was guilty no more, but was justified, and the sentence of justification was declared by his resurrection.[88]

He had no sin of His own, but as surety for those upon whom He set His love in eternity past, He took their guilt and met the law's requirements on their behalf. He was justified in answering the requirement of the law on behalf of those for whom He was surety. Indeed, having freely bound Himself to the terms of the covenant of redemption, He bound Himself to the perfect obedience required by God's rule of righteousness, apart from which Christ Himself would not have been justified. Thus, "when Christ was raised from the dead, he was justified," including "acquittance from our guilt, and his acceptance to the exaltation and glory that was the reward of his obedience."[89] Believers partake of this justi-

---

[87] "John 10:17," *Works* 24:945-6. Edwards references John 14:21 and Proverbs 8:17.
[88] "The Threefold Work of the Holy Ghost," *Works* 14:396.
[89] "Justification by Faith Alone," *Works* 19:191. See also "The Threefold Work of the Holy Ghost," *Works* 14:392-3: "Therefore Christ's going to the Father is here mentioned as the finishing stroke, as what crowns all that he did as our

fication, including Christ's reward, for "he was 'raised again for our justification' (Rom. 4:25)."[90]

> The Scripture teaches us that he is exalted, and gone to heaven, to take possession of glory in our name, as our forerunner (Heb. 6:20). We are as it were both "raised up together with Christ, and also made to set together with Christ, in heavenly places, and in him" (Eph. 2:6).[91]

Thus, in His justification of Christ, God "did not only release him from his humiliation for sin…but admitted him to that eternal and immortal life, and to the beginning of that exaltation, that was the reward of what he had done."[92] If Christ did not rise from the dead, it "would be an argument of his insufficiency as a Savior."[93]

> We are to be saved no otherwise than in him and with him as members of him, and so to be justified in his justification, which was his resurrection, to be delivered in his deliverance, to have victory in his victory, to triumph with

---

righteousness, and the last thing needful to be done by the Mediator in order to the making his righteousness ours: a crowning thing that renders him a complete object of the faith of believers, the last thing needed in order to there being sufficient grounds for the world's being convinced of the sufficiency of his righteousness. Therefore it is he shall convince the world of righteousness, 'because I go to my Father.'" Edwards' reference is to John 16:8-10.

[90] "Justification by Faith Alone," *Works* 19:191.
[91] "Justification by Faith Alone," *Works* 19:191-2.
[92] "Justification by Faith Alone," *Works* 19:151.
[93] "1 Corinthians 5:17," *Works* 24:1059. See also M 47, *Works* 13:226-7; and "The Threefold Work of the Holy Ghost," *Works* 14:393: "Christ's going to the Father is mentioned as being a principal argument whereby he does convince men of Christ's righteousness, not only as the means of our justification before the Father, but a principal means of convincing of 'em of the sufficiency of Christ's righteousness.

Christ's exaltation, viz. his rising from the dead and his ascending into heaven, is often insisted on in the gospel as being the great evidence that what Christ had done and suffered was sufficient for us. So it is, Rom. 8:34, 'Who is he that condemneth? It is Christ that died, yea rather, that is risen again, who is even at the right hand of God, who also maketh intercession for us.' So it is said, 'Christ was manifest in the flesh, justified in the Spirit' (I Tim. 3:16)."

him, to be raised up together with him, and made to sit together in heavenly places in him.[94]

"This resurrection of Christ is the most joyful event that ever came to pass, because hereby Christ rested from the great and difficult work of purchasing [redemption] and received God's testimony that it was finished."[95] Justification for the believer, then, is "being admitted to communion in, or participation of the justification of this head and surety of all believers."[96]

> Christ suffered the punishment of sin, not as a private person, but as our surety, so when after this suffering he was raised from the dead, he was therein justified, not as a private person, but as the surety and representative of all that should believe in him; so that he was raised again not only for his own, but also for our justification, according to the Apostle. Rom. 4:25, "Who was delivered for our offenses, and raised again for our justification." And therefore it is that the Apostle says as he does in Rom. 8:34, "Who is he that condemneth? it is Christ that died, yea rather that is risen again."[97]

As "Christ did not rise as a private person but as head of all the elect church," the church did "all rise in him."[98] "The day of Christ's resurrection" is "the birth day of the whole church of God to eternal glory."[99] Having finished His redemptive "labors and sufferings" on behalf of His church, He rose from the dead, ascended into heaven, and entered into "a state of most blessed, perfect, and ever-

---

[94] "1 Corinthians 5:17," *Works* 24:1059.
[95] *HWR*, *Works* 9:359.
[96] "Justification by Faith Alone," *Works* 19:151.
[97] "Justification by Faith Alone," *Works* 19:151.
[98] *HWR*, *Works* 9:358-9. See also "Matthew 28:2-4," *Works* 24:877: "Christ arose as the head of believers, to deliver them from a state of death, spiritual, temporal, and eternal. He as their head and captain of salvation broke the prison, set the doors wide open, broke the seal, rolled away the stone, laid the keeper dead, and left the sepulcher open, that all the dead that he has redeemed may come forth."
[99] "Job 3:6," *Works* 24:427.

lasting peace" with them.[100] As united to Christ, saints participate in the same justification of Christ, as they are accepted by God for the same righteousness. They participate in the same love of God by the same Holy Spirit, and will share in the same heavenly and eternal rest and glory.[101] United to Christ they participate in the accomplishment and rewards of Christ's redemptive work.

Additionally, as clothed in the justifying righteousness of Christ by which the requirement of God's rule of righteousness has been fulfilled, the justice of God now stands on the side of the believer. As the law was not abrogated but fulfilled on behalf of those for whom Christ died,[102] the stipulations of the law are thereby rendered favorable to believers. In fact, "the justice of God is not only

---

[100] "The Peace Which Christ Gives His True Followers," *Works* 25:544.

[101] "The Peace Which Christ Gives His True Followers," *Works* 25:544-5. "'Tis a participation of the same justification; for believers are justified with Christ, as he was justified when he rose [from the dead], as free from our guilt, which he had as our surety....'Tis as being accepted of God in the same righteousness; 'tis in the favor of the same God and heavenly Father [that we are at peace]. 'I ascend to my Father, and your Father' [John 20:17]. 'Tis a participation of the same Spirit, [for believers] have the Spirit of Christ....'Tis as being united to Christ and living by a participation of his life, as a branch lives by the life of the vine. 'Tis as partaking of the same love of God; John 17, last [verse], 'That the love wherewith thou hast loved me may be in them.' 'Tis as having a part with him in his victory over the same enemies, and 'tis also as having an interest in the same land of eternal rest and peace. Eph. 2:5-6, 'Even when we were dead in sins, hath quickened us together in Christ, and hath raised us up together, and made us sit together in heavenly places.'"

[102] In commenting on Romans 7:1-4, Edwards writes: "Thus we may understand the connection between this and the following verse. The law has dominion over a woman so long as she liveth, and in those commands that relate to her husband, so long as her husband liveth. For when her husband is dead, she is dead to him with respect to that part of the law that respects the relation between her and her husband. She is dead, for her living, with respect to those precepts, consists in the living of the relation between them. The woman is freed from that part of the law that related to her husband, not by any abrogating or disannulling of the law, but because she is in that matter dead, and the law don't any longer reach her. So is the law as a covenant of works dead with respect to us, and we are dead to it by Christ's body, i.e. by the dying of his body, whereby the law was satisfied and fulfilled. The law did as it were die as a covenant of works with respect to the people of Christ when Christ's body died." "Romans 7:1-4," *Works* 24:1002.

186 *The Infinite Merit of Christ*

appeased to those who have an interest in him, but stands up for them; is not only not an enemy but a friend, every whit as much as mercy."[103] Thus, by virtue of Christ's perfect righteousness, the strict and unchanging rule of God's righteousness, by which all sinners are infinitely condemned, becomes the very strict and unchanging rule that *requires* the justification of those believers for whom Christ died.

> Justice demands adoption and glorification, and importunes as much for it, as ever it did before for misery; in every respect that it is against the wicked, it is as much for the godly. Yea, it is abundantly more so than it would have been for Adam: for him it would be only because He graciously promised; but it is obliged to believers on the account of the absolute agreement between God and his Son.[104]

As noted in chapter four, God's perfect justice stands against the justification of any on the basis of any personal righteousness. The only basis of acceptance before God is the righteousness of Christ "received by faith."[105] At the same time, faith itself has no meritorious righteousness by which one is justified. Rather, "in the act of that faith which God requires in order to a sinner's justification, he looks on himself wholly as a sinner, or ungodly," and therefore "seeks justification of himself, as in himself ungodly and unrighteous, by the righteousness of another."[106] "He has no consideration of any goodness or holiness of his own in that affair, but merely and only the righteousness of Christ."[107]

> And so it is that God looks on him in justifying him. God has no consideration of any goodness in him when he justifies by faith, as that faith by which he has justified has no consideration of any goodness in him. And as justifying

---

[103] M 38, *Works* 13:221.
[104] M 38, *Works* 13:221.
[105] "Justification by Faith Alone," *Works* 19:237.
[106] M 1162, *Works* 23:84.
[107] M 1162, *Works* 23:83-4.

Christ Satisfies God's Rule of Righteousness 187

faith has respect only to the righteousness of another, so has he that justifies by faith.[108]

As justification is by the righteousness of Christ alone, so the very nature of faith is consistent with this principle.

Therefore, from the incarnation to the resurrection, Christ's purchase of the elect was complete by virtue of Christ's accomplishment alone. Though Christ was appointed and began His work as mediator before the incarnation, "no part of the purchase was made," or "no price was offered" until the incarnation, "but as soon as Christ was incarnate, then the purchase began immediately without any delay."[109] The entire life of Christ's humiliation, "from the morning that Christ began to be incarnate till the morning that he rose from the dead, was taken up in this purchase. And then the purchase was entirely and completely finished."[110]

> As you have heard, this work of purchasing salvation was wholly finished during the time [of Christ's humiliation]. So here is need of nothing more: the servants are now sent forth with the message which we have account of in Matt. 22:4 ["Behold, I have prepared my dinner: my oxen and my fatlings are killed, and all things are ready: come unto the marriage"]. Are your sins many and great, here is enough. There is no need of any righteousness of yours; come freely without money and without price; come naked; come as a poor condemned [sinner]; come cast yourself down at Jesus' feet, as one just condemned and most utterly helpless. Here is complete salvation.[111]

---

[108] M 1162, *Works* 23:83-4.
[109] *HWR*, *Works* 9:295.
[110] *HWR*, *Works* 9:295, also 331. Christ's purchase was of both New and Old Testament saints, as "there is the same Mediator, under both old testament and new." "That some of the old testament saints rose from the dead with Christ, their graves being opened by his death, shows that the old testament saints are entitled to the benefit of Christ's death, and are saved from death by his dying for 'em." Edwards references Turretin, 2:213. M 874, *Works* 20:117-8. Edwards lists numerous Scriptural references as support.
[111] *HWR*, *Works* 9:342.

Christ has purchased His bride and now invites sinners to the marriage. He "stands as the tree of life," and "we are immediately invited and called to Christ, to come to him, to take and eat, without any other terms, because the condition of righteousness is fulfilled already by our surety."[112]

Lastly, Christ's obedience as surety achieved the righteousness of justification for the elect *in particular*. In other words, having set His love on particular sinners from eternity past, He undertook to stand in their place as individuals. "He knew every one of them when he actually came into the world and when he laid down his life. He had the names of every one of them upon his heart. Every one was as it were set before his eyes."[113] "He had the names of all his people upon his heart when he went through those things as the high priest was to have the names of the children of Israel on his breastplate."[114] His "dying love" was to "every particular believer,"[115] and "his heart glowed with love to everyone of them when he stood before Pilate and when he hung upon the cross."[116] How much more, then, should believers "admire the grace of God towards them," in that they are the special recipients of God's grace, "than if they were only common partakers of a general kindness to mankind."[117]

Christ's Perfect Obedience Purchases a "Full Capacity," as Would Have Adam's Perfect Obedience

Justification by the righteousness of Christ alone, without consideration of any righteousness of the believer, raises the question with respect to differing degrees of blessing in heaven and the giving of rewards for believers' good works. With respect to the latter,

---

[112] M 498, *Works* 13:540.
[113] "Galatians 2:20," *WJEO*, L. 3r. See also L. 8v.–9r. This sermon is an in-depth and poignant treatment of the particular nature of Christ's love toward sinners.
[114] "Galatians 2:20," *WJEO*, L. 4v.
[115] "Galatians 2:20," *WJEO*, L. 3v.
[116] "1 John 4:19," *WJEO*, L. 6r.
[117] "Galatians 2:20," *WJEO*, L. 7v.

Christ Satisfies God's Rule of Righteousness 189

if the best works of a believer possess infinite demerit (as noted in chapter four), how then are they acceptable and worthy of reward, and on what basis do the degrees of reward differ? With respect to degrees of glory, on what basis could there be differing degrees of glory in heaven if all of the glory was earned by Christ alone, or "how is it said that our happiness is the reward of holiness and good works, and yet that we are made happy wholly and solely for the sake of Christ?"[118]

To begin, Edwards held to differing degrees of glory for saints redeemed by the righteousness of Christ alone and saw no contradiction between the two principles. "Christ by his righteousness purchased for everyone, complete and perfect happiness," but each "according to his capacity."[119] The happiness of every saint, regardless of capacity, is "fruit of Christ's purchase" alone, but "'tis left to God's sovereign pleasure to determine the largeness of the vessel; Christ's righteousness meddles not with this matter."[120] So also would have been the case with Adam had he obeyed.

> If Adam had persevered in perfect obedience, he and his posterity would have had perfect and full happiness; everyone's happiness would have so answered his capacity, that he would have been completely blessed; but God would have been at liberty to have made some of one capacity, and others of another as he pleased.[121]

Angels, who obtained "a state of confirmed glory by a covenant of works, whose condition was perfect obedience," have differing degrees of glory according to God's "sovereign pleasure."[122] And

---

[118] M 168, *Works* 13:322.
[119] "Justification by Faith Alone," *Works* 19:218. See also M 367, *Works* 13:437-8. With respect to degrees of glory, Edwards apparently drew upon M 367 for much of what he wrote in "Justification by Faith Alone."
[120] "Justification by Faith Alone," *Works* 19:218-9. Edwards cites Ephesians 4:4-7.
[121] "Justification by Faith Alone," *Works* 19:219.
[122] "Justification by Faith Alone," *Works* 19:219. See also "None Are Saved by Their Own Righteousness," *Works* 14:338-9.

so it is with the saints, the criteria for the degree of glory being the grace and fruitfulness of the saint on earth.

> So that it being still left with God, notwithstanding the perfect obedience of the second Adam, to fix the degree of each one's capacity, by what rule he pleases, he hath been pleased to fix the degree of capacity, and so of glory, by the proportion of the saint's grace and fruitfulness here. He gives higher degrees of glory, in reward for higher degrees of holiness and good works, because it pleases him; and yet all the happiness of each saint is indeed the fruit of the purchase of Christ's obedience.[123]

"Indeed, it can't be properly said that Christ purchased any particular degree of happiness"; rather, "he purchased eternal life, that is, perfect happiness, or which is the same thing, that everyone's capacity should be filled."[124] Nonetheless, God has established "this further constitution, that everyone's capacity shall be determined according to his holiness and his good works here in the world."[125] "God's respect to their holiness and good works shall be testified in the particular manner and degree of the reward," for "their happiness will be according to the degree of their holiness and good works."[126]

The happiness of the saint in heaven will consist of enjoying the view of the excellent perfections of the Father, as well as those

---

[123] "Justification by Faith Alone," *Works* 19:219. Edwards cites 1 Corinthians 12:18.

[124] M 367, *Works* 13:437. See also M 589, *Works* 18:122. "Christ and believers all have a right in that righteousness that Christ wrought out; it is a good common among them. And it being imputed to all, they all are entitled to benefit by it, by virtue of that original and eternal rule of righteousness which we call the law, or covenant of works; and the benefit of it that they are all entitled to by virtue of that rule, is eternal life, or a full and perfect and eternal happiness; and one to whom that righteousness belongs is entitled to no more benefit by that rule simply, than another. The case may be so, that one can challenge more than another can, because his capacity may be larger, and he may need more; but what each one's capacity shall be is a thing that the law determines not."

[125] M 589, *Works* 18:122-3.

[126] M 671, *Works* 18:227.

Christ Satisfies God's Rule of Righteousness 191

of the Son as displayed in the work of redemption (as noted in chapter one). Accordingly, the degree of happiness will consist not only of the "extent and strength of the faculty" to enjoy God, including the "degree of notional knowledge," but of the "degree and manner of those spiritual views that God lets into their minds, and the particular manifestations that he is pleased to make of himself," and by "enlarging the appetite" and "opening the heart" to enjoy God to a greater extent.[127] The degree of such glory enjoyed by saints in heaven will be according to four things: 1) "the degrees of grace and holiness here; not only the degree of the principle, but of the exercises and fruits" in good works; 2) "the degree of glory to the name of God, and the degree of good done to men, especially to the household of faith"; 3) "self-denial and suffering in the exercises and fruits of grace…especially to the glory of God"; and 4) "eminency in humility."[128] Thus, while heaven itself is purchased by the righteousness of Christ alone, differing degrees of joy are by differing capacities distributed according to God's sovereign design, according to the four criteria above. No one in heaven will be dissatisfied, as all will have a perfect happiness and be full of joy to the utmost of their capacity.[129] Christ's righteousness alone purchased eternal life and "a sea of happiness, where every vessel is full," though it is "left to God's sovereign pleasure to determine the largeness of the vessel."[130]

> And God determines that place and capacity he pleases: he makes whom he pleases the feet, and whom he pleases the hand, and whom he pleases the lungs, etc.; I Cor. 12:18, "But now hath God set the members [every one

---

[127] M 822, *Works* 18:533.
[128] M 817, *Works* 18:527-8.
[129] M 367, *Works* 13:437-8. Indeed, none will be jealous of others with a greater capacity, but happy for it. "The exaltation of some in glory above others, will be so far from diminishing anything of the perfect happiness and joy of the rest that are inferior, that they will be the happier for it. Such will be the union of all of them, that they will be partakers of each other's glory and happiness. I Cor. 12:26, 'If one of the members be honored, all the member rejoice with it.'" M 431, *Works* 13:482.
[130] "Justification by Faith Alone," *Works* 19:219.

of them in the body, as it hath pleased him]." And God efficaciously determines the place and capacity of every member here in this world, by giving different degrees of his Spirit: them that he intends for the highest place in the body, he gives them, while in this world, most of his Spirit, the greatest share of the divine nature of the Spirit, and nature of Christ Jesus the Head, whereby they perform the most excellent works.[131]

Thus the measure of fruit and the corresponding capacity for joy in heaven are by God's sovereign pleasure.

Secondly, with respect to God accepting and rewarding the sinful works of the saints, how can God accept and reward sinful works, as even the best works of the saints are accompanied by sin and infinitely sinful considered by themselves? Edwards answers that God does not view the good works of the saints "separately and by themselves, but as in Christ."[132] Viewed apart from Christ, all the works of believers are unacceptable to God. Viewed in Christ, however, the good works of saints are worthy of reward for two reasons: "First, the guilt of their persons is all done away, and the pollution and hatefulness" in and attending the good works is hidden. "Second, their relation to Christ adds a positive value and dignity to their good works, in God's sight."[133] God views the obedience of the "members of Christ" as belonging to Christ, "as the suffering of the members of Christ, are looked upon, in some respect, as the sufferings of Christ."[134]

> According to the tenor of the first covenant, the person was to be accepted and rewarded, only for the work's sake; but by the covenant of grace, the work is accepted and rewarded, only for the person's sake; the person being beheld antecedently, as a member of Christ, and clothed with his righteousness. So that though the saints' inher-

---

[131] M 403, *Works* 13:467-8.
[132] M 627, *Works* 18:155.
[133] "Justification by Faith Alone," *Works* 19:213-4.
[134] "Justification by Faith Alone," *Works* 19:215.

> ent holiness is rewarded, yet this very reward is indeed, not the less founded on the worthiness and righteousness of Christ: none of the value that their works have in his sight, nor any of the acceptance they have with him, is out of Christ, and out of his righteousness; but his worthiness as Mediator, is the prime and only foundation on which all is built, and the universal source whence all arises.[135]

Thus, with respect to the good works of believers, "all the value that is set upon them, and all their connection with the reward, is founded in, and derived from Christ's righteousness and worthiness."[136] God respects the righteousness of Christ "for its own sake, as worthy in itself," while He has "respect to the saint's own holiness for Christ's sake, as being dependently and derivatively worthy, or as deriving value from Christ's merit or righteousness."[137] Indeed, Christ purchased the very good works for which the believer is rewarded.

> The reward of Christ's righteousness includes both the holiness of the saints, and the reward of it; and it includes their justification, which makes way for their good works being rewardable, and also the reward itself. Salvation in the sum of it is only the reward of Christ's righteousness. The sum of salvation includes the saints' conversion, and justification, and holiness, and good works, and also their consequent happiness.[138]

"His righteousness not only purchased the holiness itself, but also purchased that it should be rewardable."[139] As noted in chapter one, the very fruits of grace themselves were purchased by Christ and communicated in the giving of the Holy Spirit to dwell in believers. Thus, as the Holy Spirit produces His fruits in the life of the believer, including good works done to the glory of God, God

---

[135] "Justification by Faith Alone," *Works* 19:214.
[136] "Justification by Faith Alone," *Works* 19:215.
[137] M 671, *Works* 18:225.
[138] M 671, *Works* 18:224.
[139] M 671, *Works* 18:224.

delights in those works as they are a manifestation of His own glory communicated to and manifest in the saints. God then rewards the fruit of the Holy Spirit in the manifestation of His own glory in the good works of the saints. As "the bringing men into a state of salvation and justification, and favor with God and right to eternal life, is the reward of Christ's righteousness alone,"[140] so also is the giving of the Holy Spirit to believers to produce the good works that God is pleased to reward, as He was purchased by Christ's righteousness and given to believers. Thus, rewards are given for works produced by believers already justified by virtue of being clothed in the righteousness of Christ.[141] As noted in chapter four, only those works done in Christ, by those already justified by the righteousness of Christ, are acceptable to God. For Christ purchased for the saints both the perfect righteousness by which they are justified, as well as the Holy Spirit to dwell within them by whom the saint loves and honors God by the fruit of the Spirit's work within them.[142] And as differing rewards correspond to differing capacities among saints to view and delight in God's glory in heaven and not to justification according to the perfection required by God's rule of righteousness, differing rewards for good works are thereby compatible with justification by Christ's righteousness alone. Again, as Christ's perfect obedience to God's rule of righteousness purchased justification for the elect, so His perfect obedience also purchased the Holy Spirit to be given to them so that both justification and the love of God manifest in good works are by the perfect redemptive work of Christ alone. Sinners will be perfect in God's sight by virtue of being clothed in Christ's righteousness and will see and love the glory of God for eternity by virtue of the Holy Spirit within them, the bond of union between Christ and the elect believers.[143] The Holy Spirit

---

[140] M 671, *Works* 18:224.
[141] See "Justification by Faith Alone," *Works* 19:214, quoted above.
[142] Note, the twelve signs of a true work of God in Edwards' treatise *Religious Affections* are the fruit of sign number one, the indwelling Holy Spirit manifesting His own character in and through the justified believer. See *Works* 2:197ff.
[143] See the brief discussion in chapter four regarding the Holy Spirit as the bond of union between Christ and believers.

within the believer on earth will produce the fruit of His own character for which the believer will be rewarded with greater degrees of happiness in heaven, though all are justified by the perfect righteousness of Christ alone and will be filled to capacity with the love and happiness of God in heaven by virtue of that justification. "Thus God has such a peculiar favor to his saints that he rewards them infinitely above the proportion of the goodness of what they do, and that he has such a favor for them is owing [to] the merits of Jesus Christ."[144]

Christ's Obedience to Death Is Infinitely Meritorious and the "Most Exalted Part of Christ's Positive Righteousness"

Thus far we have seen Edwards' understanding of Christ's redemptive work of perfect obedience as fulfilling the requirement of God's rule of righteousness. Having freely bound Himself to the terms of the covenant of redemption, Christ obligated Himself to its requirements, though the entirety of His redemptive work was undertaken voluntarily on behalf of others and thereby meritorious. Christ meritoriously performed the required righteousness of God's rule by His voluntary and perfect obedience to all of God's laws on behalf of the elect. Thus, the righteousness by which God justifies the believer is the very righteousness of Christ's own obedience by which He fulfilled God's requirement for eternal life.

We turn now to an examination of Edwards' understanding of the *extent* of the merit earned by Christ's redemptive work. Not only did Christ satisfy God's rule of righteousness by His perfect obedience, *He infinitely exceeded it.* For the death of Christ not only satisfied the required penalty of God's rule of righteousness, but also constituted an infinitely meritorious act of obedience. Indeed, Christ voluntarily condescended from infinite glory to suffer infinite humiliation, to suffer the greatest trial of obedience ever experienced, and to bear the infinite wrath of God for the benefit of infinitely undeserving and hateful creatures. In so doing, Christ

---

[144] M 671, *Works* 18:228.

accrued infinitely greater merit on behalf of those for whom He died than Adam would have merited for His posterity had he obeyed. The death of Christ is the apex of Christ's redemptive work, His greatest act of obedience, and the greatest display of God's excellent perfections ever accomplished.[145] In this one act of obedience the positive and negative righteousness required by God's rule of righteousness are satisfied and infinitely exceeded on behalf of sinners. In this way Christ's obedience to death was infinitely meritorious and "the most exalted part of Christ's positive righteousness."[146]

Christ's Obedience to Death Makes Atonement and Merits Eternal Life

Christ's obedience to the Father, in willingly subjecting Himself to infinite suffering and death in payment of the infinite debt of sinners, met both the negative and positive requirements of God's rule of righteousness.

> He has procured for them peace and reconciliation with God, and his favor and friendship, in that he satisfied for their sins, and laid a foundation for the perfect removal of the guilt of sin, and the forgiveness of all their trespasses, and wrought out for them a perfect and glorious righteousness, most acceptable to God and sufficient to recommend them to God's full acceptance and to the adoption of children, and to the eternal fruits of his fatherly kindness.[147]

---

[145] "It was the most glorious act of righteousness; and he has also by the same offered to man the strongest inducement to man to love God, as it was the most glorious manifestation of his amiable holiness, and winning grace, and mercy." M 772, *Works* 18:421.

[146] "The Threefold Work of the Holy Ghost," *Works* 14:400. "It was the main instance of Christ's obedience." M 483, *Works* 13:527.

[147] "The Peace Which Christ Gives His True Followers," *Works* 25:542.

"Christ's blood is not only a propitiation for sin—a satisfactory price to save from hell—but 'tis also to be considered as the price of happiness and glory."[148] "Christ's sufferings themselves may be considered as part of Christ's active obedience and positive righteousness," for in dying He not only procured "negative righteousness or mere freedom from guilt," but also "positive righteousness."[149] He came to lay down His life in obedience to the Father's will and command according to the terms of the covenant of redemption.[150]

Many Scripture texts that speak of Christ's blood and death as the means of satisfaction and salvation for sin are not exclusively with reference to satisfaction for guilt alone. Rather, Christ's death and blood "are very often spoken of in Scripture as saving, as a righteousness, or as meritorious, and as sweet and acceptable

---

[148] "Christ's Sacrifice an Inducement to His Ministers," *Works* 25:666. Also, "the blood of Christ was not only a price to pay a debt, but it was also a price to buy positive blessings with. Christ hath purchased the church with his blood (Acts 20:28); the purchased possession is purchased by Christ's blood." "The Sacrifice of Christ Acceptable," *Works* 14:454.

[149] "The Threefold Work of the Holy Ghost," *Works* 14:400. Edwards interpreted the red goat skins of the tabernacle as typical of the righteousness of Christ's death: "Of the skins of the sacrifices seems to signify the same thing as the skins that God clothed Adam and Eve with, which are also supposed to be skins of sacrifices, which signified the righteousness of Christ, the great sacrifice. These skins were to be dyed red to denote that Christ's righteousness was wrought out through the pains of death, under which he, in obedience to God, yielded up his life and shed his precious blood....Our covering of the righteousness of Christ is obtained by laying down his life. He could give us that righteousness no otherwise than by giving us his own life, and as it were giving us his own skin for our covering. See Gen. 3:21." "Exodus 26:14," *Works* 24:241-2.

[150] "He had received this command of the Father, that he should lay down his life. John 10:17-18, 'Therefore doth my Father love me, because I lay down my life, that I might take it again. No man taketh it from me, but I lay it down of myself. I have power to lay it down, and I have power to take it again. This commandment have I received of my Father.'

Christ came into the world to do the will of his Father. Christ says, 'Lo, I come: I delight to do they will, O God' (Ps. 40:8); and John 6:38, 'For I came down from heaven, not to do mine own will, but the will of him that sent me.' And this was a part of his Father's will which he did, that he should lay down his life for his people." "The Threefold Work of the Holy Ghost," *Works* 14:400.

to God's holiness, perhaps not less frequently than as a propitiation." For instance, Isaiah 53:12 speaks of positive merit: "'Therefore will I divide him a portion with the great, and he shall divide the spoil with the strong, because he hath poured out his soul unto death.'"[151] Also John 10:17-18:

> "Therefore doth my Father love me, because I lay down my life that I might take it up again. No man taketh it from me, but I lay it down of myself: I have power to lay it down, and I have power to take it again. This commandment received I of my Father." If the Father loves Christ because he laid down his life, he doubtless also loves those that are his, on the same account.[152]

In Acts 20:28: "'Take heed, feed the church of God, which he has purchased with his own blood,'" the text "certainly signifies something more than being set at liberty from hell." It also speaks of "being brought into a relation to God as his, into a covenant relation, whereby he is their God and they are his people, as appears by the scope of the place."[153] Ephesians 5:2 speaks of Christ having "'given himself for us, an offering and a sacrifice to God for a sweet smelling savor,' something positively pleasing, amiable and delightful to God, and therefore a price to purchase positive good from God."[154] Concerning the Old Testament sacrifices, "the typical sacrifices are so very often said to be a sweet savor to God; the places are too many to be mentioned."[155] In Hebrews 10:5-7 and Psalm 40:6-8, "Christ's dying is spoken of as what he did as a servant doing God's will, with delight and cheerfulness obeying his command." According to John 6:51-55, "Christ's body broken

---

[151] M 845, *Works* 20:65.
[152] M 845, *Works* 20:65.
[153] M 845, *Works* 20:65. "So in the fifth chapter of Romans, v. 9, we are said to be 'justified by his blood.' In the second chapter of Ephesians, v. 13, we are said to be 'made nigh by the blood of Christ,'" 65-6.
[154] M 845, *Works* 20:66.
[155] M 845, *Works* 20:66.

and his blood shed don't only deliver us from eternal misery, but procures for us eternal life" and entrance into heaven.[156]

> Though the redemption of Christ does consist in his positive righteousness as much as his propitiation, he entered into the holiest of all with his whole ransom, or price of redemption; but half of this consisted in his obedience. But upon this supposition, the reason is plain: the blood of Christ did as much show his righteousness as his propitiation, and appeared as mainly in his blood as his propitiation did.[157]

With respect to Revelation 5:12, "Christ's dying or being slain not only satisfied for sins, but also merited as a righteousness, for he was worthy upon the account of his being 'slain to receive power and riches,' etc." Christ not only merited these rewards for Himself, but for the elect, as He was slain as a "public person."[158]

Therefore, according to Edwards' two-fold definition of justification, in accordance with the positive and negative righteousness required by God's rule of righteousness, wherever Scripture speaks of Christ's death or blood procuring eternal blessings beyond deliverance from the penalty of the law, reference is to both propitiation and the positive merits of Christ's obedience as earning those blessings on behalf of the believer.

---

[156] M 845, *Works* 20:66. Edwards also cites John 6:55, Matthew 26:29, Hebrews 6:20, 10:19-20.
[157] M 845, *Works* 20:65-6. Edwards also cites Hebrews 13:20-21, 10:14, 10:29, 9:15-20, 12:2, 12:24; Genesis 4:10-12; 1 Peter 1:2, 3:18; Revelation 5:9, 7:14. In commenting on John 20:17, Edwards writes: "That familiarity and full enjoyment of Christ is not allowed before his ascension, for this great blessedness of the saints in the enjoyment of Christ, though it be purchased by Christ's death, is obtained to be bestowed by his ascension into heaven, and entering into the holiest of all with his own blood, by his appearing for us before God, and representing his satisfaction and obedience." "John 20:17," *Works* 24:964.
[158] "Revelation 5:12," *Works* 24:1214.

Christ's Obedience to Death Is an Infinite, Holy Act of Love and Honor to the Father and His Law

As discussed in chapter three, God's original design with respect to Adam's trial of obedience in the garden was that His creatures would not be confirmed to eternal life apart from the positive display of honor to God's authority and law by an act of positive obedience to His rule of righteousness. Therefore, by the terms of the covenant of redemption, honor to God's authority and law would be accomplished by Christ's perfect obedience to God's rule of righteousness. As Adam was surety for mankind, the requirement that mankind honor God's authority and law went unanswered and, as we have seen in chapter four, could only be met by Christ as surety for mankind. Christ, however, would perform by His obedience unto death an infinite act of love to the Father and His law. Thus, Christ "more than repaired" the honor due to God's authority and law while displaying a respect "so worthy and glorious" that His respect to it "was a greater honor than men's contempt of it."[159] Christ's sacrifice in obedience to the Father "was an expression of an infinite regard to the holiness" and "majesty" of God.[160]

As will be observed below with respect to the infinite merit of Christ's obedience, the love and honor shown to God's authority and law is not only according to the perfection of the obedience, but owing to the glory of the one who performed the act of honor and respect and the infinite expense of it. Christ "stooped infinitely low in becoming incarnate" and willingly shed His blood, the "blood of the Son of God."[161] Christ, the "absolute sovereign

---

[159] "Even As I Have Kept My Father's Commandments," *MDM*, 221.
[160] M 451, *Works* 13:498. See also M 449 and M 452, *Works* 13:496-7, 498.
[161] "Even As I Have Kept My Father's Commandments," *MDM*, 221. Also *Works* 9:312: "He performed his obedience with much greater love than the angels do theirs, even infinite love. For though the human nature of Christ was not capable of love absolutely infinite, yet Christ's obedience that performed in that human nature is not to be looked on as merely the obedience of the human, but the obedience of his person as God-man, and there was infinite love of the person of

of heaven and earth," performed "the most wonderful instance of submission to God's sovereignty that ever was."[162]

> Christ's love in making him willing to offer himself up on the fire of God's wrath, and carrying him through the torments of that flame, even till it was extinguished, did as it were conquer and quench it. Never was there such a gift of love and labor of love as this. It as more exceeds all the expressions of love in any man or angel, than the treasures of the most wealthy prince exceed the stores of the meanest peasant.[163]

His love and honor for God's authority is seen in His prayer at Gethsemane: "'Nevertheless, not my will, but thine be done.'"[164] Christ chose to suffer "from love to God and a regard to his will and glory," according to John 12:27-28: "'Now is my soul troubled; and what shall I say? Father, save me from this hour: but for this cause came I unto this hour. Father, glorify thy name.'"[165] According to Psalm 40:7-8: "'Then said I, Lo, I come: in the volume of the book it is written of me, I delight to do thy will, O my God: yea, thy law is within my heart,'" Christ showed "an infinite regard to

---

Christ manifest in that obedience. And this together with the infinite dignity of the person that obeyed rendered his obedience infinitely meritorious."

[162] "Luke 22:44," *Works* (Hickman), 2:870.

[163] M 791, *Works* 18:490-1. Also "Justification by Faith Alone," *Works* 19:188: "But now Christ by the subjecting himself to the law and obeying of it, has done great honor to the law, and to the authority of God who gave it: that so glorious a person should become subject to the law, and fulfill it, has done much more to honor it, that if mere man had obeyed it."

[164] "Luke 22:44," *Works* (Hickman), 2:870-1. "When he had such a view of the terribleness of his last sufferings, and prayed if it were possible that that cup might pass from him, i.e. if there was not an absolute necessity of it in order to the salvation of sinners, yet it was with a perfect submission to the will of God. He adds, 'Nevertheless, not my will, but thine be done.' He chose rather that the inclination of his human nature, which so much dreaded such exquisite torments, should be crossed, than that God's will should not take place. He delighted in the thought of God's will being done; and when he went and prayed the second time, he had nothing else to say but, 'O my Father, if this cup may not pass from me except I drink it, thy will be done'; and so the third time."

[165] "Christ's Sacrifice an Inducement to His Ministers," *Works* 25:666-7.

the will or the command of God," in willingly giving his life in "an infinite trial of his obedience."[166]

> Christ by that act testified an infinite regard to God, that when he desired to save sinners, he had rather die than that that salvation should be any injury to his majesty, justice and law. He had rather be at infinite expense, for it was an infinite expense that Christ was at; it was an infinite price that he paid. And this he paid that men's salvation might not be with any injury to the glory of God's attributes, and thereby not only testified his love to men, but an infinite regard to the glory of God, and showed his infinite love to God. And therefore as Christ's act of offering up himself a sacrifice was an exercise of so great love to God, so it was a transcendently holy act.[167]

"His obedience was of infinite value, because he was at infinite expense to obey," for the "greater the cost" of obedience, "so much the greater respect to God's authority."[168]

Additionally, Christ had respect to God's glory, "as all God's perfections have their most glorious display in that way of salvation," as in Isaiah 50:5-6: "'The Lord hath opened mine ear, and I was not rebellious, neither turned away back.'"[169] In John 12:28, Christ prayed that God would glorify His name.[170] Christ "greatly rejoiced to think how God would be glorified in his sufferings,

---

[166] "Christ's Sacrifice an Inducement to His Ministers," *Works* 25:667. Also, "Christ speaks of his obedience as chiefly consisting in his voluntary undergoing [of] his last sufferings and as a great manifestation of his love to the Father, and the end of his sufferings being his openly honoring God by such a manifestation of his love, in John 14:30-31. 'Hereafter I will not talk much with you: for the prince of this world cometh, and hath nothing in me. But that the world may know that I love the Father; and as the Father gave me commandment, even so I do.'" M 1146, *Works* 20:518.
[167] "The Sacrifice of Christ Acceptable," *Works* 14:450. See also "Hebrews 1:5," *YMSS*, L. 7r.
[168] M 447, *Works* 13:495.
[169] "Christ's Sacrifice an Inducement to His Ministers," *Works* 25:667.
[170] "Matthew 16:21-23," *WJEO*, L. 6v.

how this would be an occasion of showing forth his perfections to the views of men and angels."[171]

Christ's Death Is Infinitely Meritorious as Voluntary and "Active"

As discussed above, the voluntary nature of Christ's obedience is the basis of its merit. Thus, the suffering and death of Christ would not be meritorious if Christ did not undertake them voluntarily, or if such were necessary for Christ's own account. As the merit of all of Christ's humiliation and redeeming work is founded upon the voluntary nature of Christ's undertaking the terms of the covenant of redemption with the Father, so also the merit of Christ's death. For Edwards, the death of Christ is the supreme display and accomplishment of the infinite merit of Christ's perfect obedience to the Father, the apex of Christ's redemptive work. And while *any* humiliation of Christ from His infinite glory is an infinite humiliation, Christ's voluntary suffering unto death for infinitely unworthy people displays the infinite depth and extent of His humiliation and merit more pointedly than any other work of Christ. Thus, having shown the voluntary nature of Christ's redeeming work to be the overarching *basis* of His merit, we turn now to examine the specific aspects of Christ's obedience that render the *extent* of His merit *infinite*. Briefly, the *extent* of this merit, including the merit of His death, was infinite as "active" and voluntary, and performed by one of infinite dignity and worth, in condescension for those of infinite unworthiness, in the most difficult of trials and circumstances, and with the most excellent demeanor and virtue.

Christ was moved to bind himself to freely suffer on behalf of unworthy sinners by love and pity and not from personal need or obligation, for such was of "no profit" to one of infinite self-sufficiency.[172] As noted in chapters one and two, the Son set His

---

[171] "Matthew 16:21-23," *WJEO*, L. 7v.
[172] "The Threefold Work of the Holy Ghost," *Works* 14:431. See also "Christ's Sacrifice an Inducement to His Ministers," *Works* 25:663: "This also appears by

love upon His undeserving bride from all eternity, as it pleased Him to bring "such a miserable, deplorable company" from her misery "to the highest heights of happiness."[173] "He knew that if he did not suffer, sinners could not be delivered from hell and obtain that great glory which he would have them enjoy." For this reason, "when Peter said this shall not be to thee, Christ replied 'get thee behind me Satan, thou art an offense to me.'"[174] "It was love that made Christ freely to choose to suffer for sinners," and "it was love" that made Peter's suggestion offensive to Christ.[175] From love He "waded through a sea of blood" and "ran through the flames of God's wrath to relieve us."[176] The love of Christ flows "as the waters of a river run easily and freely," so the blood He freely shed "flowed as freely from his wounds as water from a spring," while "all the good things that Christ bestows on his saints come to 'em as freely as water runs down in a river."[177] "It was exceedingly pleasant to him to think how the justice of God would be satisfied and perishing souls would have safety and deliverance through his suffering."[178]

Christ's obedience unto death, therefore, was "active" and meritorious. In Edwards' earlier writings he sometimes utilized the customary terminology of "active" and "passive" in distinguishing between Christ's meritorious acts of obedience and Christ's death.[179] Nevertheless, he always understood Christ's laying down

---

what has been already observed of God's self-sufficiency and Christ's infinite happiness in the person of the Father; that happiness that is infinite cannot be added to. In that Christ was God, it appears that he is above all capacity of being requited. [His state is] immutable. In that he is God, he can't be profited by us because he is one on whom we are universally and absolutely dependent: [we] derive all [from him]." Nonetheless, having set his love upon unworthy sinners, their salvation became to Christ a thing of great joy.

[173] "The Threefold Work of the Holy Ghost," *Works* 14:431.
[174] "Matthew 16:21-23," *WJEO*, L. 8v.
[175] "Matthew 16:21-23," *WJEO*, L. 13r.
[176] "Matthew 21:5," *YMSS*, L. 11r.
[177] "Christ Is to the Heart Like a River to a Tree Planted by It," *Works* 25:602.
[178] "Matthew 16:21-23," *WJEO*, L. 8r.
[179] See M 278, *Works* 13:377-8; "Quaestio," *Works* 14:60; "The Threefold Work of the Holy Ghost," *Works* 14:398-9.

His life in obedience unto death as an "active," voluntary, and meritorious act of obedience to the Father, according to the terms of the covenant of redemption. He later entirely rejected terminology distinguishing "active" from "passive" obedience, preferring "active" as descriptive of all of Christ's obedience, including His obedience unto death. Edwards' interpretation of Romans 5:18-19, again, is instructive, "'by the righteousness of one, the free gift came upon all men unto justification of life. For as by one man's disobedience many were made sinners, so by the obedience of one shall many be made righteous,'" Edwards writes:

> 'Tis scarce possible anything should be more full and determined: the terms, taken singly, are such as do fix their own meaning, and taken together, they fix the meaning of each other: the words show that we are justified by that righteousness of Christ, that consists in his obedience, and that we are made righteous or justified by that obedience of his, that is his righteousness, or moral goodness before God.[180]

A "possible objection" to this interpretation by those who rejected "justification by the righteousness and obedience of Christ" might be that justification is by "Christ's passive obedience," or his suffering *only*. But regardless of the terminology used to describe Christ's death, the text speaks of more than "an atonement for disobedience, or a satisfaction for unrighteousness," but includes "the notion of a positive obedience, and a righteousness, or moral goodness, that it justifies us, or makes us righteous." The terms "*righteousness*, and *obedience* are used, and used too as the opposites to *sin* and *disobedience*, and an *offense*."[181]

> Now what can be meant by righteousness, when spoken of as the opposite to sin, or moral evil, but only moral goodness? What is the righteousness that is the opposite of an offense, but only the behavior that is well pleas-

---
[180] "Justification by Faith Alone," *Works* 19:193.
[181] "Justification by Faith Alone," *Works* 19:193-4.

ing? and what can be meant by obedience, when spoken of as the opposite of disobedience, or going contrary to a command, but a positive obeying and an actual complying with the command?[182]

Thus, the "invented distinction of active and passive" cannot alter the meaning of the text that "believers are justified by the righteousness and obedience of Christ under the notion of his moral goodness, and his positive obeying, and actual complying with the commands of God," and that such "conformity to his commands, was well-pleasing in his sight."[183] The terms "*righteousness* and *obedience*" imply more than "propitiation" and include Christ's "voluntary submitting and yielding himself to those sufferings" as "an act of obedience to the Father's commands," and are therefore "a part of his positive righteousness, or moral goodness."[184] So according to John 10:17-18, Christ's death was an "active" and meritorious choice of Christ: "'Therefore doth my Father love [me], because I lay down my life, that I might take it again. No man taketh it from me, but I lay it down of myself.'"[185]

Moreover, the relative difficulty of the task alters not the case with respect to an action being "active" or "passive," for "all obedience considered under the notion of obedience or righteousness, is something active, something done in active and voluntary compliance with a command."[186] Indeed, as will be seen in the following discussion, the greater the difficulty associated with a free act of obedience only serves to increase its merit and praiseworthiness.

Thus, while affirming the intent of the distinction of "active" and "passive" in asserting the entirety of Christ's work as an act of

---

[182] "Justification by Faith Alone," *Works* 19:194.
[183] "Justification by Faith Alone," *Works* 19:194. "There may in some sense be said to be a conformity to the law in a person's suffering the penalty of the law; but no other conformity to the law is properly called obedience to it, but an active voluntary conformity to the precepts of it: the word *obey* is often found in Scripture with respect to the law of God to man, but never in any other sense," 195.
[184] "Justification by Faith Alone," *Works* 19:194.
[185] "Christ's Sacrifice an Inducement to His Ministers," *Works* 25:659.
[186] "Justification by Faith Alone," *Works* 19:194.

obedience, Edwards addresses two problems with the terminology. First, the distinction could be improperly used to divide and separate the obedience of Christ for the purpose of rejecting His life-long obedience as included in His righteousness imputed to believers, contrary to the original intent of the distinction. And second, though the term "passive" refers to the suffering of Christ, its juxtaposition to the term "active" is confusing, given that all of Christ's obedience is "active," including the totality of His suffering. Given these potential problems with the terminology and that "there is no appearance of any such distinction ever entering into the hearts of any of the penmen of Scripture,"[187] Edwards rejected the "active" and "passive" terminology, preferring to describe the totality of Christ's life and death as "active" obedience. He thus affirmed the traditional intent of the "active" and "passive" distinction in affirming Christ's death as "active" and meritorious obedience.[188]

Christ's Obedience to Death Is Infinitely Meritorious by Virtue of Christ's Infinite Dignity and Worth

The basis of the merit of Christ's obedience is the voluntary nature of that obedience, whereas the extent of that same merit includes the glory of the One performing that obedience. The free

---

[187] "Justification by Faith Alone," *Works* 19:195.
[188] Turretin makes essentially the same point: "The Scripture nowhere appears to distinguish the obedience of Christ into parts, but sets it before us as a unique thing by which he has done everything which the law could require of us. Again, as Christ by the obedience of his life has rendered what was due from us (and to which we were otherwise personally bound), by that very obedience he has satisfied for us the demands of the law. As his passive obedience proceeded from unspeakable love to us (which is the fulfilling of the law), we cannot deny that it was meritorious, as it had the relation of a *lytrou* and *timēs* (or price) by which a right to life has been acquired for us. Therefore these things should not be curiously distinguished because both these benefits conjointly depend upon the entire virtue of the cause—the obedience of Christ. For neither could sin be expiated before the law was perfectly fulfilled, nor could a right to life be acquired before the guilt of sin was removed. Therefore he merited by making satisfaction and by meriting made satisfaction." Turretin, *Institutes of Elenctic Theology*, 2:13.12.

and perfect obedience of Christ to God's rule of righteousness is infinitely meritorious as performed by one of infinite dignity and glory. Deeds of love and respect to God are of greater worth to God according to the greater dignity and excellence of the one performing them.[189] "The dignity of the person gives value to his action, to his obedience," so the obedience of Christ has great value to God by virtue of His infinite delight in Christ.[190] The divinity and infinite holiness of Christ "gives this sacrifice an infinite value in the sight of God,"[191] so the blood of Christ is "infinitely precious" as the blood of God.[192] And as the blood was "infinitely precious" by virtue of the "infinite dignity and glory" of Christ, so "what was done in shedding of it for sinners was a thing infinitely great—infinitely greater than if the greatest earthly potentate had shed his blood," or if all the "princes" of the world or highest created angel had shed theirs, for "it was the blood of God, it was the blood of him before whom all the kings of the earth are as grasshoppers, and the blood of one that was the great creator and king of angels," the blood of the creator of all things.[193] By the dignity of Christ's person, the value of the virtues He exercised in His suffering "infinitely exceed the virtue of all men and angels."[194] And, as the blood shed is the very blood of God, it is "utterly impossible" that the beneficiary of Christ's obedience unto death could ever "requite him for such a benefit, the benefit is so great."[195]

Accordingly, the infinite value of Christ's sacrifice meets the need of sinners, as the infinite demerit or guilt of sin is deserving of eternal suffering. "We needed one, the worthiness of whose obedience might be answerable to the unworthiness of our disobedience, and therefore needed one who was as great and worthy

---

[189] "Hebrews 1:5," *YMSS*, L. 6r.
[190] "Even As I Have Kept My Father's Commandments," *MDM*, 220-1.
[191] "The Sacrifice of Christ Acceptable," *Works* 14:450.
[192] "1 Peter 1:19," *WJEO*, L. 4r. – 4v.
[193] "Christ's Sacrifice an Inducement to His Ministers," *Works* 25:661. Edwards cites Colossians 1:16-17.
[194] M 791, *Works* 18:493.
[195] "Christ's Sacrifice an Inducement to His Ministers," *Works* 25:663.

as we were unworthy.[196] "And though Christ's sufferings were but temporal, yet they were equivalent to our eternal sufferings by reason of the infinite dignity of his person," and because the suffering was an "infinite expense."[197] "Christ's divinity and the infinite dignity of his person" is "the precious foundation of everything that belongs to the salvation of Christ, the foundation on which stands the infinite merit and sufficiency of his righteousness."[198]

Christ's Obedience to Death Is Infinitely Meritorious as an Infinite Condescension

Corresponding to the infinite merit of Christ's obedience by virtue of His dignity and divinity is the infinite merit of His obedience as an infinite condescension. Specifically, the merit of Christ's condescension is a function of the height from which Christ humbled himself to perform His obedience, the infinite unworthiness and hatefulness of those for whom He performed His obedience, the greatness of the wickedness for which Christ humbled himself to atone, and the great sense of the vileness that Christ had of those for whom He was to suffer.

To begin, as the dignity and worth of Christ as God is infinite, so His humiliation is infinite in view of the "height of dignity and glory that he originally possessed."[199] He lowered Himself to take upon Himself a "finite crooked nature." "He came into a world that was spoiled by sin…and took our nature with all those infirmities which sin had brought upon it, except such as partook of the nature of sin."[200] His self-denial was the greatest as He descended from the highest happiness to subject Himself to man's reproach.[201]

---

[196] M 713, *Works* 18:344. See also "Justification by Faith Alone," *Works* 19:162.
[197] "The Sacrifice of Christ Acceptable," *Works* 14:452.
[198] "Canticles 3:9-10," *Works* 24:616.
[199] "Hebrews 1:5," *YMSS*, L. 6v.
[200] "Luke 2:14 (Christ's Appearing)," *WJEO*, L. 3v.
[201] "Christ's Sacrifice an Inducement to His Ministers," *Works* 25:661.

He was least, as he descended lowest in his humiliation; none in the kingdom of heaven ever descended so low. He did as it were descend into the depths of hell. He suffered most; he suffered shame. He was made a curse. He went lower in those things than ever any of his people did; and this he did as a servant, not only to God, but to men, for he "came not to be ministered to, but to minister."[202]

Furthermore, the highest of all humbled Himself to suffer on behalf of the lowest, the most unworthy, the most wicked and vile of sinners. "The unspeakableness of the gift may appear if we consider to whom this gift is given," to "infinitely inferiour and unworthy creatures."[203] What is more, such "worthless" recipients of Christ's gift are "defiled," "filthy," "full of abomination," who have set themselves in hateful and murderous opposition to him.[204] Christ "spent his life and spent his spilt blood for the good of miserable men,"[205] He shed His blood for enemies.[206] Yet, "the more sinful and unworthy those are that are freed by his death… the more fully is this design accomplished, the more is the grace of God glorified."[207]

Further, not only did Christ obey on behalf of the most wicked, He also obeyed to atone for the greatest wickedness.

> The wonderfulness of Christ's dying love appears: (1) in that he died for those that were so wicked and unworthy in themselves; (2) in that he died for those who were not only so wicked, but whose wickedness consists in being enemies to him, so that [Christ] did not only die for the wicked, but for his own enemies; (3) in that [he] was willing to die for his enemies at the same time that he was

---

[202] "Matthew 11:11," *Works* 24:846.
[203] "2 Corinthians 9:15," *WJEO*, L. 5v.
[204] "2 Corinthians 9:15," *WJEO*, L. 5v. – 6r. See also "Matthew 16:21-23," *WJEO*, L. 11v.
[205] "Matthew 21:5," *YMSS*, L. 5r.
[206] "Christ's Sacrifice an Inducement to His Ministers," *Works* 25:663.
[207] "Matthew 16:21-23," *WJEO*, L. 12r.

subject to the utmost exertions and efforts of their enmity, in the greatest possible contempt and cruelty towards him, and at the same time that he was feeling the utmost effects of it in his own greatest ignominy, torment and death; (4) in that he was willing to atone for their being his enemies in those very sufferings, by that very ignominy, torment and death that was the fruit of it.[208]

As we saw earlier, the merit of Christ's obedience is grounded in the voluntary nature of His obedience. In a similar way, the merit of Christ dying for infinitely wicked enemies is magnified by the clear sense He had of their vileness when He undertook to die for them. The greater and clearer picture Christ possessed of the wickedness of those for whom He would suffer, and the more He felt the effect of that wickedness, the more meritorious would be His willingness to suffer despite that awful understanding.

It was the corruption and wickedness of men that contrived and effected his death; it was the wickedness of men that agreed with Judas, it was the wickedness of men that betrayed him, and that apprehended him, and bound him, and led him away like a malefactor; it was by men's corruption and wickedness that he was arraigned, and falsely accused, and unjustly judged. It was by men's wickedness that he was reproached, mocked, buffeted, and spit upon. It was by men's wickedness that Barabbas was preferred before him. It was men's wickedness that laid the cross upon him to bear, and that nailed him to it, and put him to so cruel and ignominious a death. This tended to give Christ an extraordinary sense of the greatness and hatefulness of the depravity of mankind.[209]

At the time of Christ's sufferings, "he had that depravity set before him as it is, without disguise," in its "true nature" and "utmost hatred and contempt of God," "in its ultimate tendency and desire,

---

[208] M 653, *Works* 18:194. See also p. 193.
[209] "Luke 22:44," *Works* (Hickman), 2:870.

which is to kill God." "He felt the fruits of that wickedness. It was then directly levelled [sic] against himself, and exerted itself against him to work his reproach and torment," giving "a stronger sense of its hatefulness on the human nature of Christ."[210] Yet,

> He was willing to die for his enemies at the same time that he was feeling the fruits of their enmity, while he felt the utmost effects and exertions of their spite against him in the greatest possible contempt and cruelty towards him in his own greatest ignominy, torments, and death; and partly in that he was willing to atone for their being his enemies in these very sufferings, and by that very ignominy, torment, and death that was the fruit of it. The sin and wickedness of men, for which Christ suffered to make atonement, was, as it were, set before Christ in his view.[211]

Indeed, "Christ set his heart upon suffering for some of his crucifiers, for some of those that had wickedly and cruelly imbued their hands in his blood."[212]

Further, as knowing all things, "he is acquainted with every individual sinner all over the world and in all ages, and he perfectly knows all their sins of heart, lip, and life," and "in secret, in darkness or in the light." And in "having a perfect view of all the sins of the whole world and of all the odiousness, vileness, and ill dessert that there is in sin," His shedding His blood for them "is on this account more wonderful."[213] It was "fitting" that Christ should know fully "the dreadful evil and odiousness of that sin that he suffered for—that he might know how much it deserved that punishment," and "a clear sight of the dreadfulness of the punishment that he

---

[210] "Luke 22:44," *Works* (Hickman), 2:870.
[211] "Luke 22:44," *Works* (Hickman), 2:870.
[212] "Matthew 16:21-23," *WJEO*, L. 11v. See also "Luke 22:44," *Works* (Hickman), 2:870: "It is probable that Christ died to make atonement for that individual actual wickedness that wrought his sufferings, that reproached, mocked, buffeted, and crucified him."
[213] "Christ's Sacrifice an Inducement to His Ministers," *Works* 25:665.

suffered to deliver 'em from—otherwise he would not know how great a benefit he vouchsafed 'em in redeeming them from this punishment." Both of these are requisite "that it might be real and actual grace in him that he undertook and suffered such things," and not from ignorance in giving so great a gift.[214]

Christ Endured the Greatest Trial of Obedience Ever

What has been said thus far with respect to Edwards' understanding of the extent of the merit of Christ's obedience is also intimately related to the difficult nature of Christ's trial of obedience. For one of infinite glory to submit to infinite humiliation on behalf of unworthy and infinitely wicked enemies contributed greatly to the difficulty of Christ's trial. The most important and difficult facet of Christ's trial of obedience, however, is Christ's willing submission to the infinite wrath of God in the place of sinners.

> Christ's laying down his life….was doubtless Christ's main act of obedience, because it was obedience to a command that was attended with immensely the greatest difficulty, and so to a command that was the greatest trial of his obedience; his respect shown to God in it, and his honor to God's authority, was proportionably great: it is spoken of in Scripture as Christ's principal act of obedience.[215]

In this utmost act of Christ, to which all of Christ's acts were ultimately directed, Edwards saw the greatest display of Christ's love to God and to man, and the most monumental display of God's glory. In confronting the prospect of taking upon himself the infinite wrath of God, Christ suffered the most difficult aspect of His trial of obedience, a trial beyond the ability of finite creatures to fully comprehend. But in the many circumstances and experi-

---

[214] M 1005, *Works* 20:329-0.
[215] "Justification by Faith Alone," *Works* 19:198. Edwards cites Philippians 2:7-9 and Hebrews 5:8.

ences related to this ultimate trial, the greatness of Christ's trial of obedience is compounded as it is attended with the greatest of difficulties.

For instance, Christ was tried with the temptations by which man and angels were tried. In His temptation in the wilderness, following forty days without food, Christ was tempted by the Devil according to "the importunate desires and inclinations of animal nature" to "take an unlawful course to gratify that appetite."[216] Far greater, however, was the trial of His human inclinations "which so exceedingly dreaded and shrunk at those torments that it was to undergo, and solicited to be delivered from the bitterness of that cup" of suffering He was given to drink. In contrast to the deceptively pleasing prospect presented to Adam in "the sweetness of the forbidden fruit," Christ fully understood the nature of the suffering He was to undergo.[217] With respect to the trial of angels, who fell from their exalted position in their refusal to submit to their proposed role in God's plan of salvation (i.e., to be ministering servants to the objects of salvation), Christ did not shrink back from His role, despite His infinite dignity as God.[218]

Also, the depth of Christ's humiliation as compared to the height of His glory was the greatest, as was the deprivation He suffered of the infinite love of God that He had enjoyed for all eternity. As noted above, Christ's condescension on behalf of sinners was from the infinite height of His glory. In both the prospect of His suffering, as well as His actual suffering, Christ was well-aware of His own honor and dignity, and so was tried not only with respect to "a principle of love of his own ease and his aversion to pain, but also as an humiliation, or as they affected a principle of regard to his own honor and dignity." As the "proportion" of humiliation was greater for Christ as one of infinite dignity, "so it was proportionately a greater trial."[219] The "greater than Solomon,"

---

[216] M 791, *Works* 18:493.
[217] M 791, *Works* 18:493-4.
[218] M 791, *Works* 18:494.
[219] M 664b, *Works* 18:204-5.

"infinitely glorious Son of God," suffered a death so heinous that even the Romans would not allow their own worst citizens to be so treated.[220]

Closely related to the depth of humiliation suffered is the infinite degree of happiness from which Christ descended. "In order rightly to judge of the degree of Christ's self-denial for the salvation of souls, we must take our measure from the height of happiness he was in before, to the depth of sorrow, pain, and contempt he descended to." Christ's self-denial was thereby "unmeasurable, incomprehensible, and truly infinitely great."[221] For as God, Christ dwelled in "infinite happiness" and the infinite "blessedness in the love and communion with God."[222] "The Father's love was infinite to him," and "he had actually been infinitely happy in the enjoyment of the Father's love, so that he knew more by experience of the worth of it, than any angel or saint in heaven."[223] Thus, Christ's suffering was the greatest when God hid His face from Him in His bearing sin on the cross, a suffering far greater than the physical torments.[224] The strength of the suffering of His soul was such that "Christ's heart did as it were break, and his vitals were rent with torment and amazement."[225]

Christ descended from the highest glory, from the greatest dignity and the greatest happiness, to a suffering so great that it transcends human understanding. Thus, in the darkest moment of Christ's trial of obedience, in the garden of Gethsemane, His clear view of what He was to suffer "overwhelmed him and amazed him."

---

[220] "Matthew 16:21-23," *WJEO*, L. 15v. – 16r.
[221] "Christ's Sacrifice an Inducement to His Ministers," *Works* 25:662.
[222] M 265, *Works* 13:371.
[223] M 516, *Works* 18:62.
[224] M 664b, *Works* 18:205.
[225] "John 19:34," *Works* 24:962. Edwards refers here to the separation of the water and blood in the heart of Christ as being the result of the extreme torment of Christ's soul affecting His body.

The very sight of these last sufferings was so very dreadful as to sink his soul down into the dark shadow of death; yea, so dreadful was it, that in the sore conflict which his nature had with it, he was all in a sweat of blood, his body all over was covered with clotted blood, and not only his body, but the very ground under him with the blood that fell from him, which had been forced through his pores through the violence of his agony. And if only the foresight of the cup was so dreadful, how dreadful was the cup itself, how far beyond all that can be uttered or conceived![226]

As Christ had such a clear understanding of the terrors He would endure, so His obedience would be the more meritorious in that He understood the cost.[227] Christ was faced with circumstances and temptations that tended "in the highest degree to hinder his going on to offer himself in the heavenly flames of divine charity, and voluntarily presenting himself to suffer the flames of divine wrath."[228] "These were like floods of great waters that were then thrown upon him to quench his love and to prevent his going on to endure those extreme torments in the fire of God's wrath."[229] Yet, "nothing could move him away from his steadfast obedience to God, but he persisted in saying, 'Thy will be done.'"[230] "His strong cries, his tears, and his blood, were all offered up together to God, and they were all offered up for the same end, for the glory of God in the salvation of the elect."[231] "His obedience was attended

---

[226] "Luke 22:44," *Works* (Hickman), 2:869. See also M 664b, *Works* 18:204.
[227] M 621, *Works* 18:152-3. "God saw fit to give Christ a very full understanding what his approaching sufferings were, just before they came, before he was apprehended, when he had yet opportunity to flee; that his choosing them and abiding them might be his own act as man, that it might not be said that he undertook to suffer he knew not what. It was the will of God that that should be the act of Christ, both of the divine and human nature, that it might be a glorious manifestation of the love of both natures towards man, and it might be a more meritorious act of obedience."
[228] "1 Kings 18:33-35," *Works* 24:384.
[229] "1 Kings 18:33-35," *Works* 24:385.
[230] "Luke 22:44," *Works* (Hickman), 2:871.
[231] "Luke 22:44," *Works* (Hickman), 2:875.

with the greatest difficulties, and most extreme abasement and sufferings, that ever any obedience was; which was another thing that rendered it more meritorious and thankworthy."[232] Edwards summarizes this heading best:

> God had given him this cup to drink, and had commanded him to drink it, and that was reason enough with him to drink it; hence he says, at the conclusion of his agony, when Judas came with his band, "The cup which my Father giveth me to drink, shall I not drink it?" John 18:11. Christ, at the time of his agony, had an inconceivably greater trial of obedience than any man or any angel ever had. How much was this trial of the obedience of the second Adam beyond the trial of the obedience of the first Adam! How light was our first father's temptation in comparison of this! And yet our first surety failed, and our second failed not, but obtained a glorious victory, and went and became obedient unto death, even the death of the cross. Thus wonderful and glorious was the obedience of Christ, by which he wrought out righteousness for believers, and which obedience is imputed to them.[233]

Thus, the death of Christ is a meritorious act of His will in obedience to the Father on behalf of the elect for their justification, in fulfillment of the terms of the covenant of redemption, and in meeting the requirement of God's rule of righteousness to an infinite degree.[234]

---

[232] *HWR, Works* 9:312.

[233] "Luke 22:44," *Works* (Hickman), 2:871.

[234] "He has purchased us to be a peculiar people to himself, for him forever to rule over. Never any king obtained his kingdom at so dear a rate. Many kings have gone through many dangerous battles and great hardships and vast difficulties to obtain their kingdom, but never any did or endured such great things to obtain their kingdom as Christ to obtain his kingdom of grace. Acts 20:28, 'The church of God, which he hath purchased with his own blood.'" "The Threefold Work of the Holy Ghost," *Works* 14:431.

Christ Exercised Perfect Virtue in His Greatest Trial of Obedience

Christ "exercised every possible virtue and grace" in His work of redemption. And as "strict virtue shines most when most tried," never did virtue so shine as in the obedience of Christ in the greatest of all trials.[235]

> It was chiefly under those trials that Christ underwent in the close of his life that his love to God, his honor of God's majesty, and his regard to honor of his law, and his spirit of obedience, and his humility, and contempt of the world, and his patience, and his meekness, and spirit of forgiveness, and love towards men appeared.[236]

"Christ's virtue was not only perfect, but was exercised in those circumstances, and under those trials, that rendered his virtuous acts vastly the most amiable of any that ever appeared in any creature whether man or angel."[237] He shed His blood "in the exercise of a spirit of filial obedience to his heavenly Father. He did it in the exercise of a holy submission and entire resignation to the will of God," in "the most wonderful patience."[238] He exercised "the most wonderful condescension" and "superlative charity and benevolence" and "most admirable meekness towards his most injurious, spiteful, and contemptuous enemies, when they were in the highest exercise of their cruelty."[239] And "though he was the most excellent and honorable of all men, yet was the most humble." And though He knew of His own exalted status and privilege, "he did not disdain to be abased and depressed down into lower and viler circumstances and sufferings than ever any other elect creature was; so that he became least of all and lowest of all."[240]

---

[235] *HWR, Works* 9:320.
[236] *HWR, Works* 9:324.
[237] "Christ the Great Example of Gospel Ministers," *Works* 25:342.
[238] "Christ's Sacrifice an Inducement to His Ministers," *Works* 25:671.
[239] "Christ's Sacrifice an Inducement to His Ministers," *Works* 25:671.
[240] *HWR, Works* 9:321-2.

He knew his infinite worthiness of honor, and of being honored ten thousand times as much as the highest prince on earth, or angel in heaven, yet he did not think it too much when called to it to be bound as a cursed malefactor, and to be the laughing stock and spitting stock of the vilest of men, and to be crowned with thorns and a mock robe and crucified like a slave and malefactor and one of the meanest and worst of vagabonds and miscreants, and a cursed enemy of God and men that was not fit to live on the earth, and that not for himself but for some of the meanest and vilest of creatures, some of those cursed wretches that crucified [him]. Was not this a wonderful manifestation of humility when he cheerfully and most freely complied with this abasement.[241]

Notice that the "wonderful" nature of Christ's humility is founded upon the freeness of it, for Christ "cheerfully and most freely complied with this abasement." As noted earlier, Edwards saw all the acts of Christ in His life and death as "active," voluntary, and meritorious.

Christ exercised the most "wonderful" meekness and forgiving spirit in the midst of the greatest provocations "from the vilest of men," such that He cried for their forgiveness when He suffered on the cross. According to Isaiah 53:7, "'as a sheep before his shearers is dumb, so he opened not his mouth.'"[242] "The flame of love in which Christ offered up the sacrifice of himself" included "love to God and love to man," for "both these flames did as it were overcome the flame of wrath."[243]

---

[241] *HWR, Works* 9:322.
[242] *HWR, Works* 9:322-3. See also "Matthew 21:5," *YMSS,* L. 8r; M 791, *Works* 18:491.
[243] M 791, *Works* 18:491.

Christ's Death Is His Highest Act of Love to the Elect

Much of what has been said above equally applies to Christ's death as His highest act of love to the elect, so the present section will be brief. As the merit of Christ's obedience to the Father is founded on the voluntary nature of that obedience, and the extent of that merit is a function of the level of difficulty and suffering of His obedience, so also is the nature of Christ's love to the elect. The foundation of the love manifest in Christ's sufferings for the elect is in the voluntary undertaking of those sufferings, while the depth of that same love is seen in the infinite extent of the difficulties and suffering Christ willingly undertook on their behalf.

As surety for the object of His love, His elect bride, Christ "stood for them" in His suffering, He "fixed the idea of them in his mind, as if he had really been they, and fixed their calamity in his mind, as though it really was his."[244] His great love carried Him through the dreadful suffering.

> The heart of Christ at that time was full of distress, but it was fuller of love to vile worms: his sorrows abounded, but his love did much more abound. Christ's soul was overwhelmed with a deluge of grief, but this was from a deluge of love to sinners in his heart sufficient to overflow the world, and overwhelm the highest mountains of its sins. Those great drops of blood that fell down to the ground were a manifestation of an ocean of love in Christ's heart.[245]

When given a full view of the fiery furnace in which He was to enter, He was "overwhelmed with the thought; his feeble human nature shrunk at the dismal sight. It put him into this dreadful agony…but his love to sinners held out." Such would not be undertaken by Christ "needlessly" if the salvation of His elect could be accomplished another way, for "he desired that the cup might pass from him." Yet, "if sinners, on whom he had set his love, could

---

[244] M 1005, *Works* 20:331-2.
[245] "Luke 22:44," *Works* (Hickman), 869.

not, agreeably to the will of God, be saved without his drinking it, he chose that the will of God should be done." He chose the furnace "rather than those poor sinners whom he had loved from all eternity should perish."[246] He did not grasp His glory "when the dreadful cup was before Him," He did not claim His Father's love to avoid it, nor retreat on account of the vile nature of His enemies for whom the cup would be consumed. "On the contrary, his love held out, and he resolved even then, in the midst of his agony, to yield himself up to the will of God, and to take the cup and drink it."[247] Moreover, even when His own disciples and friends forsook Him in His darkest hour, "the wonderful freeness, strength, and constancy of the love of Christ" persevered unto death on their behalf.[248] Thus, the depth and constancy of Christ's love for the elect is displayed in His willingness to suffer.[249]

As we noted earlier, Christ is perfect and cannot profit from His creatures. Nonetheless, having set His love upon His bride from eternity, the promised reward of salvation for the elect according to the terms of the covenant of redemption became to Christ the "joy that was set before Him," a true reward, a motive for the success of His redeeming work.[250] "Let us consider at how great a price Christ purchased his spouse: he did not redeem her with corruptible things as silver and gold, but with his own precious blood; yea he gave *himself* for her."[251]

> When he offered up himself to God in those extreme labors and sufferings, this was the joy that was set before him, that made him cheerfully to endure the cross, and despise the pain and shame, in comparison of this joy; even that rejoicing over his church, as the bridegroom rejoiceth over the bride, that the Father had promised him,

---

[246] "Luke 22:44," *Works* (Hickman), 869.
[247] "Luke 22:44," *Works* (Hickman), 869.
[248] "Mark 14:50," *Works* 24:889-0.
[249] M 762, *Works* 18:408.
[250] "Hebrews 12:2-3," *YMSS*, L. 2r. – 2v.
[251] "The Church's Marriage to Her Sons, and to Her God," *Works* 25:188.

and that he expected when he should present her to himself in perfect beauty and blessedness.[252]

The obtaining of His bride "supported him in the midst of the dismal prospect of his sufferings, at which his soul was troubled," as stated in John 12:27: "'Now is my soul troubled: and what shall I say? Father save me from this hour: but for this cause came I unto this hour.'"[253]

All Christ's Acts as Mediator Are Propitiatory and Meritorious.

We have just observed that Edwards held Christ's suffering unto death as both a propitiation for sin and meritorious act of obedience, constituting the greatest aspect of Christ's justifying righteousness. The merit of this great act of obedience is founded upon the freeness of it, ultimately traced to the Son's voluntary acceptance of the terms of the covenant of redemption. The Son freely undertook to do all that was required for the redemption of the elect. Accordingly, as all of Christ's acts in His state of humiliation as mediator are founded upon His voluntary acceptance of the terms of the covenant of redemption and constitute parts of the one great work of redemption, so also all of Christ's works in His state of humiliation are meritorious. In a similar way, all of Christ's suffering and humiliation are propitiatory, as all of Christ's humiliation entailed bearing the effects of sin upon Himself as compared to His infinite state of glory.

> We are as much saved by the death of Christ, as his yielding himself to die was an act of obedience, as we are, as it was a propitiation for our sins: for as it was not the only act of obedience that merited, he having performed meritorious acts of obedience through the whole course of his life; so neither was it the only suffering that was

---
[252] "The Church's Marriage to Her Sons, and to Her God," *Works* 25:188.
[253] "The Church's Marriage to Her Sons, and to Her God," *Works* 25:188.

propitiatory; all his suffering through the whole course of his life being propitiatory, as well as every act of obedience meritorious: indeed this was his principal suffering; and it was as much his principal act of obedience.[254]

Thus, Christ both propitiated for sins and merited eternal life in the same act of dying for sinners. And, as noted above, there is no proper distinction between an "active" and "passive" aspect of Christ's redeeming life and death, as all aspects of His redeeming work are both propitiatory and meritorious. Moreover, there can be no separating Christ's death from Christ laying down His life, or willingly "drinking the cup" of God's wrath, or loving the elect to the uttermost. Christ *gave* His life for His bride. Indeed, in the voluntary and willful nature of His obedience unto death is seen the infinite merit and love of the act itself.

Also, Christ's purchase of redemption includes satisfaction and merit in the identical payment of the identical price, for "it pays our debt and so it satisfies by its intrinsic value and agreement between the Father and Son," and "it procures a title for us to happiness and so it merits." Thus, "the satisfaction of Christ is to free us from misery, and the merit of Christ is to purchase happiness for us," both in the same act of obedience.[255]

Edwards defines an act of Christ as propitiatory "by virtue of the suffering or humiliation" in it. Or, "whatever Christ was subject to that was the judicial fruit of sin had the nature of satisfaction for sin," including suffering and "all abasement and depression of the state or circumstance of mankind below its primitive honor and dignity."[256] At the same time, "all that Christ did in his state

---

[254] "Justification by Faith Alone," *Works* 19:198. See also M 497, *Works* 13:540, wherein Edwards cites Hebrews 5:8 and John 18:11, respectively: "Yet learned he obedience by the things that he suffered," and, "the cup which my Father hath given me, shall I not drink?"
[255] *HWR, Works* 9:304.
[256] *HWR, Works* 9:305. Therefore the Holy Spirit's subjection to the Son in His redeeming work, "though it be in some respect new, and be for our sakes, yet is not meritorious for us," for it does not entail any humiliation and is not a new

of humiliation that had the nature of obedience, or moral virtue, or goodness in it in one respect or another, had the nature of merit in it, and was part of the price with which he purchased happiness for the elect." In each case, respect is to God's rule of righteousness, for the satisfaction of Christ answers the penalty or demand of the law "consequent on the breach of the law," while the merit of Christ answers the obedience demanded by the law "prior to man's breach of the law."[257] So also the death of Christ was both propitiatory and meritorious in that it met the penalty of the law as well as the positive requirement of obedience. And as every act of Christ involved suffering and humiliation as compared to the glory of His exalted state, and was performed in perfect obedience to the Father's will in every aspect of His redemptive work, so also every act of Christ in His humiliation was propitiatory and meritorious. Thus, the "satisfaction and purchase of Christ were not only both carried on through the whole time of Christ's humiliation, but they were both carried on by the same things." "Thus his going about doing good, preaching the gospel, and teaching disciples, was part of righteousness and purchase of heaven as it was done in obedience to the Father," while each of the very same works, in that "he did it with great labor, trouble, and weariness, and under great large labor, exposing himself thereby to reproach and contempt," was propitiatory.[258]

With respect to Christ's incarnation, "it had the nature of satisfaction by reason of the humiliation that was in it; and also of righteousness, as it was the act of his person in obedience to the Father."[259] When Christ came into the world, "though he was perfectly free from any personal guilt," He came into the world as the representative of sinners "with guilt upon his soul."[260] He began to bear the burden of the iniquities of mankind in the humiliation

---

subjection or obedience beyond "the economical order of the persons of the Trinity," M 1062, *Works* 20:441.
[257] *HWR*, *Works* 9:305.
[258] *HWR*, *Works* 9:307.
[259] *HWR*, *Works* 9:308.
[260] "The Threefold Work of the Holy Ghost," *Works* 14:395.

of His incarnation.[261] And as He bore the imputation of Adam's sin throughout His life, He was thereby subject to "a mean and low and suffering state," for "these were the things that divine justice required and that imputed guilt was an obligation to."[262] Yet He bore all this willingly, and thus meritoriously, throughout the whole course of His earthly life.

> And so all his sufferings in his infancy and childhood, and all that labor, and contempt, and reproach, and temptation, and difficulty of some kind or other that he suffered through the whole course of his life, was of a propitiatory and satisfactory nature. And so his purchase of happiness by his righteousness was also carried on through the whole time of his humiliation till his resurrection, not only in that obedience he performed through the course of his life, but also the obedience he performed in laying down his life.[263]

In concluding this brief section, it is worth noting Edwards' awareness of the difficulties in the use of ambiguous terminology with respect to Christ's satisfaction and merits. In the parlance of "divines" (i.e., theologians), the term "purchase" is sometimes used more narrowly to denote the merit of Christ and more broadly with respect to Christ's satisfaction and merit. "Indeed most of the words that are used in this affair are used ambiguously."[264] Sometimes "satisfaction" is used "not only for his propitiation but for his meritorious obedience. For in some sense not only suffering the penalty but positively obeying is needful to satisfy the law." The ambiguity in the usage of terms "seems to be" that merit and satisfaction "don't differ so much really as relatively."[265] Each pays an infinite price. Satisfaction concerns payment of a debt, while merit concerns payment for "a positive good to be obtained."[266]

---

[261] "Hebrews 9:28," *WJEO*, L. 5r.
[262] "Hebrews 9:28," *WJEO*, L. 8v.
[263] *HWR, Works* 9:306-7.
[264] *HWR, Works* 9:304.
[265] *HWR, Works* 9:304.
[266] *HWR, Works* 9:304.

The differences between paying a debt and making a positive purchase differ more relatively than they do essentially. He that lays down a price to pay a debt, he does in some sense make a purchase, he purchases liberty from that obligation. And he that lays down a price to purchase a positive good does, as it [were], make satisfaction. He satisfies the conditional demands of him to whom he pays it. This may suffice concerning what is meant by the purchase of Christ.[267]

Thus, in saying Christ purchased redemption, respect may be to the narrow understanding of Christ's merits purchasing eternal life, or more broadly to both merit and satisfaction. In speaking of Christ's satisfaction, respect may be to the narrow understanding of Christ's payment of the penalty of sin, or more broadly to the satisfaction of the penalty and positive requirement of perfect obedience.

Christ's Obedience Merits the Rewards of the Covenant of Redemption

To review the brief discussion in chapter two of the nature of the rewards promised in the covenant of redemption, the Son freely bound Himself to the terms of the covenant and became subject to the penalty for disobedience or the reward for obedience. The Father promised the Son a reward commensurate with the "merit," "gloriousness," "difficulty," and "expense" of the work.[268] And though the Son in His glory was not capable of the reward of exaltation promised in the covenant, He was so capable in His humiliation as mediator. Further, He would be rewarded with the

---

[267] *HWR, Works* 9:304. Nonetheless, Edwards maintained that Christ's merit and satisfaction of punishment for sin should be distinguished, the former being of "some excellency or worth," while the later satisfies by fulfillment by an equivalent representative. "If the law be fulfilled, there is no need of any excellency or merit to satisfy it, because 'tis satisfied by taking place and having its course." For more detail on this finely nuanced point, see M 846, *Works* 20:67-8.
[268] "Isaiah 53:10," *YMSS*, L. 2r.

salvation of His bride, and power and authority to give the Holy Spirit to them, for Christ's perfect obedience as surety for the elect met and infinitely exceeded the standard of God's rule of righteousness, meriting the promised rewards on their behalf. And though Christ as God could not be profited by anything, especially sinful unworthy creatures, the salvation of His bride became to Him a joy and reward in that He had set His love upon them from eternity.

All of Christ's redeeming work on earth was undertaken on behalf of His bride for whom He acted as surety and representative. The Son freely undertook to stand for His bride in binding Himself to the covenant terms and took upon Himself a human nature and body that He might stand as their proper substitute and representative. In every propitiatory and meritorious act of His entire life of humiliation He acted on her behalf, and willingly drank the cup of God's wrath in her place. In all this, Christ succeeded in meeting and infinitely exceeding the requirement of God's rule of righteousness for which Christ and His bride would be rewarded. Therefore, Christ's perfect obedience merited the salvation and exaltation of the elect.

Christ as surety for the salvation and exaltation of the elect is seen in many "types" or examples in the Old Testament. For instance, as God worked out Joseph's exaltation for the deliverance of His people, so also Christ was exalted for the deliverance of His people.[269] In the same way, "Abraham, Isaac, and Jacob herein are types of Christ," for "God saves us, not for our righteousness, but that he may perform the promise which he made to Christ, our spiritual father, in the covenant of redemption."[270]

---

[269] For a lengthy and detailed description and comparison of Joseph as a type of Christ, see "Genesis 41:40-57," *Works* 24:189-194.

[270] "Deuteronomy 9:5," *Works* 24:291. In commenting on Zechariah 6:14, Edwards writes: "The crowns are all represented as being set on Joshua (v. 11), because they are crowned in and with him as partakers of his glory. So believers are crowned in Christ as partaking of the glory which the Father hath given. Christ's glory is their glory, and the glory of the whole church is the reward of Christ." "Zechariah 6:14," *Works* 24:814.

Moreover, the exaltation of the elect to glory as a participation in the exaltation of Christ is a common teaching of the New Testament. With respect to Ephesians 1:19-23, Edwards writes:

> It seems manifest by these verses that the saints shall partake with Christ, not only in his resurrection and ascension into heaven, but also in his exaltation there, "far above all principality, and power, and might, and dominion," and having "all things put under his feet" [Eph. 1:21-22]. And the reason of it is couched in the last verse, viz. that the church is his body.[271]

"To sit down with Christ in his throne, as he is set down with his Father in his throne," is "obtained only by Christ's purchase… by that victory that he obtained."[272] As God, Christ possessed the right to reign in glory forever as "the Father's proper heir," but also by virtue of His perfect righteousness in His work of redemption.[273] So also the elect "have that eternal life given to them in their measure which Christ himself possesses." They participate in Christ's life, they live "because he lives," and "they inherit his kingdom, the same kingdom which the Father appointed unto him. Luke 22:29: 'The Father hath appointed unto me a kingdom.'"[274] "They have his glory given to them (John 17:[22])," and "they shall reign on his throne (Rev. 3:21)," for "all things are Christ's, so in Christ all things are also the saints' (I Cor. 3:21-22)."[275] For when Christ "obeyed and died," He "did not obey and

---

[271] "Ephesians 1:19-23," *Works* 24:1095.
[272] M 809, *Works* 18:514. Edwards references Revelation 3:21. With respect to Ephesians 1:10, he writes: "The only way that ever has been contrived for the gathering together angels and men into one society, and one place of habitation, is by Christ. Eph. 1:10, 'That in the dispensation of the fullness of times he might gather together in one all things in Christ, both which are in heaven, and which are on earth; even in him,'" 515.
[273] M 609, *Works* 18:144.
[274] "The Peace Which Christ Gives His True Followers," *Works* 25:540.
[275] "The Peace Which Christ Gives His True Followers," *Works* 25:541. Commenting on John 20:17, Edwards writes: "When Christ ascended, then was the reward given to Christ into his hands, to be bestowed on his disciples. Then he received the promise of the Father to bestow on those that are his. Christ aims

die as private person but as our representative, so when he was exalted it was not as a private person but as our head."[276] He was glorified "in our name," as "he is risen and ascended as the first fruits."[277] Indeed, "the whole reward that was promised for what Christ did and suffered may be summed up in this, viz., the exaltation of Christ mystical," including "the whole reward for what he did in his humiliation." In this the "whole Christ" is exalted, "both the head and the members."[278]

> This will be the improvement Christ will make of his own glory, to make his beloved friends partakers with him, to glorify them in his glory; as Christ says to his Father, John 17:22-23, "And the glory which thou has given me have I given them; that they may be one, even as we are one: I in them, and thou in me, that they may be made perfect in one." For we are to consider that though Christ be greatly exalted, yet he is exalted not as a private person for himself only, but he is exalted as his people's head; he is exalted in their name and upon their account, and as one of them, as their representative, as the firstfruits.[279]

"By virtue of the union between Christ and believers, it follows that believers must be partakers of all Christ's glorification."[280] "By virtue of their union with Christ, they also shall rule over all," from the same throne, "over the same kingdom, as his spouse and his body, and shall [have] all things disposed according to their will, for the will of the head will be the will of the whole body."[281] "Souls espoused to Christ must reign over the world, because Christ reigns over the world," and "must sit down in his

---

in all his discourses with his disciples before his death, and still his aim is the same after his death, to possess his followers with an apprehension that it will be profitable for them for him to go away, and go to his Father." *Works* 24:964.
[276] "Hebrews 1:5," *YMSS*, L. 9v.
[277] "Hebrews 1:5," *YMSS*, L. 10r. Edwards references 1 Corinthians 15:23.
[278] "Hebrews 1:5," *YMSS*, L. 10r.
[279] M 571, *Works* 18:107.
[280] M bb, *Works* 13:179.
[281] M 1072, *Works* 20:455.

throne because he is set down on his Father's throne, Rev. 3:21." As Christ rules the nations "with a rod of iron," so "they also shall have power over the nations, and 'shall rule them with a rod of iron.'"[282] As "Christ is God's Son and heir of all God's estate, believers must be sons and heirs of all God's estate."[283] As "Jesus Christ is possessor of heaven earth and sea, sun moon and stars, so believers must be possessors of heaven earth and sea, sun, moon and stars."[284] And, "because Christ rose from the dead, which was a great part of his glorification, so shall saints rise from the dead too, which is a great part of their glorification."[285] They shall share in Christ's glory as promised by the Father in the covenant of redemption. Indeed, "the happiness of the saints in heaven consists much in that, that they are with Christ and are partakers with him in that glory and reward."[286]

> Christ shall enter into heaven with his glorious church every way completed, and shall present them before the Father without spot or {blemish}, having given them that perfect beauty and crowned them with that glory and honor and happiness which was stipulated in the covenant of redemption before the world was, and which he died to procure for them.[287]

The saints will "in the most endearing manner and with the sweetest expressions of love" be invited by Christ to share in His kingdom at the right hand of God: "'Come, ye blessed of my Father, inherit the kingdom prepared for you from the foundations of the world.'"[288] He will bid them "to go where he goes, to dwell where he dwells, to enjoy him and to partake with him." Christ "puts them in mind that God was pleased to set his love upon them

---

[282] M bb, *Works* 13:179. Edwards cites Revelation 2:26-27.
[283] M bb, *Works* 13:179. Edwards cites Romans 8:17.
[284] M bb, *Works* 13:179. Edwards cites Revelation 21:7, 2 Corinthians 6:10, 1 Corinthians 8:22.
[285] M bb, *Works* 13:179.
[286] M 529, *Works* 18:71-2.
[287] "The Day of Judgment," *Works* 14:531.
[288] "The Day of Judgment," *Works* 14:530. A reference to Matthew 25:34.

Christ Satisfies God's Rule of Righteousness

from all eternity, long before ever they had a being, and that God made heaven on purpose for them, fitted it for their delight and happiness." God's "sovereign and eternal love" is "the source of their blessedness."[289]

In addition to the benefit of Christ's heavenly glory, the elect participate in the success of Christ's ministry of the Gospel, in "the glorious flourishing of the church and success of the gospel after he is gone to heaven."[290] Christ and the members of His body have "prayed and labored for the advancement of Christ's kingdom, and have suffered for it, and therein been made partakers with their head in his labors and sufferings, have filled up what is lacking in the sufferings of Christ for the same end." And "as they partook in desires, and prayers, and labors, and sufferings for this, with their head and elder brother in this world," so they participate in the fruits of this labor. "Christ is our forerunner in the reward he receives. He is the first fruits and the pattern of the saints not only in deeds and sufferings, but in his reward and glory."[291] To summarize:

> Christ's success in his work of redemption, in bringing home souls to himself, applying his saving benefits by his spirit, and the advancement of the kingdom of grace in the world, is the reward especially promised to him by his Father in the covenant of redemption, for the hard and difficult service he performed while in the form of a servant; as is manifest by Is. 53:10-12. But the saints shall be rewarded with him: they shall partake with him in the joy of this reward; for this obedience that is thus rewarded, is reckoned to them, as they are his members.[292]

---

[289] "The Day of Judgment," *Works* 14:530.
[290] M 776, *Works* 18:426. Edwards cites Isaiah 49:4-6, 53:10-12.
[291] M 776, *Works* 18:426-7.
[292] "True Saints Are Present with the Lord," *Works* 25:238.

Judgment over Mankind and Angels

In the exaltation of Christ and the elect to the right hand of the Father in heaven, they shall not only rule over all; they shall judge mankind and the angels. As both God and man, in possessing the same nature, "subject to the same law," "under like weakness, frailty, and temptations, yea, infinitely greater temptations,"[293] and "having manifested infinite regard both to the honor of God's majesty and justice, and to the welfare of mankind," Christ is a fit judge of mankind.[294] Moreover, this particular honor is given to Christ "as a suitable reward for his sufferings," as part of His exaltation:

> The exaltation of Christ is given him in reward for his humiliation and sufferings. This was what was stipulated in the covenant of redemption, and we are expressly told that it was given him in reward for that. Phil. 2:8-11, "And being found in fashion as a man, he humbled himself, and became obedient unto death, even the death of the cross. Wherefore hath God highly exalted him, and given him a name above every name: that at the name of Jesus every knee should bow, of things in heaven, and things in earth, and under the earth; and that every tongue should confess that Jesus Christ is Lord, to the glory of God the Father."[295]

"As Christ died as the head of believers and in their name, and was exalted in their name, so shall he judge the world as their head and representative."[296] Thus, by "God's design," Satan will be judged by man, the object of his envy and hatred, for Christ "is appointed to this work in the name of the rest, and the rest are to be with him in it."[297] As noted in chapter three, Edwards surmised that Satan and the angels fell from God's favor in rejecting their future role as ministering spirits to the elect in God's plan of redemption.

---

[293] "John 5:27," *Works* 24:936. See also "The Day of Judgment," *Works* 14:518.
[294] M 813, *Works* 18:523.
[295] "The Day of Judgment," *Works* 14:519.
[296] M 571, *Works* 18:108.
[297] M 571, *Works* 18:108-9.

Thus, in God's wisdom, the fallen angels would be judged by those they refused to serve.[298] Moreover, "it was congruous that Christ, who was despised and rejected by a great number of the angels, should become the foundation upon which the rest should be built for eternal life," and that "God should thus honor Christ in the sight of the angels…that fell."[299] Indeed, "what the fallen angels have done for the ruin of mankind, has only proved an occasion of mankind's being exalted into their stead and to fill up that room that was left vacant in heaven by their fall."[300]

The judging of men and angels is both an integral part of Christ's work of redemption and the finishing of His great work. The great judgment will be the "finishing stroke" when the resurrected redeemed are crowned "with honor and glory" before the world and their reward is finished and perfected.[301] Christ is thereby a "complete Redeemer" in finishing all aspects of His work of redeeming sinners.[302] "Raising the saints from the dead, and judging of them and fulfilling the sentence, is part of their salvation; and therefore it was needful that Christ should be the judge of the world in order to his finishing his work."[303]

---

[298] See M 591, *Works* 18:124-5, for a discussion of Christ as the judge of good and fallen angels as the God-man. With respect to Philippians 2:9-11, that all knees shall bow to Christ includes the angels when Christ sits as judge. He also cites John 5:22, Matthew 28:18, 1 Corinthians 6:3, and Romans 14:9 in support. See also M 515, *Works* 18:58-61 for a discussion of Christ in His human nature in heaven confirming in righteousness the angels that stood against the angels that fell in the rebellion of Lucifer.

[299] M 515, *Works* 18:58.

[300] M 616, *Works* 18:147.

[301] "The Day of Judgment," *Works* 14:520. See also "The True Excellency of a Minister of the Gospel," *Works* 25:84, wherein Edwards speaks of Christ's work of redemption as God's greatest work, a work that will not be completed until Christ's resurrection and judgment.

[302] "The Day of Judgment," *Works* 14:519.

[303] "The Day of Judgment," *Works* 14:520. In addition to Romans 8:23, Edwards cites the following: "John 6:39-40, 'And this is the Father's will which hath sent me, that of all which he hath given me I should lose nothing, but should raise it up again at the last day. And this is the will of him that sent me, that every one which seeth the Son, and believeth on him, may have everlasting life: and I will raise him up at the last day.' John 5:25-30, 'The hour is coming, and now is,

234 *The Infinite Merit of Christ*

The Day of Judgment will display the "sufficiency and excellency" of Christ as mediator "in all respects." The "exceeding purity and holiness" of Christ as judge will be displayed and "will so terrify the wicked and manifest their exceeding guiltiness to their own consciences and to the world," while giving added "confidence" to the saints in the confirmation and advancement of their joy.[304]

> The sight of that awful and pure glory will the more clearly demonstrate their perfect freedom from guilt, for it will demonstrate the value and sufficiency of the atonement that has been made for them, as it will show the dignity and excellency of the high priest and sacrifice by which the atonement was made. For this was no other than the same person that then will appear so great and glorious. He made atonement by the sacrifice of himself. The glory in which he will then appear will show the preciousness of his blood and its sufficiency to atone for the most heinous sins. And that will also demonstrate the value of his righteousness and tend to make 'em the more confident in appearing in it before the judgment seat.[305]

Christ will judge "according to a most just and righteous rule," and "those that are condemned will be most justly condemned."[306] The

---

when the dead shall hear the voice of the Son of God: and they that hear shall live. For as the Father hath life in himself; so hath he given to the Son to have life in himself; and hath given him authority to execute judgment also, because he is the Son of man.'"

[304] M 1133, *Works* 20:512. See also "John 5:27," *Works* 24:936: "It tends to confirm the faith of the saints that their near kinsman and elder brother, and himself being in the form of a servant, performed obedience for them, and wrought out the righteousness, that they depend upon for justification in the judgment, and also suffered from the same unrighteous enemies. This tends to encourage and confirm their faith and hope that he will vindicate 'em in the judgment, and plead their righteous cause against their unrighteous enemies. And it tends also to the convictions of those that shall be condemned in the judgment. Christ, being in the same nature with them, and subject to the same law, under like weakness, frailty, and temptations, yea, infinitely greater temptations, will be the fitter to rise up in judgment against them, and condemn 'em."

[305] M 1133, *Works* 20:512-3.

[306] "The Day of Judgment," *Works* 14:531.

objections of the wicked will be put to silence as God's righteous judgment will be clearly manifest, while "their own consciences will tell them that the sentence is just, and all cavils will be put to silence."[307] At the same time, the justification of sinners deserving of death will be "justified and adjudged" according to the same just and righteous rule. Consistent with Romans 3:26, "'that God may be just, and the justifier of him that believeth in Jesus,'" those "in Christ" will receive their "due proportion" according to "the reward merited by Christ's righteousness." He cannot err in judgment.[308] Indeed, the law will stand for or against everyone, for the judgment will inquire of all "whether they have a fulfillment of the Law to show."[309]

> As for the righteous, they will have this to show: they will have it to plead that the judge himself has fulfilled the Law for them; that he has both satisfied for their sins and fulfilled the righteousness of the Law for them. Rom. 10:4, "Christ is the end of the law for righteousness to every one that believeth." And as for the wicked: when it shall be found by the book of God's remembrance that they have broken the Law and have no fulfillment of the Law to plead for themselves, they shall have the sentence of the Law pronounced upon them.[310]

Thus, in destroying the wicked and rewarding those who "stand in Christ," God acts righteously in judging according to His strict rule of righteousness.[311] The Day of Judgment will be a "doleful" day of the condemnation for "wicked men and devils," but a joyful day for saints and angels. Such will be a day of "open justification"

---

[307] "The Day of Judgment," *Works* 14:531.
[308] "The Day of Judgment," *Works* 14:531-2. "His 'eyes are as a flame of fire' [Rev. 1:14], and he 'searcheth the hearts, and trieth the reins of the children of men' [Rev.. 2:23]. He can't err as to what is justice in particular cases, as human judges often do. He can't be blinded by prejudice, as human judges are very liable to be," 532.
[309] "The Day of Judgment," *Works* 14:528.
[310] "The Day of Judgment," *Works* 14:528-9.
[311] M 450, *Works* 13:498.

and "public acknowledgement" of Christ's great love to the saints, "the day of the bestowment of their consummate happiness, and their entrance on their last and most perfect and glorious state."[312] "It will be the wedding day of the church," the "marriage of the Lamb."

Further, the Day of Judgment will thereby be a vindication and display of Christ's glory.

> It will be the day of his highest exaltation, or greatest manifestation of his exaltation, which exaltation is the reward of his righteousness. It will be the day when Christ himself will be most openly and publicly and remarkably justified. He is said to be justified when God raised him from the dead. God the Father then gave an open testimony of his approbation of what he had done. But how much more will God's setting of him to be the universal judge of heaven, earth and hell be a testimony of his approbation, and an open justification of him.[313]

Christ will have accomplished "the whole work that the Father [appointed] for his glory." He will then "deliver up the kingdom to the Father, and then will he receive his reward from the Father." Christ will receive His crown on this great "day of His triumph," for "the success of his labors and sufferings in the work of redemption will be completed."[314]

> He will fully attain the joy that was set before him, in the perfecting his mystical body in every member of it, in the perfect salvation and full glory of all that the Father hath given him. These will be his joy and crown. If the saints are the joy and crown, in the day of Christ, of faithful ministers that have been the means of their salvation, how much more will they in that day be the joy and crown of

---

[312] M 664b, *Works* 18:209.
[313] M 664b, *Works* 18:209.
[314] M 664b, *Works* 18:210.

Christ, the great author of their salvation, and who has purchased them with his own blood.[315]

Consistent with Christ's prayer in John 17:24, the delivering of the kingdom to the Father will not diminish the joy of the saints in their beholding the glory of Christ. For as the glory and exaltation of Christ with His bride will be forever, so will be the bride's enjoyment of the bridegroom.[316]

Thus, in the glorious day of Christ's judgment and reward we come full circle. God created His creatures that He might give them His goodness and display His glory. Christ freely determines to accomplish God's glory in the redemption of the elect and the bestowing of His happiness to them, and receives His greatest happiness in fully honoring and glorifying the Father through His voluntary obedience and suffering, and is Himself rewarded with this great happiness for His great work. And as will be seen in the last section below, the result is the objects of God's great love dwell together in glorious happiness for all eternity by virtue of the glory of Christ's mediatorial obedience, conceived by the Father, accomplished by the Son, and applied and consummated in union by the Holy Spirit, to the glory of the great Triune God.

The Renewal and Beautification of Heaven, Earth, and the Elect

As noted briefly in chapter one, God created the heavens for the wedding celebration and eternal glory of the bride and Bridegroom, the reward for Christ's perfect obedience to God's rule of righteousness in the purchase of His bride.[317] The merit of Christ's obedience was sufficient to obtain a new heaven and earth.

> The infinitely glorious and beloved Son of God, his shedding his blood and enduring those extreme sufferings in obedience to his Father, was a thing great enough to ob-

---
[315] M 664b, *Works* 18:210.
[316] M 736, *Works* 18:360-1.
[317] See M 952, *Works* 20:212-3.

> tain this, even that the very heaven of heavens should be made new with new glory for him. It was great enough to lay the foundation for a universal refreshing, renewing or new creation of all elect things, that all spiritual and external should be immensely exalted in perfection, beauty and glory.[318]

Thus, when Christ puts on "new glory," then all of heaven puts on an equivalent new glory, for "Christ is the glory of heaven, the beauty and ornament, life and soul of all; and there is no glory there, but only the reflection of his glory, and the emanation of his brightness and life, and the diffusion of his sweetness." All the glory of heaven is "dependent on him," and a reflection of Him.[319] Therefore, "the glory of the latter house will in every respect be greater than the glory of the former house, because the Lord, the messenger of the covenant, shall come into his temple and fill the house with glory." His glory will glorify "the bodies of his saints, as though it was an immediate, visible communication of his glory and life to them, as from the head to his members."[320] And so as God entrusted the original creation of the heavens and the earth to the Son, "much more would he commit to him the creation of the new, for this is his business, to renew all things."

> The creation of the new heavens and new earth is by the work of redemption, which is his work. And 'tis a work that he works out as God-man, and therefore as God-man he will make the heavens new. All new things are by Christ. The new creature, the new name, the new covenant, the new song, the new Jerusalem, and the new heavens and new earth are all by Christ, God-man.[321]

---

[318] M 952, *Works* 20:216.
[319] M 952, *Works* 20:216.
[320] M 952, *Works* 20:216. Christ as the "messenger of the covenant" is language from Malachi 3:1.
[321] M 952, *Works* 20:221.

The work of the new creation is given to Christ as an honor "in reward of what he has done and suffered."[322] In Christ is a remedy "for every calamity that came by the fall," a remedy and restoration to "a far more glorious state of things."[323] "All is made new by Christ."[324]

According to Romans 8:29, "the sum of what the elect are predestinated to" is "'to be conformed to the image of his Son,' to be made like his Son, and to have communion with him in his holiness and in his happiness."[325] The following quotation is lengthy, but is an excellent summary of Edwards' understanding of the comprehensive nature of the elect's participation in the redemptive work of Christ.

> They are predestinated to be conformed to his Son in his death, in dying to sin and the world, and in his resurrection, by being quickened from being dead in trespasses and sins, and also in their bodies being raised, Christ the first fruits, and afterwards those that are Christ's at his coming. They are conformed to Christ in his justification. When Christ rose, he was justified; and believers in their justification do but partake with him in his justification, as v. 34. They are conformed to Christ in his relation to the Father, or in his sonship, and are made also the children of God, so that they are his brethren, only he is the firstborn among them, as the Apostle here observes. They are conformed to Christ in the Father's love to him, and are partakers with him in it as members. They are conformed to Christ in his being heir of the world, and they are joint heirs. They are conformed to Christ in his exaltation and glorification, for he and they shall be glorified together. They are conformed to him in ascension into heaven; they shall also ascend. They are conformed to him in the

---

[322] M 952, *Works* 20:222.
[323] M 806, *Works* 18:509.
[324] M 1037, *Works* 20:377.
[325] "Romans 8:29," *Works* 24:1019.

glorification of his body, for their bodies shall be made like unto his glorious body. They are conformed to him in his enjoyment of the Father in heaven; they by being members of him partake with him in his enjoyment of the Father's infinite love, and in his joy in the Father. His joy is fufulled [sic] in them, and the glory which the Father has given him, he has given them. They are conformed to him in his reigning over the world. They sit with him in his throne, and they have power over the nations, and they shall rule them with a rod of iron, and as the vessels of a potter shall they be broken to shivers, even as he received of his Father. They shall be conformed unto him in his judging the world, for the saints shall judge the world; yea, they shall sit with Christ in judging angels. This glory, this excellency and happiness that consists in the saints' being conformed to Christ, is the sum of the good that they are predestinated to; and the whole of their conformity to Christ is what the Apostle has respect [to], and not only their being made like him in conversion and sanctification.[326]

Christ's Obedience Accomplishes God's Ultimate Purpose to Display and Communicate His Glory

In His sermon on Luke 22:44, we have, perhaps, Edwards' most striking and moving portrayal of the sufferings of Christ in His agony and struggle in the moments before His capture and crucifixion.[327] For in the Garden of Gethsemane, Christ is confronted with the clear understanding of the full weight of that which He was about to endure, including the depth of the wickedness of those for whom He would suffer.[328] He would experience the agony of the undiluted wrath of the Father upon His own soul. The depth of the temptation was infinite, as He was tempted with the

---

[326] "Romans 8:29," *Works* 24:1019-0.
[327] Special thanks to Michael McClenahan for alerting me to this sermon.
[328] "Luke 22:44," *Works* (Hickman), 2:870.

desire to remain in the unbroken and infinite love of the Father, a temptation of infinite power, and a temptation inscrutable to those who would be the beneficiaries of His obedience.[329] In the agony of His prayer He sought that "*God's will might be done*," "'O my Father, if this cup may not pass from me, except I drink it, thy will be done!'"[330] Indeed, there was no other way. He understood that for sinners to be saved, He must in obedience to the Father cast Himself into the "dreadful furnace of wrath."[331]

> He obtained strength and help from God, all that he needed, and was carried through. He was enabled to do and to suffer the whole will of God; and he obtained the whole of the end of his sufferings--a full atonement for the sins of the whole world, and the full salvation of every one of those who were given him in the covenant of redemption, and all that glory to the name of God, which his mediation was designed to accomplish, not one jot or tittle hath failed.[332]

Thus, the ultimate purpose of God to display and communicate His glory was accomplished in the Father's answer to Christ's prayer in the Garden of Gethsemane.

Union and Communion of Believers with the Trinity

Christ's perfect obedience to God's rule of righteousness redeemed His bride in the accomplishment of the ultimate purpose of God. He purchased her happiness that she might dwell with Him and enjoy the glory of Himself and the Father forever. The bride is thus brought into the most intimate of communion with God and made a member of God's family.

---

[329] "Luke 22:44," *Works* (Hickman), 2:871.
[330] "Luke 22:44," *Works* (Hickman), 2:873.
[331] "Luke 22:44," *Works* (Hickman), 2:868-9.
[332] "Luke 22:44," *Works* (Hickman), 2:874.

> This was the design of Christ to bring it to pass, that he and his Father and his people might be brought to a most intimate union and communion. John 17:21-23, "That they all may be one; as thou, Father, art in me, and I in thee, that they also may be one in us: that the world may believe that thou hast sent me. And the glory which thou has given me have I given them; that they may be one, even as we are one: I in them, and thou in me, that they may be made perfect in one." Christ has brought it to pass, that those that the Father has given him should be brought into the household of God, that he and his Father and they should be as it were one society, one family; that his people should be in a sort admitted into that society of the three persons in the Godhead. In this family or household, God [is] the Father, Jesus Christ is his own natural and eternally begotten Son. The saints, they also are children in the family; the church is the daughter of God, being the spouse of his Son. They all have communion in the same spirit, the Holy Ghost.[333]

By the infinite display of God's excellent perfections in the infinitely meritorious obedience of Christ, unworthy sinners are brought into intimate communion with the persons of the Trinity. United to Christ in His humanity, the saints have an intimacy beyond which they would have enjoyed had Christ not taken upon Himself a human nature, as well as a greater intimacy with the Father in being united to Christ as the eternal Son of God.[334] God designed that through "an intimate enjoyment of the Son," saints "shall have a most intimate enjoyment of the Father," so "'our fellowship is with the Father, and with his Son Jesus Christ' (I John 1:3)."[335] As mediator, Christ will unite the church "together to their highest and consummate union with God" when He presents her "perfectly delivered, and perfectly restored, and perfectly

---

[333] M 571, *Works* 18:110.
[334] M 571, *Works* 18:109.
[335] M 741, *Works* 18:368. See 366-373 for a detailed discussion of the nature of this intimate communion.

glorified; saying, 'Here am I, and the children which thou hast given me.'" This He will do in the end "when He will deliver up the kingdom to the Father," "having finished the work which the Father gave him to do."[336]

In God's design "to communicate himself to men," He "so communicated himself to the first and chief of elect men, the elder brother and the head and representative of the rest, even so that this man should be the same person with one of the persons of the Trinity." God designed "to admit man as it were to the inmost fellowship with the deity," into the "eternal society or family in the Godhead in the Trinity of persons."[337] Saints will be "admitted into that blessed society," and will "come to the fountain of happiness" and "partake of that happiness of the Godhead," of the "infinitely sweet and glorious society of the persons of the Trinity (Prov. 8:30)."[338] Saints have been reborn as privileged children of God, to be "instructed, protected, counseled, provided [for, and] received [in] to his house [to] dwell with him" as "'heirs of God, and joint-heirs [with Christ].'"[339] In fact, "it seems to be God's design to admit the church into the divine family as his son's wife, so that which Satan made use [of] as a temptation to our first parents, *Ye shall be as gods*,' shall be fulfilled contrary to his design."[340]

---

[336] M 772, *Works* 18:422. Edwards quotes Hebrews 2:13 and 1 Corinthians 15:24.
[337] M 741, *Works* 18:367.
[338] "Of God the Father," *Works* 25:153.
[339] "Of God the Father," *Works* 25:153. Edwards cites Romans 8:17 and Revelation 21:7 with respect to being heirs, and 1 John 3:1, 5:1, and John 1:12-13 with respect to being reborn as God's children.
[340] M 741, *Works* 18:367. Reference is to Genesis 3:5. Though creatures are exalted to intimate fellowship with God, I have not found in Edwards' works that creatures are ever anything other than *creatures*. In fact, in discussing the dwelling of the Holy Spirit in believers, he qualifies the believer's participation in the holiness of God by maintaining a clear distinction between the Creator and the creature as follows: "Not that the saints are made partakers of the essence of God, and so are "Godded" with God, and "Christed" with Christ, according to the abominable and blasphemous language and notions of some heretics." See *Works* 2:203.

They shall be exalted to a greater privilege and closer union with God than the angels.[341]

Moreover, those united to Christ will have the great happiness of having Christ as their own possession, just as they are His, for "Christ rejoices over the church as the bridegroom rejoiceth over the bride, and she rejoices in him as the bride rejoices in the bridegroom." "They rejoice in each other, *as those that they have chosen above others, for their nearest, most intimate, and everlasting friends and companions.* The church is Christ's chosen." He chose them "'in the furnace of affliction.'"[342] And the infinite glory of Christ's redeeming work "leaves nothing to hinder our highest exaltation, and the utmost intimacy and fullness of enjoyment of God," for His blood removed the hindrance of our guilt, while His obedience obtained "the highest perfection and glory."[343] The church is Christ's "special" possession, His "portion and inheritance."[344] As bride and Bridegroom, they "rejoice in each other," and are "the objects of each others' most tender ardent love." Christ's love to His church "is altogether unparalleled: the height and depth and length and breadth of it pass knowledge: for he loved the church, and gave himself for it; and his love to her proved stronger than death."[345] They "*rejoice in each other's beauty*," as "the church rejoices in Christ's divine beauty and glory,"[346] and they "rejoice *in each others' love*."[347] "United in their happiness" and "fellowship," the bride and bridegroom "rejoice together at the wedding feast,"

---

[341] M 893, *Works* 20:153.
[342] "The Church's Marriage to Her Sons, and to Her God," *Works* 25:178. Edwards cites Isaiah 41:9, 48:10; John 15:15; Psalm 122:8, 132:13-14, 135:4; Hebrews 2:16; Canticles 6:9.
[343] M 741, *Works* 18:366.
[344] "The Church's Marriage to Her Sons, and to Her God," *Works* 25:179. Edwards cites Revelation 14:4; James 1:18; Isaiah 65:19; Canticles 2:16, 6:3, 7:10.
[345] "The Church's Marriage to Her Sons, and to Her God," *Works* 25:180. Edwards cites Zephaniah 3:17, 1 Peter 1:7-8.
[346] "The Church's Marriage to Her Sons, and to Her God," *Works* 25:180. Edwards cites Isaiah 2:5; Canticles 1:3, 4:9; 1 Peter 3:4; Psalm 45:11.
[347] "The Church's Marriage to Her Sons, and to Her God," *Works* 25:180. Edwards cites Psalm 104:15; Canticles 1:4, 4:10.

and thereafter will be "joint partakers of each others' comforts and joys."[348]

Believers are assured of both the propriety and greatness of their future intimacy and enjoyment of God by the greatness of the price given on their behalf to obtain it. "Nothing so much confirms these things as the death and sufferings of Christ. He that hath not withheld his own Son, but hath freely delivered him up for us all in death, how shall he not with him also freely give us all things?"[349] "He had in the eternal covenant of redemption given his life to them, and so looked upon it theirs, and laid it down for them when their good required it."[350]

> He looked on his blood theirs and so spilt it for them when it was needed for their happiness. He looked on his flesh theirs, and so gave it for their life. John 6:51, "The bread I will give is my flesh." His heart was theirs; he had given [it] to them in the eternal covenant; and therefore, he yielded it up to be broke for them, and to spill out his heart's blood for them, being pierced by the wrath of God for their sins. He looked on his soul to be theirs; and therefore, he poured out his soul unto death, and made his soul an offering for their sins. Thus he from eternity gave himself to them, and looked on them as having so great a propriety in him, as amounted to his thus spending and being spent for them; and as he gave himself to them from eternity, so he is theirs to eternity.[351]

Therefore, there can be no greater encouragement or foundation of the proper right for believers "to come boldly to Christ."[352] "The awful majesty of God" is no longer a hindrance to the "freedom

---

[348] "The Church's Marriage to Her Sons, and to Her God," *Works* 25:181. Edwards cites Revelation 3:20; John 15:11, 17:13; Psalm 36:8-9; Canticles 5:1, 2:16, 7:13, 4:16.
[349] M 741, *Works* 18:368. Edwards quotes Romans 8:32 here.
[350] M 741, *Works* 18:369.
[351] M 741, *Works* 18:369-70.
[352] M 741, *Works* 18:370.

and intimacy in the enjoyment of God, any more than if God were our equal, because that majesty has already been fully displayed, vindicated and glorified in Christ's blood." The honor due to "God's awful majesty" has been "abundantly answered" by the sufferings of Christ. "All the ends of divine majesty are already answered fully and perfectly, so as to prepare the way for the most perfect union and communion, without the least injury to the honor of that majesty."[353] God so ordered salvation that its validity, benefits, comforts and joys are dependent and founded upon the sufferings of Christ, "for the joy and glory of heaven shall be enjoyed as in Christ, as the members of the Lamb slain, and the divine love and glory shall be manifested through him." The understanding of the punishment required of the affront to God's majesty, as well as God's love manifested in answering that punishment, produce an appreciation of God's "awful majesty" with the concurrent benefit of intimate communion and enjoyment of God.[354] No higher assurance can be found than Christ spending Himself "in the furnace of God's wrath" on one's behalf, and "no greater argument of the exceeding greatness of the happiness and glory" of those redeemed can be found "than the greatness of the price paid" and "the excellency of that righteousness."[355]

Deliverance of the Kingdom to the Father

We come now to the culmination and completion of the great Trinitarian work of redemption in fulfillment of God's ultimate purpose to display and communicate His glory. Having successfully completed His task in obedience to the Father in perfect execution of the terms of the covenant of redemption, Christ delivers the kingdom to the Father. As noted above, Christ presents to the Father His bride, the church, in her spotless perfection, the children given Him by the Father to redeem. "Then shall the Father, with infinite manifestations of endearment and delight, testify his

---

[353] M 741, *Works* 18:371.
[354] M 741, *Works* 18:371.
[355] "Christ's Sacrifice an Inducement to His Ministers," *Works* 25:666.

acceptance of Christ and of his church thus presented to him," and reward them with "the joys of their eternal wedding."[356] The Father "will dress his Son in his wedding robes," and the Son shall be glorified with an "infinitely sweet divine love, grace, gentleness and joy, and shall shine with this sweet light far more brightly than ever he did before; he shall be clothed with those sweet robes in a far more glorious manner than ever before." Therein Psalm 21:6 (and the verses preceding) shall be fulfilled: "'For thou hast made him most blessed forever: thou hast made him exceeding glad with thy countenance.'" Thus, according to Psalm 21:2, The Father gives the Son His "heart's desire," that the Son "might express his infinite love to his elect spouse full and freely," crowned by the Father "with a crown of love," arrayed "in the brightest robes of love and grace as his wedding garments," in which he will "embrace his dear redeemed spouse, now brought home to her everlasting rest in the house of her husband."[357]

In delivering the kingdom to the Father, Christ relinquishes the reward of His rule as God-man, as the Father's representative, in accordance with the economy of the Trinity, for "the Father is properly the lawgiver and judge of the world." Christ was constituted the Father's "delegate" or "representative" in "the Father's economical work…of governing as lawgiver and judge," for "a season." In delivering the kingdom to the Father, the order of the economic Trinity is thus returned to its eternal order.[358] Nonetheless, such is no reduction of Christ's glory. To the contrary, "when the glory of the members is perfected, and brought to its highest pitch, without doubt the glory of the head will not be diminished, but greatly increased."[359] Moreover, Christ's "mediatorial kingdom" will never be given to the Father.[360] Christ will continue

---
[356] M 957, *Works* 20:231-2.
[357] M 957, *Works* 20:232.
[358] M 742, *Works* 18:373.
[359] M 742, *Works* 18:375.
[360] M 742, *Works* 18:373. See also M 86, *Works* 13:250-1; and, M 609, *Works* 18:143-5. In M 86 Edwards writes that "there will be no more need of a mediatorial government of the universe," and that "Christ Jesus shall govern the universe no more as Mediator." In M 742, Edwards further refines his description

as the mediator and "middle person between the Father and the saints to all eternity, and as the bond of union with the Father, and of derivation from him, and of all manner of communication and intercourse with the Father."[361] Thus, the ultimate purpose of God in displaying and communicating His glory is accomplished, the eternal economic relationships of the persons of the Trinity are restored to their original order, and Christ and His bride are exalted together in infinite glory and happiness for all eternity.

---

of the kingdom delivered to the Father as the "representative kingdom" as distinguished from the "mediatorial kingdom" which remains. This is not a change in his view, but a more careful and narrow defining of the nature of the kingdom delivered to God as "representative," thus distinguishing Christ's role as ruler of the universe in the place of the Father from His ongoing and eternal role as mediator between the Father and the elect.

[361] M 742, *Works* 18:374.

CONCLUSION

The center of Jonathan Edwards' theology is the person and meritorious work of Christ in redeeming sinners, in perfect and free obedience to God's unalterable rule of righteousness, in the accomplishment of the ultimate Trinitarian purpose of the display and communication of God's glory. Such is both the foundation and unifying thread throughout his writings. Indeed, it is difficult to conceive of any aspect of Edwards' thought that is not directly or indirectly dependent upon or related to the person and work of Christ in His accomplishment of God's ultimate purpose.

With respect to revisionist treatments of Edwards' soteriology, proper consideration of Christ's redeeming work in His perfect meritorious obedience to God's unchanging rule of righteousness is necessary for an accurate exposition of Edwards' understanding of the nature of justification, sanctification, regeneration, and the place of good works with respect to each. For instance, the rendering of Edwards' soteriology as either inclusivistic (McClymond, McDermott, Morimoto) or Catholic (Hunsinger, Morimoto) would require a complete re-write of the whole of Edwards' theology, as the entire ultimate Trinitarian purpose to display and communicate His glory would be overthrown. Moreover, neo-orthodox interpretations of Edwards, insofar as they neglect the legal foundation of the whole of Edwards' theology, cannot properly account for the God-centered nature of his thought. As we have seen, Edwards understood that God would not be God if a single soul were saved apart from the perfect satisfaction of God's unchanging rule of righteousness. And, as the glory of God consists in the excellence of His perfections, there could be no display or communication of the excellence of His perfections if God were not perfectly righteous and just. In fact, as Edwards understood the perfections of God as mutually interdependent upon each other, God would neither be holy, good, wise, omniscient, etc.

Further, Edwards' metaphysics cannot be presented accurately in abstraction from the pre-temporal, historical and earthly ministry of Christ in His humiliation, crucifixion, and resurrection. An accurate understanding of the Triune God depends upon an accurate understanding of the pre-temporal and earthly ministry of Christ in satisfying the positive and negative demands of God's unchanging rule of righteousness, as revealed in Scripture. The Trinity is not an abstract concept divorced from the person and work of Christ. Apart from Christ's perfect obedience in accomplishment of the Trinitarian purpose of God, there could be no salvation of sinners and no true knowledge and love of the Triune God, as such constitute the purpose and accomplishment of the redemptive work of Christ.

My brief and narrow treatment of Edwards leaves much to be examined with respect to the present topic. Further research might include an examination of the relationship of God's rule of righteousness to the consideration of works in the revelation of God's righteous judgment in the final judgment of sinners. The relationship of justification, regeneration, and works in light of the unchanging and strict nature of God's rule of righteousness and Christ's perfect satisfaction of the same would be a useful undertaking. Given the depth and breadth of Edwards' writings, there will be no lack of opportunity for fresh research. In any event, my hope is that this meager contribution to Edwards scholarship will prove a helpful catalyst to that end, and in some small way be used of God in His ultimate purpose to display and communicate His glory in the person and work of Christ, to whom belongs all glory.

BIBLIOGRAPHY

Aldridge, Alfred Owen. *Jonathan Edwards*. New York: Washington Square Press, 1964.

Allen, Alexander V. G. *Jonathan Edwards*. 1889 ed. Reprint, New York: Burt Franklin, 1974.

Ames, William. *The Marrow of Theology*. Translated by John Dykstra Eusden. First Baker Books ed. Grand Rapids: Baker Books, 1997.

Asselt, Willem J. van. *The Federal Theology of Johannes Cocceius (1603-1669)*. Translated by Raymond A. Blacketer. Vol. 100 of *Studies in the History of Christian Thought*. Boston: Brill, 2001.

Atchison, Thomas F. "Towards Developing a Theology of Christian Assurance from 1 John with Reference to Jonathan Edwards." *DAI* 65, no. 02A (2004): 567.

Bebbington, D. W. *Evangelicalism in Modern Britain: A History from the 1730s to the 1980s*. Grand Rapids: Baker Book House, 1992.

Beeke, Joel R. *Assurance of Faith: Calvin, English Puritanism, and the Dutch Second Reformation*. Vol. 89 of *American University Studies*. Series vii, Theology and Religion. New York: Peter Lang, 1994.

Bell, Richard H. "On Trusting One's Own Heart: Scepticism in Jonathan Edwards and Soren Kierkegaard." *History of European Ideas* 12, no. 1 (1990): 105-116.

Berkouwer, G. C. *The Work of Christ*. Translated by Cornelius Lambregtse. 1965. Reprint, Grand Rapids: W. B. Eerdmans, 1984.

Bogue, Carl W. *Jonathan Edwards and the Covenant of Grace*. Cherry Hill, NJ: Mack Publishing Company, 1975.

Bombaro, John J. "Jonathan Edwards's Vision of Salvation." *The Westminster Theological Journal* 65 (2003): 45-67.

———. "Dispositional Peculiarity, History, and Edwards's Evangelistic Appeal to Self-Love." *The Westminster Theological Journal* 66 (2004): 121-158.

———. "The Formulation of Jonathan Edwards' Theocentric Metaphysics: Part One of Four." *The Clarion Review* 1 (2004): 8-19.

———. "God in Us, Us in God; Part Two of Four: The Formulation of Jonathan Edwards' Theocentric Metaphysics." *The Clarion Review* 2 (2004): 7-16.

Bos, Frans Lukas. *Johann Piscator: Ein Beitrag Zur Geschichte Der Reformierten Theologie*. Kampen: J. H. Kok, 1932.

Brand, David C. *Profile of the Last Puritan: Jonathan Edwards, Self-Love, and the Dawn of the Beatific*. American Academy of Religion Academy Series. Edited by Susan Thistlewaite. Atlanta: Scholars Press, 1991.

Brown, Robert E. "Edwards, Locke, and the Bible." *Journal of Religion* 79 (1999): 361-384.

———. *Jonathan Edwards and the Bible*. Bloomington: Indiana University Press, 2002.

Buchanan, James. *The Doctrine of Justification: An Outline of Its History in the Church and of Its Exposition from Scripture*. Edinburgh; Carlisle, PA: Banner of Truth Trust, 1984.

Caldwell, Robert W., III. *Communion in the Spirit: The Holy Spirit as the Bond of Union in the Theology of Jonathan Edwards*. Studies in Evangelical History and Thought. Carlisle, U.K.: Paternoster, 2007.

Calvin, John. *Institutes of the Christian Religion*. Translated by Ford Lewis Battles. Edited by John T. McNeill. 2 vols. Philadelphia: Westminster Press, 1960.

Carse, James P. *Jonathan Edwards & the Visibility of God*. New York: Scribner, 1967.

Chamberlain, Mary Ava. "Jonathan Edwards Against the Antinomians and Arminians." *DAI* 52, no 02A (1990): 572.

Chemnitz, Martin. *Examination of the Council of Trent.* Translated by Fred Kramer. Vol. 1. St. Louis: Concordia Publishing House, 1971.

Cherry, Conrad. "The Puritan Notion of the Covenant in Jonathan Edwards' Doctrine of Faith." *Church History* 34 (1965): 328-341.

_____. *The Theology of Jonathan Edwards: A Reappraisal.* 1990 ed. Bloomington: Indiana University Press, 1966.

_____. Review of "Jonathan Edwards and the Covenant of Grace." *Church History* 46 (1977): 251-252.

Clifford, Alan C. *Atonement and Justification: English Evangelical Theology, 1640-1790: An Evaluation.* Oxford: Oxford University Press, 1990.

Coffin, David F. *A Select Bibliography of Jonathan Edwards's Background Reading*, 1988.

Colwell, John E. "The Glory of God's Justice and the Glory of God's Grace: Contemporary Reflections on the Doctrine of Hell in the Teaching of Jonathan Edwards." *Evangelical Quarterly* 67 (1995): 291-308.

Conforti, Joseph A. *Jonathan Edwards, Religious Tradition & American Culture.* Chapel Hill: University of North Carolina Press, 1995.

Copan, Paul. "Jonathan Edwards's Philosophical Influences: Lockean or Malebranchean?" *Journal of the Evangelical Theological Society* 44 (2001): 107-124.

Crisp, Oliver D. "Jonathan Edwards on Divine Simplicity." *Religious Studies* 39, no. 1 (2003): 23-41.

_____. "On the Theological Pedigree of Jonathan Edwards's Doctrine of Imputation." *Scottish Journal of Theology* 56, no. 3 (2003): 308-327.

_____. *Jonathan Edwards and the Metaphysics of Sin.* Aldershot, Hants, England; Burlington, VT: Ashgate, 2005.

Cunningham, W. *Historical Theology: A Review of the Principal Doctrinal Discussions in the Christian Church since the Apostolic Age*. Students' Reformed Theological Library. 1960. Reprint, Edinburgh; Carlisle, PA: Banner of Truth Trust, 1994.

Danaher, William J., Jr. *The Trinitarian Ethics of Jonathan Edwards*. Columbia Series in Reformed Theology. Louisville: Westminster John Knox Press, 2004.

Daniel, Stephen H. "Postmodern Concepts of God and Edwards's Trinitarian Ontology." In *Edwards in Our Time: Jonathan Edwards and the Shaping of American Religion*. Edited by Sang Hyun Lee and Allen C. Guelzo, 45-64. Grand Rapids: W. B. Eerdmans, 1999.

Davidson, Edward H. *Jonathan Edwards: The Narrative of a Puritan Mind*. Cambridge: Harvard University Press, 1968.

De Jong, Peter Y. *The Covenant Idea in New England Theology, 1620-1847*. Grand Rapids: W. B. Eerdmans, 1945.

De Prospo, R. C. *Theism in the Discourse of Jonathan Edwards*. Newark: University of Delaware Press, 1985.

Delattre, Roland A. *Beauty and Sensibility in the Thought of Jonathan Edwards: An Essay in Aesthetics and Theological Ethics*. New Haven: Yale University Press, 1968.

_____. "Recent Scholarship on Jonathan Edwards." *Religious Studies Review* 24 (1998): 369-375.

_____. "Review Essays – Recent Scholarship on Jonathan Edwards." *Religious Studies Review* 24, no. 4 (1998): 8.

_____. "Aesthetics and Ethics: Jonathan Edwards and the Recovery of Aesthetics for Religious Ethics." *Journal of Religious Ethics* 31, no. 2 (2003): 277-297.

Edwards, Jonathan. *The Works of Jonathan Edwards*. 2 vols. Edited by Edward Hickman. 1834. Reprint, Edinburgh: Banner of Truth Trust, 1974.

_____. *Selections from the Unpublished Writings of Jonathan Edwards, of America*. Edited by Alexander Balloch Grosart.

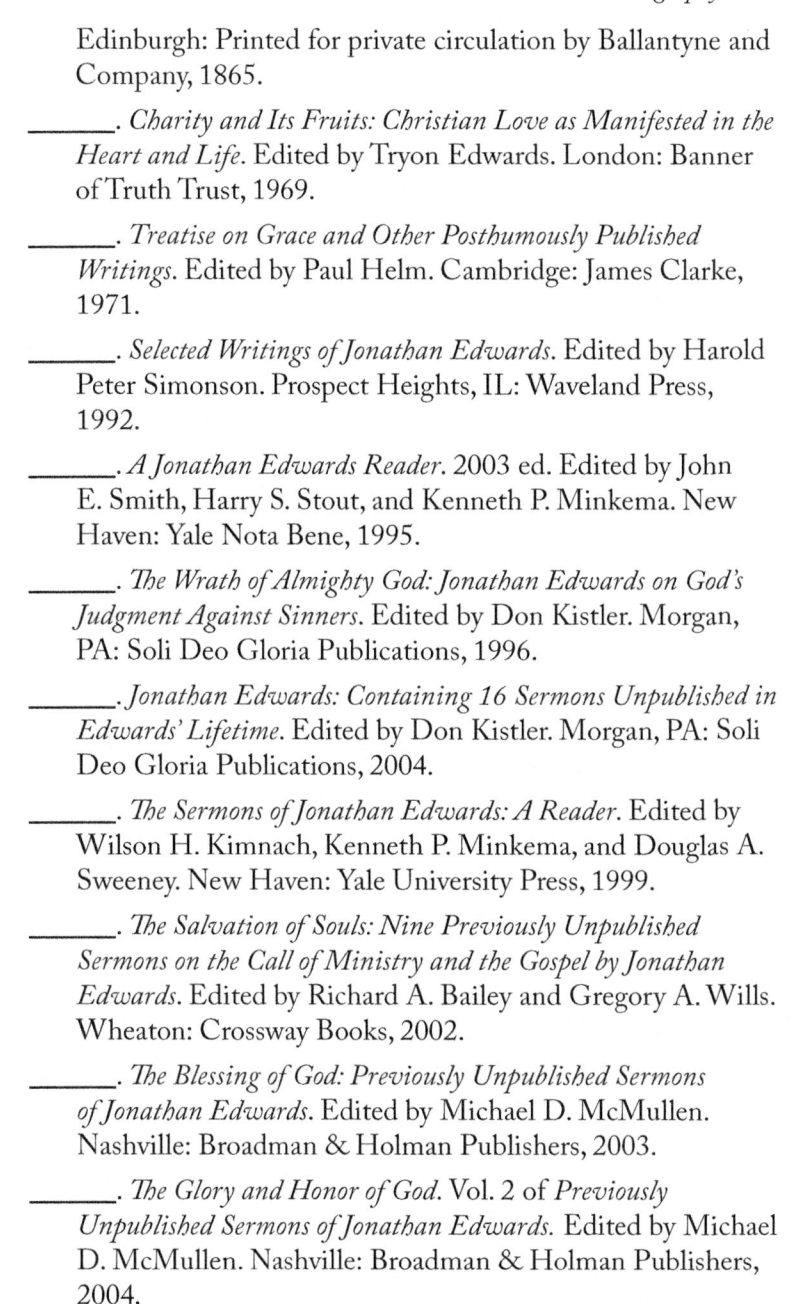

Edinburgh: Printed for private circulation by Ballantyne and Company, 1865.

———. *Charity and Its Fruits: Christian Love as Manifested in the Heart and Life*. Edited by Tryon Edwards. London: Banner of Truth Trust, 1969.

———. *Treatise on Grace and Other Posthumously Published Writings*. Edited by Paul Helm. Cambridge: James Clarke, 1971.

———. *Selected Writings of Jonathan Edwards*. Edited by Harold Peter Simonson. Prospect Heights, IL: Waveland Press, 1992.

———. *A Jonathan Edwards Reader*. 2003 ed. Edited by John E. Smith, Harry S. Stout, and Kenneth P. Minkema. New Haven: Yale Nota Bene, 1995.

———. *The Wrath of Almighty God: Jonathan Edwards on God's Judgment Against Sinners*. Edited by Don Kistler. Morgan, PA: Soli Deo Gloria Publications, 1996.

———. *Jonathan Edwards: Containing 16 Sermons Unpublished in Edwards' Lifetime*. Edited by Don Kistler. Morgan, PA: Soli Deo Gloria Publications, 2004.

———. *The Sermons of Jonathan Edwards: A Reader*. Edited by Wilson H. Kimnach, Kenneth P. Minkema, and Douglas A. Sweeney. New Haven: Yale University Press, 1999.

———. *The Salvation of Souls: Nine Previously Unpublished Sermons on the Call of Ministry and the Gospel by Jonathan Edwards*. Edited by Richard A. Bailey and Gregory A. Wills. Wheaton: Crossway Books, 2002.

———. *The Blessing of God: Previously Unpublished Sermons of Jonathan Edwards*. Edited by Michael D. McMullen. Nashville: Broadman & Holman Publishers, 2003.

———. *The Glory and Honor of God*. Vol. 2 of *Previously Unpublished Sermons of Jonathan Edwards*. Edited by Michael D. McMullen. Nashville: Broadman & Holman Publishers, 2004.

_____. *Freedom of the Will*. Vol. 1 of *The Works of Jonathan Edwards*. Edited by Paul Ramsey. New Haven: Yale University Press, 1957.

_____. *Religious Affections*. Vol. 2 of *The Works of Jonathan Edwards*. Edited by John Edwin Smith. New Haven: Yale University Press, 1959.

_____. *Original Sin*. Vol. 3 of *The Works of Jonathan Edwards*. Edited by Clyde A. Holbrook. New Haven: Yale University Press, 1977.

_____. *Apocalyptic Writings*. Vol. 5 of *The Works of Jonathan Edwards*. Edited by Stephen J. Stein. New Haven: Yale University Press, 1977.

_____. *Scientific and Philosophical Writings*. Vol. 6 of *The Works of Jonathan Edwards*. Edited by Wallace E. Anderson. New Haven: Yale University Press, 1980.

_____. "Dissertation Concerning the End for Which God Created the World." In *Ethical Writings*, Vol. 8 of *The Works of Jonathan Edwards*. Edited by Paul Ramsey, 403-536. New Haven: Yale University Press, 1989.

_____. *A History of the Work of Redemption*. Vol. 9 of *The Works of Jonathan Edwards*. Edited by John F. Wilson. New Haven: Yale University Press, 1989.

_____. *Sermons and Discourses, 1720-1723*. Vol. 10 of *The Works of Jonathan Edwards*. Edited by Wilson H. Kimnach. New Haven: Yale University Press, 1992.

_____. *Typological Writings*. Vol. 11 of *The Works of Jonathan Edwards*. Edited by Wallace E. Anderson, Jr., Mason I. Lowance, and David H. Watters. New Haven: Yale University Press, 1993.

_____. *The "Miscellanies," a-500*. Vol. 13 of *The Works of Jonathan Edwards*. Edited by Thomas A Schafer. Corrected ed. New Haven: Yale University Press, 2002.

_____. *Sermons and Discourses, 1723-1729*. Vol. 14 of *The Works of Jonathan Edwards*. Edited by Kenneth P. Minkema. New Haven: Yale University Press, 1997.

_____. *Notes on Scripture*. Vol. 15 of *The Works of Jonathan Edwards*. Edited by Stephen J. Stein. New Haven: Yale University Press, 1998.

_____. *Letters and Personal Writings*. Vol. 16 of *The Works of Jonathan Edwards*. Edited by George S. Claghorn. New Haven: Yale University Press, 1998.

_____. *Sermons and Discourses, 1730-1733*. Vol. 17 of *The Works of Jonathan Edwards*. Edited by Mark Valeri. New Haven: Yale University Press, 1999.

_____. *The "Miscellanies," 501-832*. Vol. 18 of *The Works of Jonathan Edwards*. Edited by Ava Chamberlain. New Haven: Yale University Press, 2001.

_____. *Sermons and Discourses, 1734-1738*. Vol. 19 of *The Works of Jonathan Edwards*. Edited by M. X. Lesser. New Haven: Yale University Press, 2001.

_____. *The "Miscellanies," 833-1152*. Vol. 20 of *The Works of Jonathan Edwards*. Edited by Amy Plantinga Pauw. New Haven: Yale University Press, 2002.

_____. *Sermons and Discourses, 1739-1742*. Vol. 22 of *The Works of Jonathan Edwards*. Edited by Harry S. Stout, Nathan O. Hatch, and Kyle P. Farley. New Haven: Yale University Press, 2003.

_____. *Writings on the Trinity, Grace, and Faith*. Vol. 21 of *The Works of Jonathan Edwards*. Edited by Sang Hyun Lee. New Haven: Yale University Press, 2003.

_____. *The "Miscellanies," 1153-1360*. Vol. 23 of *The Works of Jonathan Edwards*. Edited by Douglas A. Sweeney. New Haven: Yale University Press, 2004.

_____. *The "Blank Bible"*. Vol. 24 of *The Works of Jonathan Edwards*. Edited by Stephen J. Stein. New Haven: Yale University Press, 2006.

———. *Sermons and Discourses, 1743-1758*. Vol. 25 of *The Works of Jonathan Edwards*. Edited by Wilson H. Kimnach. New Haven: Yale University Press, 2006.

———. *Sermon Manuscripts*. New Haven: The Jonathan Edwards Center at Yale University, 2005. http://edwards.yale.edu/archive/ (accessed 2006).

Elwood, Douglas J. *The Philosophical Theology of Jonathan Edwards*. New York: Columbia University Press, 1960.

Erdt, Terence. *Jonathan Edwards: Art and the Sense of the Heart*. Amherst: University of Massachusetts Press, 1980.

Evans, William Borden. "Imputation and Impartation: The Problem of Union with Christ in Nineteenth Century American Reformed Theology." *DAI* 57, no. 04A (1996): 1682.

Faust, Clarence H. *Jonathan Edwards's View of Human Nature*. New York, 1935.

Faust, Clarence H., and Thomas H. Johnson. *Jonathan Edwards: Representative Selections, with Introduction, Bibliography, and Notes*. American Century Series. 1962 ed. New York: Hill and Wang, 1935.

Fiering, Norman. *Jonathan Edwards's Moral Thought and Its British Context*. Published for the Institute of Early American History and Culture, Williamsburg, Virginia. Chapel Hill: University of North Carolina Press, 1981.

———. "The Rationalist Foundations of Jonathan Edwards." In *Jonathan Edwards and the American Experience*, 73-101. New York: Oxford University Press, 1988.

Foster, Frank Hugh. *A Genetic History of the New England Theology*. Chicago: The University of Chicago Press, 1907.

Gay, Peter. *A Loss of Master: Puritan Historians in Colonial America*. Jefferson Memorial Lectures. Berkeley: University of California Press, 1966.

―――. "Jonathan Edwards: An American Tragedy." In *Jonathan Edwards: A Profile*. Edited by David Levin. New York: Hill and Wang, 1969.

Gerstner, John H. Review of "Tragedy in Eden: Original Sin in the Theology of Jonathan Edwards." *Trinity Journal* 7 (1986): 92-93.

―――. *Jonathan Edwards: A Mini-Theology*. Wheaton: Tyndale House, 1987.

―――. *The Rational Biblical Theology of Jonathan Edwards*. 3 vols. Powhatan, VA: Berea Publications, 1991-3.

Gilbert, Greg D. "The Nations Will Worship: Jonathan Edwards and the Salvation of the Heathen." *Trinity Journal* 23 (2002): 53-76.

Goen, Clarence Curtis. "Jonathan Edwards: A New Departure in Eschatology." *Church History* 28 (1959): 25-40.

Grudem, Wayne A. *Systematic Theology: An Introduction to Biblical Doctrine*. Grand Rapids: Zondervan, 2000.

Haroutunian, Joseph. *Piety Versus Moralism*. New York: Harper & Row, 1970.

Hart, D. G., Sean Michael Lucas, and Stephen J. Nichols. *The Legacy of Jonathan Edwards: American Religion and the Evangelical Tradition*. Grand Rapids: Baker Academic, 2003.

Hatch, Nathan O., and Harry S. Stout. *Jonathan Edwards and the American Experience*. New York: Oxford University Press, 1988.

Heimert, Alan. *Religion and the American Mind: From the Great Awakening to the Revolution*. Cambridge: Harvard University Press, 1966.

Helm, Paul. "John Locke and Jonathan Edwards: A Reconsideration." *Journal of the History of Philosophy* 8 (1969): 51-61.

―――. *Calvin and Calvinists*. Edinburgh; Carlisle, PA: Banner of Truth Trust, 1982.

_____. "A Forensic Dilemma: John Locke and Jonathan Edwards on Personal Identity." In *Jonathan Edwards: Philosophical Theologian*. Edited by Paul Helm and Oliver D. Crisp, 45-59. Burlington, VT: Ashgate, 2003.

Helm, Paul, and Oliver D. Crisp. *Jonathan Edwards: Philosophical Theologian*. Aldershot: Ashgate, 2003.

Hindson, Edward E. *Introduction to Puritan Theology: A Reader*. Grand Rapids: Baker Book House, 1976.

Hodge, Charles. *Systematic Theology*. Peabody, MA: Hendrickson Publishers, 1999.

Holbrook, Clyde A. "Jonathan Edwards and His Detractors." *Theology Today* 10 (1953): 384-396.

_____. "Original Sin and the Enlightenment." In *Heritage of Christian Thought: Essays in Honor of Robert Lowry Calhoun*, 142-165. New York: Harper & Row, 1965.

Holifield, E. Brooks. *Theology in America: Christian Thought from the Age of the Puritans to the Civil War*. New Haven: Yale University Press, 2003.

Holmes, Oliver Wendell. *Pages from an Old Volume of Life: A Collection of Essays, 1857-1881*. Boston: Houghton Mifflin and Co., 1883.

Holmes, Stephen R. *God of Grace and God of Glory: An Account of the Theology of Jonathan Edwards*. Grand Rapids: W. B. Eerdmans, 2001.

_____. "Does Jonathan Edwards Use a Dispositional Ontology? A Response to Sang Hyun Lee." In *Jonathan Edwards: Philosophical Theologian*. Edited by Paul Helm and Oliver D. Crisp, 99-114. Burlington: Ashgate, 2003.

Hoopes, James. "Jonathan Edwards's Religious Psychology." *Journal of American History* 69 (1982-83): 849-865.

Hopkins, Samuel. *The Works of Samuel Hopkins*. American Religious Thought of the 18th and 19th Centuries. 3 vols. New York: Garland, 1987.

Hunsinger, George. "Dispositional Soteriology: Jonathan Edwards on Justification by Faith Alone." *The Westminster Theological Journal* 66 (2004): 107-120.

Jenson, Robert W. *America's Theologian: A Recommendation of Jonathan Edwards.* New York: Oxford University Press, 1992.

Jinkins, Michael. "The 'Being of Beings': Jonathan Edwards' Understanding of God as Reflected in His Final Treatises." *Scottish Journal of Theology* 46, no. 2 (1993): 161-190.

_____. *A Comparative Study in the Theology of Atonement in Jonathan Edwards and John Mcleod Campbell: Atonement and the Character of God.* San Francisco: Mellen Research University Press, 1993.

Johnson, Thomas Herbert. *The Printed Writings of Jonathan Edwards, 1703-1758: A Bibliography.* New York: B. Franklin, 1970.

Kang, Kevin Woongsan. "Justified by Faith in Christ: Jonathan Edwards' Doctrine of Justification in Light of Union with Christ." *DAI* 64, no. 04A (2003): 1303.

Kearney, John. "Jonathan Edwards' Account of Adam's First Sin." *Scottish Bulletin of Evangelical Theology* 15 (1997): 127-141.

Kidd, Thomas S. "The Edwards at 300 Symposium and the Future of Jonathan Edwards Studies." *Early American Literature* 39 no. 2 (2004): 405-407.

Kling, David William, and Douglas A. Sweeney. *Jonathan Edwards at Home and Abroad: Historical Memories, Cultural Movements, Global Horizons.* Columbia: University of South Carolina Press, 2003.

Kuklick, Bruce. *Churchmen and Philosophers: From Jonathan Edwards to John Dewey.* New Haven: Yale University Press, 1985.

_____. "Review Essay: An Edwards for the Millennium." *Religion and American Culture* 11 (2001): 116-117.

Lambert, Frank. *Inventing the "Great Awakening".* Princeton: Princeton University Press, 1999.

Lee, Sang Hyun. *The Philosophical Theology of Jonathan Edwards*. Princeton: Princeton University Press, 1988.

_____. "Grace and Justification by Faith Alone." In *The Princeton Companion to Jonathan Edwards*. Edited by Sang Hyun Lee, 130-145. Princeton: Princeton University Press, 2005.

Lee, Sang Hyun, ed. *The Princeton Companion to Jonathan Edwards*. Princeton: Princeton University Press, 2005.

Lee, Sang Hyun, and Allen C. Guelzo. *Edwards in Our Time: Jonathan Edwards and the Shaping of American Religion*. Grand Rapids: W. B. Eerdmans, 1999.

Lesser, M. X. *Jonathan Edwards: A Reference Guide*. Edited by Everett Emerson. Boston: G. K. Hall, 1981.

_____. *Jonathan Edwards: An Annotated Bibliography, 1979-1993*. Bibliographies and Indexes in Religious Studies, no. 30. Westport, CT: Greenwood Press, 1994.

Lesser, M. X. and Thomas Herbert Johnson. *The Printed Writings of Jonathan Edwards, 1703-1758: A Bibliography*. Rev. ed. Princeton: Princeton Theological Seminary, 2003.

Levin, David. *The Puritan and the Enlightenment: Franklin and Edwards*. Berkeley Series in American History. Chicago: Rand McNally, 1968.

_____. *Jonathan Edwards: A Profile*. American Century Series. New York: Hill and Wang, 1970.

Lewis, Paul. Review of "The Philosophical Theology of Jonathan Edwards." *Christian Scholar's Review* 19 (1989): 90-91.

Locke, John. *The Reasonableness of Christianity*. A Library of Modern Religious Thought. Edited by Ian T. Ramsay. Palo Alto: Stanford University Press, 1967.

_____. *Philosophical Works*, ed. James Augustus St. John. Freeport, NY: Books for Libraries Press, 1969.

———. *The Locke Reader: Selections from the Works of John Locke: With a General Introduction and Commentary*. Edited by John W. Yolton. New York: Cambridge University Press, 1977.

Loeb, Louis E. *From Descartes to Hume: Continental Metaphysics and the Development of Modern Philosophy*. Ithaca, NY: Cornell University Press, 1981.

Logan, Samuel T. "The Doctrine of Justification in the Theology of Jonathan Edwards." *Westminster Theological Journal* 46 (1984): 26-52.

———. Review of "Tragedy in Eden: Original Sin in the Theology of Jonathan Edwards." *Westminster Theological Journal* 48 (1986): 398-404.

Lowance, Mason I. "Images or Shadows of Divine Things: The Typology of Jonathan Edwards." *Early American Literature* 5 (1970): 141-181.

Lucas, Sean Michael. "Jonathan Edwards between Church and Academy." In *The Legacy of Jonathan Edwards: American Religion and the Evangelical Tradition*. Edited by D. G. Hart, Sean Michael Lucas, and Stephen J. Nichols, 228-247. Grand Rapids: Baker Academic, 2003.

Luther, Martin. "Two Kinds of Righteousness." In *The Career of the Reformer I*, vol. 31 of *Luther's Works*. Edited by Harold J. Grimm, 297-306. Philadelphia: Muhlenberg Press, 1957.

Manspeaker, Nancy. *Jonathan Edwards: Bibliographical Synopses*. New York: E. Mellen Press, 1981.

Marsden, George M. "Perry Miller's Rehabilitation of the Puritans: A Critique." *Church History* 39 (1970): 91-105.

———. "The Edwardsian Vision." *The Reformed Journal* 39, June (1989): 23-25.

———. *Jonathan Edwards: A Life*. New Haven: Yale University Press, 2003.

Mastricht, Peter van. *A Treatise on Regeneration*. Morgan, PA: Soli Deo Gloria Publications, 2002.

May, Henry F. "The Recovery of American Religious History." *American Historical Review* 70 (1964): 79-92.

_____. "Jonathan Edwards and America." In *Jonathan Edwards and the American Experience*. Edited by Nathan O. Hatch and Harry S. Stout, 19-33. New York: Oxford University Press, 1988.

_____. *The Divided Heart: Essays on Protestantism and the Enlightenment in America*. New York: Oxford University Press, 1991.

McClymond, Michael J. *Encounters with God: An Approach to the Theology of Jonathan Edwards*. Religion in America. New York: Oxford University Press, 1998.

_____. "A Different Legacy" In *Jonathan Edwards at Home and Abroad: Historical Memories, Cultural Movements, Global Horizons*. Edited by David William Kling and Douglas A. Sweeney, 16-39. Columbia: University of South Carolina Press, 2003.

McDermott, Gerald R. *Jonathan Edwards Confronts the Gods: Christian Theology, Enlightenment Religion, and Non-Christian Faiths*. New York: Oxford University Press, 2000.

_____. "Response to Gilbert: 'The Nations Will Worship: Jonathan Edwards and the Salvation of the Heathen'." *Trinity Journal* 23 (2002): 77-80.

McGiffert, Arthur Cushman. *Jonathan Edwards*. Philosophy in America. New York: AMS Press, 1980.

McGrath, Alister E. *Iustitia Dei: A History of the Christian Doctrine of Justification*. 2nd ed. New York: Cambridge University Press, 1998.

Miller, Perry. *Jonathan Edwards*. 1949. Reprint, Amherst: The University of Massachusetts Press, 1981.

_____. *The New England Mind: From Colony to Province*. Cambridge: Harvard University Press, 1953.

_____. *Errand into the Wilderness*. Cambridge: Belknap Press of Harvard University Press, 1956.

_____. *The New England Mind: The Seventeenth Century.* Cambridge: Harvard University Press, 1967.

Minkema, Kenneth P. "The Other Unfinished 'Great Work': Jonathan Edwards Messianic Prophecy, and 'the Harmony of the Old and New Testaments.'" In *Jonathan Edwards's Writings: Text, Context, Interpretation.* Edited by Stephen J. Stein, 52-68. Bloomington: Indiana University Press, 1996.

_____. "Jonathan Edwards in the Twentieth Century." *Journal of the Evangelical Theological Society* 47 (2004): 659-687.

Morimoto, Anri. *Jonathan Edwards and the Catholic Vision of Salvation.* University Park: Pennsylvania State University Press, 1995.

Morris, Kenneth R. "The Puritan Roots of American Universalism." *Scottish Journal of Theology* 44 (1991): 457-487.

Morris, William Sparkes. "Genius of Jonathan Edwards." In *Re-Interpretation in American Church History*, 29-65. Chicago: University of Chicago Press, 1968.

_____. *The Young Jonathan Edwards: A Reconstruction.* Vol. 14 of *Chicago Studies in the History of American Religion.* Brooklyn, NY: Carlson Publishing, 1991.

Mulder, John M., and John Frederick Wilson. *Religion in American History: Interpretive Essays.* Englewood Cliffs, NJ: Prentice-Hall, 1978.

Muller, Richard A. "Covenant and Conscience in English Reformed Theology: Three Variations on a 17th Century Theme." *Westminster Theological Journal* 42 (1980): 308-334.

_____. *Christ and the Decree: Christology and Predestination in Reformed Theology from Calvin to Perkins.* Grand Rapids: Baker Book House, 1988.

_____. "Calvin and the 'Calvinists': Assessing Continuities and Discontinuities between the Reformation and Orthodoxy." *Calvin Theological Journal* 31(1996): 125-160.

_____. *After Calvin: Studies in the Development of a Theological Tradition.* Oxford Studies in Historical Theology. New York; Oxford: Oxford University Press, 2003.

Murray, Iain H. *Jonathan Edwards: A New Biography.* 1987. Reprint, Edinburgh: The Banner of Truth Trust, 1988.

Murray, John. *The Imputation of Adam's Sin.* Grand Rapids: W. B. Eerdmans, 1959.

_____. *Collected Writings of John Murray: Professor of Systematic Theology, Westminster Theological Seminary, Philadelphia, Pennsylvania, 1937-1966.* Edinburgh; Carlisle, PA: Banner of Truth Trust, 1976.

Nichols, Stephen J. *An Absolute Sort of Certainty: The Holy Spirit and the Apologetics of Jonathan Edwards.* Phillipsburg, NJ: P & R Publishing, 2003.

Niebuhr, H. Richard. *The Kingdom of God in America.* New York: Harper, 1959.

_____. "The Anachronism of Jonathan Edwards." *Christianity Century* 113 (1996): 480-485.

Noll, Mark A. "The Contested Legacy of Jonathan Edwards." In *Reckoning with the Past.* Edited by D. G. Hart, 200-220. Grand Rapids: Baker Book House, 1983.

_____. "Jonathan Edwards and Nineteenth-Century Theology." In *Jonathan Edwards and the American Experience.* Edited by Nathan O. Hatch and Harry S. Stout, 260-287. New York: Oxford University Press, 1988.

_____. *America's God: From Jonathan Edwards to Abraham Lincoln.* New York: Oxford University Press, 2002.

Oberg, Barbara O., and Harry S. Stout. *Benjamin Franklin, Jonathan Edwards, and the Representation of American Culture.* New York: Oxford University Press, 1993.

Oliphint, K. Scott. "Jonathan Edwards: Reformed Apologist." *Westminster Theological Journal* 57 (1995): 165-186.

Opie, John. *Jonathan Edwards and the Enlightenment.* Problems in American Civilization. Lexington, MA: Heath, 1969.

Otto, Randall E. "Justification and Justice: An Edwardsean Proposal." *Evangelical Quarterly* 65 (1993): 131-145.

Owen, John. *The Doctrine of Justification by Faith: Through the Imputation of the Righteousness of Christ, Explained, Confirmed, and Vindicated.* Edited by Carl R. Trueman. Grand Rapids: Reformation Heritage Books, 2006.

Parkes, Henry Bamford. *Jonathan Edwards: The Fiery Puritan.* New York: Minton, Balch, & Company, 1930.

Parrington, Vernon Louis. *The Colonial Mind, 1620-1800.* Vol. 1 of *Main Currents in American Thought.* New York: Harcourt Brace and Co., 1927.

Pauw, Amy Plantinga. "'Heaven Is a World of Love': Edwards on Heaven and the Trinity." *Calvin Theological Journal* 30 (1995): 392-401.

———. *The Supreme Harmony of All: The Trinitarian Theology of Jonathan Edwards.* Grand Rapids: W. B. Eerdmans, 2002.

———. "'One Alone Cannot Be Excellent': Edwards on Divine Simplicity." In *Jonathan Edwards: Philosophical Theologian.* Edited by Paul Helm and Oliver D. Crisp, 115-125. Burlington, VT: Ashgate, 2003.

Piper, John. *Desiring God: Meditations of a Christian Hedonist.* 2nd ed. Sisters, OR: Multnomah Press, 1986.

———. *The Supremacy of God in Preaching.* Grand Rapids: Baker: 1990.

———. *The Pleasures of God.* 2nd ed. Sisters, OR: Multnomah Press, 1991.

———. *God's Passion for His Glory: Living the Vision of Jonathan Edwards.* Wheaton: Crossway, 1998.

Piper, John, and Justin Taylor. *A God Entranced Vision of All Things: The Legacy of Jonathan Edwards.* Wheaton: Crossway Books, 2004.

Reid, James. *Memoirs of the Westminster Divines.* Edinburgh; Carlisle, PA: Banner of Truth Trust, 1982.

Reid, Jasper. "The Trinitarian Metaphysics of Jonathan Edwards and Nicolas Malebranche." *The Heythrop Journal* 43, no. 2 (2002): 152-169.

Ricketts, Allyn Lee. "The Primacy of Revelation in the Philosophical Theology of Jonathan Edwards." *DAI* 56, no. 05A (1995): 1843.

Riforgiato, Leonard R. "The Unified Thought of Jonathan Edwards." *Thought* 47 (1972): 599-610.

Rudisill, Dorus Paul. *Doctrine of Atonement in Jonathan Edwards and His Successors.* New York: Poseidon Books, 1971.

Schafer, Thomas A. "Jonathan Edwards and Justification by Faith." *Church History* 20 (1951): 55-67.

──────. "The Role of Jonathan Edwards in American Religious History." *American Theological Library Association Summary of Proceedings* 21 (1967): 153-165.

Scheick, William J. *Critical Essays on Jonathan Edwards.* Critical Essays on American Literature. Boston: G. K. Hall, 1980.

Shea, Daniel. "Jonathan Edwards: The First Two Hundred Years." *Journal of American Studies* 14 (1980): 181-197.

Simonson, Harold Peter. *Jonathan Edwards: Theologian of the Heart.* Grand Rapids: W. B. Eerdmans, 1974.

Stagg, John W. *Calvin, Twisse and Edwards on the Universal Salvation of Those Dying in Infancy.* Richmond, VA: Presbyterian Committee of Publication, 1902.

Stein, Stephen J. "Quest for the Spiritual Sense: The Biblical Hermeneutics of Jonathan Edwards." *Harvard Theological Review* 70 (1977): 99-113.

———. "The Spirit and the Word: Jonathan Edwards and Scriptural Exegesis." In *Jonathan Edwards and the American Experience*. Edited by Nathan O. Hatch and Harry S. Stout, 118-130. New York: Oxford University Press, 1988.

———. *Jonathan Edwards's Writings: Text, Context, Interpretation*. Bloomington: Indiana University Press, 1996.

Stephens, Bruce M. "An Appeal to the Universe: The Doctrine of the Atonement in American Protestant Thought from Jonathan Edwards to Edwards Amasa Park." *Encounter* 60 (1999): 55-72.

Stoddard, Soloman. *The Safety of Appearing at the Day of Judgment, in the Righteousness of Christ, Opened and Applied*. Morgan, PA: Soli Deo Gloria, 1995.

Storms, C. Samuel. *Tragedy in Eden: Original Sin in the Theology of Jonathan Edwards*. Lanham, MD: University Press of America, 1985.

Stout, Harry S. "The Puritans and Edwards." In *Jonathan Edwards and the American Experience*, 142-159. New York: Oxford University Press, 1988.

Stout, Harry S., Kenneth P. Minkema, and Caleb J. D. Maskell. *Jonathan Edwards at 300: Essays on the Tercentenary of His Birth*. Lanham, MD: University Press of America, 2005.

Studebaker, Steven Michael. "Jonathan Edwards' Social Augustinian Trinitarianism: A Criticism of and an Alternative to Recent Interpretations." *DAI* 64, no. 05A (2003): 1718.

Sweeney, Douglas A. "Edwards and His Mantle: The Historiography of the New England Theology." *New England Quarterly* 71, no. March (1998): 97-119.

———. *Nathaniel Taylor, New Haven Theology, and the Legacy of Jonathan Edwards*. New York: Oxford University Press, 2003.

———. " A Plentiful Harvest." *Books and Culture*, November/December (2003): 16, 40-42.

―――. "'Longing for More and More of It'? The Strange Career of Jonathan Edwards's Exegetical Assertions." In *Jonathan Edwards at 300: Essay on the Tercentenary of His Birth*. Edited by Harry S. Stout, Kenneth P. Minkema, and Caleb J. D. Maskell., 25-37. Lanham, MD: University Press of America, 2005.

Taylor, John. *The Scripture Doctrine of Original Sin Proposed to Free and Candid Examination: In Three Parts*. 4th ed. Newcastle: J. Barker, 1845.

Tracy, Joseph. *The Great Awakening*. New York: Arno Press, 1969.

Tracy, Patricia J. *Jonathan Edwards: Pastor*. New York: Hill and Wang, 1980.

Turnbull, Ralph G. *Jonathan Edwards the Preacher*. Grand Rapids: Baker Book House, 1958.

Turrettin, Francis. *Institutes of Elenctic Theology*. Translated by George Musgrave Giger. Edited by James T. Dennison. 3 vols. Phillipsburg, NJ: P & R Publishing, 1992-7.

Valeri, Mark R. *Law and Providence in Joseph Bellany's New England: The Origins of the New Divinity in Revolutionary America*. New York: Oxford University Press, 1994.

Vetö, Miklos, and Michael J. McClymond. "Spiritual Knowledge According to Jonathan Edwards." *Calvin Theological Journal* 31 (1996): 161-181.

Warren, William Fairfield. "The 'Edwardsean' Theory of Atonement." *Methodist Review* 42 (1860): 386-402.

Webber, Richard M. "The Trinitarian Theology of Jonathan Edwards: An Investigation of Charges Against Its Orthodoxy." *Journal of the Evangelical Theological Society* 44 (2001): 297-318.

Weber, Donald. "The Recovery of Jonathan Edwards." In *Jonathan Edwards and the American Experience*. Edited by Nathan O. Hatch and Harry S. Stout, 50-70. New York: Oxford University Press, 1988.

Whitefield, George. *George Whitefield's Journals.* Edinburgh: Banner of Truth Trust, 1960.

Wilson-Kastner, Patricia. "Jonathan Edwards: History and the Covenant." *Andrews University Seminary Studies* 15 (1977): 205-216.

_____. *Coherence in a Fragmented World: Jonathan Edwards' Theology of the Holy Spirit.* Washington, DC: University Press of America, 1978.

Wilson, John F. "History, Redemption, and the Millennium." In *Jonathan Edwards and the American Experience.* Edited by Nathan O. Hatch and Harry S. Stout, 131-141. New York: Oxford University Press, 1988.

_____. Review of "The Philosophical Theology of Jonathan Edwards." *Theology Today* 46 (1989): 101-102.

Winiarski, Douglas L. "Seeking Synthesis in Edwards Scholarship." *William and Mary Quarterly* 61, no. 1 (2004): 135-151.

Winslow, Ola Elizabeth. *Jonathan Edwards, 1703-1758.* 1940. Reprint, New York: Octagon, 1979.

Withrow, Brandon. "Jonathan Edwards and Justification by Faith." *Reformation & Revival* 11 (2002): 93-109.

Youngs, Fred William. "The Place of Spiritual Union in the Thought of Jonathan Edwards." *DAI* 47, no. 05A (1986): 1768.

Zakai, Avihu. *Jonathan Edwards' Philosophy of History: The Re-Enchantment of the World in the Age of Enlightenment.* Princeton: Princeton University Press, 2003.

Printed in Great Britain
by Amazon